An American

Bride in Kabul

An American Bride in Kabul

A MEMOIR

Phyllis Chesler

palgrave
macmillan

AN AMERICAN BRIDE IN KABUL
Copyright © Phyllis Chesler, 2013.
All rights reserved.

First published in 2013 by PALGRAVE MACMILLAN® in the United
States—a division of St. Martin's Press LLC, 175 Fifth Avenue, New
York, NY 10010.

Where this book is distributed in the UK, Europe, and the rest of the
world, this is by Palgrave Macmillan, a division of Macmillan Publishers
Limited, registered in England, company number 785998, of Houndmills,
Basingstoke, Hampshire RG21 6XS.

Palgrave Macmillan is the global academic imprint of the above
companies and has companies and representatives throughout the world.

Palgrave® and Macmillan® are registered trademarks in the United
States, the United Kingdom, Europe, and other countries.

ISBN 978-0-230-34221-7

Library of Congress Cataloging-in-Publication Data

Chesler, Phyllis.
  An American bride in Kabul : a memoir / Phyllis Chesler.
    pages   cm
  ISBN 978-0-230-34221-7 (alk. paper)
    1. Chesler, Phyllis. 2. Jewish women—Afghanistan—Kabul. 3. Brides—
Afghanistan—Kabul. 4. Men—Afghanistan—Kabul. 5. Afghanistan—
Social life and customs. I. Title.
HQ1172.C44   2013
305.892'40581—dc23

                                                              2013008141

A catalogue record of the book is available from the British Library.

Design by Letra Libre

First edition: October 2013

10 9 8 7 6 5 4 3 2 1

Printed in the United States of America.

Contents

Preface

I once lived in a harem in Afghanistan.

I did not enter the kingdom as a diplomat, soldier, teacher, journalist, or foreign aid worker, nor did I ruggedly arrive on foot or riding a strong horse over dangerous mountain passes. I was there long before American hippies followed the old Silk Road in search of drugs.

I was in search of another kind of adventure, one that has lasted more than fifty years.

I came as the young bride of the son of one of the country's wealthiest men. To my astonishment, I was held captive—but it's not as if I had been kidnapped by wild savages and ravished. This is not a tale of a white and helpless maiden taken by Barbary pirates and sold into an imperial harem. I was not *sold* into captivity.

I walked into it of my own free will.

My Afghan bridegroom was a Westernized man I had known for nearly three years at college in America. He had never mentioned that his father had three wives and twenty-one children or that I would be expected to live under a polite form of rather posh house arrest, together with his mother and the other women—or that I would be expected to convert to Islam.

I lived behind high walls in a grand home surrounded by other such family homes. The dwellings were European in style. They had indoor plumbing, hot water, marble floors, lush carpets, and ballroom-sized living rooms.

I lived as a member of an Afghan family and as such learned about the Afghan people in a way that the great Western travelers could not. Afterward I was often able to see the West with Eastern eyes.

Afghan men and women know that life can change in an instant; that happiness is brief and illusory; that one is utterly dependent on one's faith and one's family and on the strongest man in that family; that poverty, cruelty, and tragedy are to be expected; and that no one—not even one's brother, certainly no foreign power, can ever be trusted.

Afghans believe that without a husband and sons a woman absolutely cannot survive and that women and children are a man's property. They are his to protect or abuse. They are his to kill. It is the way things are.

Most Afghan men will not admit to these truths. They will denounce anyone who says so as a liar and an enemy. Exposing these facts is considered a crime.

This is the story of a young and naive Jewish American woman who meant to rebel against tradition—but who found herself trapped in the past, stuck in the Middle Ages, without a passport back.

Eventually I escaped.

I started a diary while I was in Kabul. I have it still. Most of the first entries are too raw, poorly written, perhaps too shocking, to share just yet. Here is what I subsequently wrote about our arrival.

> *1961: Our plane is landing in Kabul. An airport official demands—and then keeps—my American passport. "Just a formality," he assures me. I never see that passport again. I am now subject to Afghan laws and customs. I am no longer a citizen of the United States. I am the property of my Afghan family.*
>
> *We will no longer be living alone as a couple. We will be living with my mother-in-law, her oldest son, his wife, their children, her two youngest sons, and with many turbaned and sometimes barefoot servants. This living arrangement is quite a surprise.*

We had no television. We had a phone, but it rarely rang and it did not always work. People mainly had each other. We were each other's entertainment. We ate together, talked, gossiped, joked, huddled under a communal *sandali* (a low bench warmed by a brazier) when it was cold, entertained relatives, drank tea, chewed nuts, ate sticky candies. The men prayed, worked in one of the family businesses, plotted, and dreamed. We lived a semitribal life.

Many years later, when I saw the first Cirque du Soleil performance in Battery Park City, in New York City, I was entranced. The audience sat in a tent in which the players rode their horses around and around hypnotically—amazing horses and amazing riders—and musicians from India and Pakistan played their drums and tiny instruments and cast a spell that threw me back into our tribal and nomadic past.

On a good day that's what it was like.

My family had servants, the latest model cars, chauffeurs, gardens, balconies, villas—and if one sat out at night, the stars were a cluster of golden grapes, close enough to pluck.

My unexpected house arrest was not as shocking as was my husband's refusal to acknowledge it as such. Similarly, when I first saw women in ghost-like burqas (called *chowdrys* in Afghanistan) huddled at the back of a bus, I was outraged and frightened; that my family treated this as normal made things worse. My husband insisted that this custom was on its way out. My relatives laughed at my discomfort.

I saw pairs of fully armed warriors walking down the street holding hands, each with a flower behind his ear. When I asked my husband and brothers-in-law about homosexuality in Afghanistan, I was dismissed as a crazy American.

I was living in a culture where extreme gender apartheid was the norm and where my reactions to it were considered abnormal and unusual.

Nevertheless my feeling of kinship with the Islamic world has not diminished in the five decades since. Even my detention in Afghanistan was not enough to quell my abiding ardor. Something about the Islamic world had called me. Like my Afghan husband, perhaps I am also multicultural and belong both to the East and West. Jews have certainly lived in Arab and Muslim countries, including Afghanistan, for thousands of years.

But I was also an independent bohemian American. I wore black leotards with ballet slippers or jeans and sneakers. I practiced yoga, wrote poetry, and was always reading a book. I purposely chose a college that had no required courses because I did not want anyone in a position of authority telling me what to do.

My religious Jewish family saw Afghanistan as the end of the earth.

"No," I stubbornly insisted, "China is farther. So are Russia and Australia." I recently went to the Metropolitan Museum in New York City in search of Moghul-era Buddhist art from Afghanistan.

Now, *that* involved going to the farthest reaches of the museum, to the last gallery on the second floor. One reaches it only by taking a series of elevators and then climbing two or three different sets of stairs.

And there they were: two beheaded pre-Islamic Buddhas from Afghanistan. One Buddha had amber-colored jeweled eyes and seemed to be looking right at me.

But my family was right. I *had* gone to the ends of the earth—culturally. For example I was not allowed to leave the family compound without a male chaperone and a female relative or two. My mother-in-law kept expecting me to wear a long and filmy kerchief (*hijab*) and a long coat when I went out. She also launched a campaign to convert me to Islam.

This book is a personal memoir about an unusual first marriage and subsequent friendship with my ex-husband and his family—one that has endured for more than fifty years.

This is not my life memoir. This is a memoir of my Afghan sojourn and what it was like to live as a wife in a Muslim country. Writing this book is not without risk. My words may shame, shock, enrage, or dishearten people who are dear to me. A writer always wrestles with this problem. I have softened many blows, but as a writer I am also committed to telling the truth.

The first seven chapters of this memoir (Section One) tell the story of my time as a bride in Kabul and my flight back to America.

But have I really escaped? The country and its people seem to have followed me into the future and right into the West. Islamic *hijab* (headscarves), *niqab* (face masks), and burqas are here in America, both in the media and on the streets.

The haunting cries of the muezzin calling the faithful to prayer may be heard all across North America and Europe. Honor killings are here too, as are forced arranged marriages, polygamy, and varieties of purdah (female seclusion). Afghanistan has landed in America, and America is still deployed in Afghanistan.

The last seven chapters (Section Two) describe what I did after I returned to America on an Afghan passport, how my husband tried to force me to return, and how he made a dramatic escape of his own, disguised as a peasant, just before the Soviet invasion. We have remained in touch ever since.

9/11 changed the direction this book would take. I had intended to use my own experience in Afghanistan as a way of reviving the more daring and often more idyllic adventures of other Western travelers to Afghanistan and to the Islamic world in general. I was especially interested in sharing the long-forgotten tales of women travelers.

Then, in my lifetime, Afghanistan literally turned into a Margaret Atwood dystopian novel—even darker and more misogynistic than *The Handmaid's Tale*. Given the increasingly barbaric persecution and subordination of Muslim women, I decided to connect my own brief brush with purdah and gender apartheid to the surreal lives of Afghan and Muslim women today. Perhaps my story will serve to bring Americans closer to the suffering of Muslim women—and Muslim women closer to an American feminism that was forged in purdah in Afghanistan.

But how could I write about Afghanistan and Muslim women without also writing about Islamic/Islamist terrorism and its war against Muslim civilians and against the West? I cannot pretend that this war is not real. It has already affected all our lives.

In my research I also stumbled upon the astounding history of Jews and Hindus in Afghanistan and how that history intimately relates to my Afghan family's wealth and social position.

These grave realities have not permitted me to write the lyrical, apolitical, strictly literary work that I had envisioned so long ago.

But I am romantic about my Afghan adventure—just not in the usual sense of romance. I love that I was there, however briefly. I love the breathtaking diversity of the people. They are the descendants of ancient Selucids, Scythians, Sassanids, Persians, Turks, Mongols, Indo-Arians, Greeks, Romans, Jews, and Arabs; their many religions have included Zoroastrianism, paganism, Buddhism, Hinduism, Judaism, Manicheanism, Christianity, and Islam.

Perhaps I once lived somewhere in Central Asia in a previous life. If so, I hope that I was a warrior, not an imprisoned concubine; a scribe, not one of many wives in a polygamous household; a court poet, not an illiterate farmer. Call me an Orientalist but I will go to my death loving such things—including the fabulously jeweled ceremonial swords and daggers of the Moghul era.

Why am I writing this book?

The subject haunts me—but also because I am a writer and the material is irresistible, wondrous.

I believe that my American feminism began in Afghanistan. It is a feminism that many Muslim and ex-Muslim feminists and dissidents welcome and support. They are my closest intellectual and political companions today. Some are religious Muslims, others are committed secularists or apostates.

We are all *anti-Islamists*: We oppose totalitarianism, terrorism, and gender and religious apartheid and support individual, human, and women's rights.

Some of my compatriots write under pseudonyms. Others live with round-the-clock bodyguards. An increasing number have been sued and impoverished for telling the truth about their lives. In the Middle East, Central Asia, the Far East, and Africa, those who think as we do have been jailed, tortured, and executed.

Their heroism is extraordinary.

Ironies abound. I fled the indoor and secluded life of the harem, but as a writer I actually lead such a life. When I write, I am usually wearing a long loose caftan.

Part of me will always long for perfumed gardens, indoor court-yards, open cooking fires, brightly glazed hookahs, highly ceremonial communal meals with a large extended family, the smells and sounds of the bazaar, snow-capped mountains, and a thrilling expanse of sky.

I am something of a sentimentalist, but make no mistake: I am also a woman who is married to her work; I require a serious measure of solitude in order to accomplish it. Living with an extended family as an obedient wife and daughter-in-law is a fantasy—a nightmare, really—for someone like me.

The Afghanistan I came to know was and still is a place where misogyny and violence are indigenous, pandemic, and considered normal. Female children are still sold into polygamous marriages to men old enough to be their grandfathers; many girls are routinely worked like animals, beaten brutally on a daily basis, sometimes tortured, even slain in honor killings. Male child orphans become the "dancing boy" sex toys of wizened warlords.

None of this is new or the result of foreign occupations. What is new is that the world knows about it. Many Western humanitarians are trying to rescue and heal such victims and hold the perpetrators lawfully accountable for their crimes. But what, if anything, can America really do to stop such indigenous barbarism? How much blood and treasure must we spend to hold back the baleful sky?

Telling the truth requires effort. Lying is far easier.

Both the passage of time and the complexity of intimate relationships make this a daunting task. Memory often fails us. It even fails writers who are trying hard to remember things exactly as they happened. If I have misremembered anything, it was not purposeful and I ask forgiveness of both my readers and of those about whom I am writing. I am trying to create a time and place that no longer exist, that remain alive only in memories. Here I am also forcing myself to remember those things that I once repressed in order to get on with my life.

Some believe *in vino veritas,* that wine loosens inhibition and allows one to speak forbidden truths. For me *in scribo veritas.* Only by writing do I discover the truth.

I am not entirely sure why I went to Afghanistan. Perhaps I am writing this book to find out.

Was I in search of a lost band of Scythian Amazon warrior women or one of the lost tribes of Israel? Scholars suggest that both groups once settled in the region. Was I a typical Western adventurer lured by "the past present," a place where a simpler time still existed? Or had life in the West already broken my young heart; was I in search of oblivion, "half in love with easeful Death"?

Really, why did I go to Afghanistan?

Why else than to be able to tell you about it now, at this moment in history. It was kismet, *bashert,* fated, written in the stars; clearly it was my destiny.

An American Bride in Kabul

SECTION ONE

In Afghanistan

ONE

From Brooklyn to Kabul

I am eighteen and I have just met my prince. He is a dark, handsome, charming, sophisticated, and wealthy foreign student. We are in college in America. I am the only woman who matters to him. I have a nineteen-inch waist and embarrassingly full lips. The whole world is mine. I believe I am invincible and will live forever.

True, he is a Muslim and I am a Jew. I am very Jewish. But he is the Agha Khan, and I am Rita Hayworth. He is Yul Brynner, and I am Gertrude Lawrence in *The King and I*.

Years later I would learn that this beloved musical is based on the chilling diary of Anna H. Leonowens. Entitled *Siamese Harem Life,* it documents the slavery, cruelty, and other practices that are considered customary in the East.

Unfortunately I fall in love before I find this extraordinary volume.

My prince, Abdul-Kareem, is from Afghanistan. He is not really a royal prince but he conducts himself like one. Everyone around him treats him with exaggerated deference—especially Americans who love to rub shoulders with royalty.

His father helped found Afghanistan's first modern banking system and owns and runs the country's largest import-export company, in addition to many farms, homes, and properties. When he visits New York, he stays at the Plaza.

I am a first-generation American on my father's side. My mother is the only one in her family who was born in the United States. Her parents and sisters came from the Austro-Hungarian empire—in other words, from Poland. I feel lucky to live in a country where a young woman on a full college scholarship can meet such an interesting person from such a faraway place.

Abdul-Kareem wears a silk handkerchief in the breast pocket of his well-made suit. He also wears designer sunglasses, even in winter. I've seen men do that only in movies. He is suave and self-assured and has thick dark hair, golden skin, and penetrating eyes. I have never met anyone like him. Years later I decide that Abdul-Kareem most resembles the Egyptian actor Omar Sharif.

The whole thing is biblical. He is Prince Shechem, I am Dina.

Some say that one of the lost tribes of Israel left Babylon for Persia and then went to Afghanistan. Maybe Abdul-Kareem is a descendent of Joseph, that most splendid Hebrew Egyptian, a figure I adore.

When I get to Kabul, it is like stepping into the Bible. Here are the nomads, caravans, fat-tailed sheep, camels, turbans, veiled and shrouded women, a pleasant confusion of ancient dust and mingled male voices.

When we meet in America, Abdul-Kareem has just returned from his first visit home in almost ten years. He tells me nothing about his trip and I do not press him for details.

I am curiously indifferent.

Afghanistan never comes up in our conversations.

Abdul-Kareem spent some time in Europe, then attended private school in the United States. He speaks English perfectly.

Apart from his appearance, there is little evidence of any real foreignness about him. We never discuss Judaism, Islam, or the role of women. It will be a long time before I learn anything about the history of his country or about its religious and tribal culture.

For now we share more bohemian interests: the new Italian and French cinema. Vittorio De Sica's *The Bicycle Thief* and *Two Women.* Federico Fellini's *La Strada, Nights of Cabiria,* and *La Dolce Vita* are quasi-religious experiences for us.

We adore Giulietta Masina, Sophia Loren, Marcello Mastroianni, and Anna Magnani. After seeing François Truffaut's *The 400 Blows* and Jean-Luc Godard's *Breathless,* we talk of nothing else. The Swedish director Ingmar Bergman is a fast-rising god to us.

Somehow life seems more romantic and certainly more serious in black and white and in a foreign language. The actors, especially the intercontinentals, Anthony Quinn, Ingrid Bergman, and Irene Papas, seem sexier and more important with their tragic outlooks on life.

We agree: Most American actors seem far too optimistic and naive. The movies all have happy endings; we are far too unconventional and too pretentious to believe in them.

I make an exception for Marlon Brando (*The Wild One, On the Waterfront*) and James Dean (*Rebel Without a Cause* and *East of Eden*).

When we see Satyajit Ray's Apu Trilogy (*Pather Panchali, Aparajito,* and *Apur Sansar*), Abdul-Kareem is uncommonly quiet. These films about the life of the poor in India speak to him in another way. India is closer to home. The on-screen, on-the-wheel-of-life suffering is endless, irredeemable, yet the people maintain enormous dignity.

This is who we think we are: film buffs, culture vultures, artists, intellectuals, bohemians. Abdul-Kareem decides that he will be a film and theater director. He suggests that I write scripts, stories, and novels upon which he'll base his films. Or, he says, maybe I should act in the productions: "That's what you once wanted to do, isn't it? Now you'll have your chance."

This sounds both unrealistic and delightful. It appeals to my vanity.

We also talk endlessly about Camus, Sartre, Dostoevsky, Strindberg, Ibsen, and Proust. We listen to jazz, ragtime, opera, show tunes, doo-wop, rock 'n' roll, and the blues.

We fancy ourselves existentialists, twin souls spinning in space without moorings, except in each other. Neither of us is Christian. We are both somewhat exotic in America. Together we are a trendy item on a campus where many students party in the Caribbean during winter break and spend summers at family homes in France or Italy.

As for me, I must succeed academically or I will lose my scholarship. I am always studying: in the coffee shop, in my room, on the lawn, in the library, even in class. Abdul-Kareem and I read side by side in the school cafeteria or at the diner down the road, where we enjoy greasy hamburgers smothered in fried onions.

We spend hours talking animatedly to each other, unaware of the world around us.

Abdul-Kareem is the first man with whom I sleep. The earth does not shudder beneath me, and I do not see God, but I still have to marry him.

I am a good Jewish woman and as such am not supposed to sleep with a man before marriage. But now that I have broken this rule, we must marry. These are the rules. The die is cast.

Abdul-Kareem and I live together in series of small furnished apartments in New York City during our winter and summer breaks.

I would rather just travel the wide, wide world together, like gypsies or abdicating aristocrats who have permanently taken to the road—but Abdul-Kareem tells me we must marry, that there is no other way for us to travel together in the Muslim world or for me to meet his family. To embark on this adventure of a lifetime, I must, ironically, embrace the tradition of marriage. Yet this marriage is not exactly traditional because I am marrying a non-Jew, a non-American—a stranger, really, from a distant land.

My parents are religious Jews; they are hysterical and terrified. My father is bereft. My mother has always viewed me as a bad seed and a changeling, and that view is now confirmed.

I believed that marriage to Abdul-Kareem would grant me all the freedoms that I never enjoyed as a child. I would be out of my family's tight grasp; I would travel to Europe, the Middle East, North Africa, Central Asia, India, and the Far East. We would live in Kabul for a while, then move on to Paris, and then back to New York so I could finish college.

The rebel that I am is a slave to romantic fantasies. Finally all those fairy tales have had their way with me. I am special, not at all provincial. My life will unwind like a foreign film. Ah, but the rebellious runaway is also a good girl who's doing precisely what the fairy tales advise: marry a prince, live in a villa, if not exactly a castle.

I was a complete fool. When I finally returned to America, I literally kissed the ground at Idlewild (Kennedy) Airport.

Abdul-Kareem believes that he is rescuing me from my savagely critical mother and from my father, who loves me but who, in Abdul-Kareem's view, cannot provide for me properly, lavishly.

Abdul-Kareem assures me that he will be able to take care of us far better as his wealthy father's son than as Mr. Muslim Foreigner in America. He convinces me that we will travel widely and lead cultured lives. He does not tell me that once we land in Kabul, I will be placed under house arrest.

I can just hear him! "House arrest—really? Phyllis, you are so dramatic. If we lived alone, how could you have managed on your own?"

His is also a rather grand rebellion. He chose to marry a dark-haired, dark-eyed American Jew whose family has no political standing. He chose to marry for love. He chose a woman as his intellectual companion. In retrospect this was madness.

I was told privately that Abdul-Kareem's older brothers were puzzled, even disappointed, because I did not have blonde hair and blue eyes and could easily pass for an Afghan girl. "He could have gotten one just like this right here at home," I heard one of them say.

Did we once really love each other? Were we soul mates? I am not sure. I dare not remember—the pain would be overwhelming and pointless.

Do photos tell the truth? I am looking at some old black-and-white photos of us holding hands and looking into each other's eyes. We look very much in love. We are in an idyllic setting, surrounded by trees. I cannot remember who took the pictures.

The truth may be more complicated. I wanted to travel. This was the only way I could do so at that time.

Twenty years later, after Abdul-Kareem and his family escaped from the Soviets, he tells me that he has never gotten over me. I remain silent. I find this hard to believe.

At the time he says this, he needs my help. He is probably trying to flatter me—or get me into bed. Have I become heartless—or have I finally learned something?

Abdul-Kareem gently chides me. He asks me how I could forget how close we were—how we once talked for twenty hours, fell asleep, woke up, and immediately continued the conversation.

I do not remember this.

I do remember how safe I felt when he was behind the wheel of his car. I remember how much he enjoyed a good Jewish joke.

Although I do not want to get married (my *parents* are married; I have never imagined myself as a bride or a wife), Abdul-Kareem never-theless persuades me. At the last minute I ask a dress designer friend, a woman who once lived in Senegal, to transform a creamy white raw silk Afghan turban into a cocktail-length wedding dress for me.

I wonder whatever happened to that lovely little dress. I never wore it again. I have no memory of what I did with it.

We marry in a civil ceremony in Poughkeepsie, New York. We have no family present. Toby, one of my college roommates, is my witness, and Hussain, an Afghan man with whom we have enjoyed many Sunday picnics, acts as Abdul-Kareem's.

Afterward we all have a glass of wine and a meal and then go home, change into jeans, pack, and leave for Europe. Europe!

We travel to Europe in nineteenth-century style on *Le Flandre*. I remember we had champagne in our stateroom and that my youngest brother came to see us off. My parents were not there. Indeed my parents tell no one what I've done. No relative or family friend was ever told that I had married a Muslim and sailed clear off to Afghanistan.

On board I feel we are starring in a black-and-white movie. Sometimes we dine at the captain's table, but I spend most of my time on deck, pondering the wide blue sea—and reading. Nestled luxuriously in a deck chair, covered by a blanket, sipping coffee, I read straight through Lawrence Durrell's *The Alexandria Quartet*. It is all very romantic.

We have a huge fight on board. I cannot remember about what. I do remember that some other passengers looked quite startled, perhaps even frightened. We are fighting as we land in Southampton.

Abdul-Kareem finally has to tell me that our stay in Europe will be a brief one, that we are expected in Kabul as soon as possible, and that his expense allowance, never large, has been curtailed—which is pro forma for all Afghan students studying abroad.

Maybe that's why we were fighting.

He did not, perhaps he could not, bring himself to tell me that we were almost broke. And so our London lodgings turned out to be a rather seedy bed-and-breakfast. I didn't care. I was finally here, in the city of the high red buses and the almost circus-like large black taxi cabs, the country of Chaucer, Shakespeare, Donne, Dickens, the Brontë sisters, George Eliot, and the queen. What did it matter that we'd be eating fish and chips rather than having tea at the Ritz? Still, our suddenly shrunken budget was a sign of more ominous things to come.

I make the proverbial tourist beeline for the British Museum, which brazenly, beautifully houses the treasures of ancient Egypt, Greece (the Elgin Marbles, the muscular but graceful Amazons), Rome, and China, together with the portraits of royalty, and of horses and dogs.

We have tea at Russell Square, where the Bloomsbury literati once gossiped and dined and scandalized. We dash off to Madame Tussaud's, Piccadilly Circus, and the West End. Abdul-Kareem is humoring me. He has done all this before. I want to stop and browse in every used and antiquarian bookstore we pass.

I like being in a city without being surrounded by towering skyscrapers. The human frame seems more the measure of things when it is not dwarfed by shining glass monuments built to scrape the very sky.

Onward we go, too quickly, to Paris. I have a photo of myself in front of a French kiosk. Was I really once that young and thin?

France: George Sand's land, Colette's land, Edith Piaf's land, too. I have listened to the Sparrow incessantly and know the words of many of her songs by heart. France means Baudelaire, Rimbaud, and

Marie-Henri Beyle—the great writer Stendhal—whose work is the subject of my nearly completed college thesis.

We visit the Louvre to ponder the enigmatic *Mona Lisa* and pay our respects to the Vermeers, Rembrandts, and Caravaggios.

I like Ingres and am entranced by his *Odalisque* and *Turkish Baths*. Ironic but telling: I am being introduced to the Muslim world through the eyes of those dreamy Western painters who expressed their own sensuality by painting their European patrons dressed in elaborate turbans, framed by large pillows and a Moorish arch or two.

We pile into the Galerie Nationale du Jeu de Paume, which houses all the riotously colorful French impressionist paintings: Monet, Manet, Renoir, Seurat, Degas, and of course my beloved madman, Van Gogh. I consider them all my friends.

Exhausted, in too much of a rush, we visit Versailles. I find it cold, very cold, and am not impressed by its vast mirrored emptiness or by the manicured formal gardens. Of course at this time we are both huge fans of the French Revolution and are not likely to be impressed by the aesthetic decisions of heartless kings and queens. (Oh, how I have changed my mind about some of this.)

But we are in Paris. We must visit the Left Bank. For me that means hours of dawdling among the bookseller stalls, never wanting to leave, but it also means visiting the cafes where, innocents that we are, we actually hope to run into a living existentialist or two. We walk for hours up and down the Champs-Élysées.

On our last night we go to a cabaret with a garish can-can show (Abdul-Kareem's choice, not mine). The women dance topless, and I am shocked, titillated, slightly disapproving.

All this time Abdul-Kareem is preoccupied, impatient, but he tries hard to hide it. He wishes to indulge my passion for art, history, books, and travel, but he obviously has some serious things on his mind.

He chooses Munich as the city from which we will leave for the Middle East. Munich frightens me, mainly because I like it. I like the large soft comforters on our bed, the homey-cozy restaurants and cafes, and the heavy rich food. But the grotesquely large municipal Hansel and Gretel clock, with its combined German exactitude and deceptively childish facade, offends me. This is the country that, not long before, put all its Jewish, gypsy, and political Hansels and Gretels right into the smoking ovens.

Chamberlain signed the Munich Pact here; it gave Hitler the Sudetenland. It was a consummate act of appeasement. The Nazis marched here only sixteen years earlier. Some areas of debris from wartime bomb-ings still are cordoned off. Why am I comfortable here at all? Years later I will have a much more disconcerting sense of familiarity and comfort in Vienna: the city of both Freud and Herzl—Hitler's city, too.

When we land in Beirut, the air is softer and oddly exciting. But we cannot stay; we are due in Teheran.

Abdul-Kareem's Iranian friends send a car and driver to meet us at the airport. We are given a brief tour of the city. We drive down Isfahan Street and Firdowsi Avenue and the grand Lalezar Avenue. Of course there is also a Pahlavi Avenue.

Our hosts—people much older than we are—pick us up for a night out on the town. I remember a room with access to its own private bal-cony. The food, the traffic, and the laughter all flow together.

Our hosts decide to entertain us by making a disabled servant boy (a musician who plays the accordion) dance for us after they get him drunk. They throw more and more money at him as he makes a fool of himself. It is a cruel spectacle that I do not entirely understand.

The women are dressed in the latest European fashions. They smoke. They drink. They wear makeup. They laugh a lot. They speak French and English. They gossip: The Shah, Mohammed Reza Pahlavi, has been forced to divorce the woman he loves (Soraya Esfandiary-Bakhtiari), be-cause she cannot give him an heir. He has recently married Farah Diba, a beautiful young woman who, it is hoped, will do just that.

The women are sympathetic to both Soraya and Farah—but are mostly sympathetic to the Shah. "Life is tragic. One's fate is what it is. One's duty cannot be shirked." I conclude that they may look European on the outside, but on the inside they seem to have different values.

I know I really am in Asia.

Here one can see enormous wealth right next to dire poverty. Bare-foot women and children work for and live with people who wear only the finest Italian leather shoes. Yes, of course we have pockets of en-trenched poverty in America, but I have never seen barefoot servants or child beggars on the streets of New York.

My family is poor, but we do not think of ourselves this way. True, I have sometimes worn hand-me-down clothes, but we have always had enough to eat, a roof over our heads, a free coed education, and private music, drama, and art lessons for me, the presumed child prodigy.

In Teheran's Grand Bazaar shopkeepers man tiny stalls. I wonder if the bazaar has looked like this for the last thousand years.

Fresh carcasses of sheep hang in the streets. One has to buy fruit in one place, vegetables in another, bread and delicious pastries elsewhere. Each stall is devoted to a single item: carpets, hammered goods, spices. Everyone specializes. This is so different from the American department store or supermarket, where one can buy almost everything in one place and all indoors. The bazaar has a public bath whose exterior resembles a palace.

The smell of the bazaar is tantalizing, familiar, energizing. Gas and kerosene mingle with such spices as saffron, cinnamon, garlic, basil, and cilantro; the smells of fresh or not-so-fresh meat and vegetables combine with the smells of dirt, human sweat, cigarette tobacco, and the latest French perfume.

I love it.

We arrive in Kabul on an early morning flight from Teheran. From the plane the notoriously treacherous mountains—the Hindu Kush, the Pamirs—look like unassuming piles of snow-whitened red-brown sand. Thirty or more relatives are waiting for us at the Kabul airport—including not one, not two, but three mothers-in-law. Before I can even ask Abdul-Kareem what this means, the entire family is upon us.

It is all very emotional. There is much excitement, many introductions. I think I have been introduced to the same people two or three times. There are tears, smiles, handshakes, bows, and Russian bear hugs.

My (real) mother-in-law, Abdul-Kareem's biological mother, is my father-in-law's *first* wife. Her name is Bebegul. She is a short, full-breasted woman. Her feet seem small. She is wearing a long, loose, comfortable dress under which I can see her Turkish-style trousers.

I immediately want a pair of trousers for my own. Yes, I am eager to go native; I will undoubtedly be more comfortable dressed as a traditional Afghan woman (or man) on the many traveling adventures I have in mind.

Bebegul's lined and weather-beaten face and shoulders are softly framed by a long chiffon veil. She steps forward and kisses me and her son on both cheeks. She searches our faces intensely.

Her husband, Ismail Mohammed, my father-in-law, is an incredibly commanding figure. He stands six feet tall and has dark velvet eyes and thick dark hair only lightly flecked with white at the temples. Ismail Mohammed (or Agha Jan, Dear Father) sports a debonair moustache, an expertly tailored European suit, and an expensive karakul cap. Unlike Bebegul, he belongs to the modern world.

The other women are wearing devastatingly fashionable Western dresses, light scarves, and long coats and are exquisitely poised on high heels. Ismail Mohammed embraces Abdul-Kareem and addresses me in English, "Was the flight pleasant? Are you well rested?" Before our modern-day caravan can set off, an airport official politely but firmly demands that I turn over my American passport.

I refuse.

Everyone stops. Both the official and my husband—whom I trust more than anyone else on Earth—assure me that this is a mere formality. It will soon be returned to me.

"Madam, we will have someone bring it to your home."

I reluctantly relinquish it.

I never see that passport again.

I am now subject to the laws and customs of Afghanistan. I am an Afghan wife. This does not mean that I enjoy the rights of an Afghan (male) citizen; rather, I now belong to one man and his family. I am their property. At the time I do not realize that I will not be able to leave Afghanistan at will or as an American citizen but only if my husband or father-in-law agrees to obtain an Afghan passport for me and allows me to travel out of the Royal Kingdom of Afghanistan.

In the weeks that followed, the Afghan government did not return my American passport to me. It was hard for me to understand and accept that Abdul-Kareem did not share my outrage and alarm. In fact he refused to discuss it. How could I have known that the loss of my American passport in Kabul might lead to further unimaginable difficulties in America?

In 1959 Edward Hunter, who had been an American intelligence agent in World War II, published a book, *The Past Present: A Year in Afghanistan*. It is a psychologically brilliant work; few people seem to have read it. Hunter writes that the only way an Afghan man could have a "love marriage" (in the 1940s and 1950s) was if he "found a foreign girl." If he did, it often constituted a scandal. According to Hunter, "The foreign wives had no idea of what sort of life they were coming into, of the discrimination they would come up against. The government made a point of seizing their foreign passports. Their children did not belong to them, but had to be brought up in accordance with the so-called customs of the country. . . . It was an open secret that many of these young wives were kept pregnant year after year under primitive conditions."

In 1961, the very year I was trapped in Kabul, British-born Robin Jenkins published a novel, *Dust on the Paw,* which describes the hands-off diplomacy practiced by European and American diplomats. Jenkins's narrator describes the fate of a foreign wife whom the British and Americans refuse to help because, as a wife, "she comes under Afghan jurisdiction; we've got no responsibility for her at all . . . by marrying this chap, she virtually put herself beyond our protection." The wife in question does not wear a burqa, "but the rest of the family do, and because she refused, they make her life a hell. She's kept more or less a prisoner. She's not allowed to visit other foreigners. She never has a penny of her own."

At the time I knew nothing about the existence of either book.

The point is this: In 1961 I am a young girl who loves and trusts my husband. I have no way of understanding what the smooth removal of my passport might mean.

I also have absolutely no idea what kind of relationship I am expected to have with my father-in-law or with each of my mothers-in-law.

I have no time to think about these matters right now. The cars are waiting. I am too tired, too wired, and far too excited. We leave the barracks-like airport in a black cavalcade of Mercedes-Benzes.

In 1937 the marvelous British traveler Rosita Forbes wrote, "Kabul has a beauty like nothing else on Earth. Around the plain there are mountains. . . . They are rugged under snow. But on a clear day they are white, and I have never looked at them without surprise. They are nearer to the city than most mountains, and more final. The country needs no other defense."

She was right about the mountains. They are majestic and as never ending as the sea. One is immediately humbled, relieved of responsibility. Here humanity is not in charge of, but is instead embraced by, eternity. Here Nature and God are the main protagonists.

Not that many cars are on the street. I see no tall modern hotels or dazzling modern restaurants. I do see a few ramshackle tea shops (*choi chanas*) along the way, filled with men. No women are on the street—not even women wearing burqas. Kabul seems at least fifty years behind Teheran and not that cosmopolitan.

As yet no nomads and no camels are in view. Small adobe mud dwellings tumble down the side of the mountain, but they are far away. We pass a lovely mosque.

The route chosen ends in a wide Western-style boulevard lined with trees. According to my husband, the high walls, one after the other, hide large and beautiful homes.

Abdul-Kareem's family has a compound, comprised of a number of whitewashed, two-story European-style houses with patios, verandas, and overflowing flower beds. There are fruit trees. A tiny picturesque garden stream runs through the property, and three cows, a cow herder, and some chickens live behind one of the dwellings.

The property also has a seemingly endless number of small one-story structures. An unheated one-room building is where the servants sleep, apparently right on the dirt floor.

My mother-in-law, Bebegul, has converted a series of unheated two-room buildings into quarters for her and her two youngest teenaged sons, Sami and Rafi.

Abdul-Kareem and I will be sleeping in the magnificent house of her oldest son, Hassan, where she once lived. We enter a large and quite formal European living room that's the size of a ballroom. Velvet drapes, vast carpets, a number of couch-like benches line the walls; there are also a few large soft armchairs and small artisan-carved wooden coffee tables.

Turbaned male servants in poorly fitting Western jackets and baggy pants pass around plates of pistachios, raisins, and candies and cups of tea. Large, Russian-style samovars are bubbling merrily.

Bebegul takes me on a tour. Every bedroom is large and is meant to function as a private family apartment, like a bed-sitting room. My brother-in-law Hassan has one. We have another. I believe a third such bed-sitting room is on the second floor—but I am not sure.

The living room, hallways, and bedroom floors are all covered with the most beautifully designed maroon Afghan wool carpets. I come to learn that the carpets are from Baluchistan, Turkmenistan, and Kazakhstan as well as from Afghanistan.

I want to take my shoes off so that I can walk on them in my bare feet.

Bebegul proudly shows me that she has a modern, utterly clean, totally electric kitchen. I will learn that no one ever uses it. The cooking is mainly done outdoors over an open fire or in a fire-breathing ancient wood stove. The house also has two all-marble bathrooms that work, although the water is not always hot.

My bedroom window on the second floor looks out on the Paghman Mountains, the foothills of the mighty Himalayas.

My second mother-in-law lives in her own house. A low fence or wall with a gate separates the first and second wives. Within the same enclosed property my father-in-law lives nearby with his younger third wife and their eight children.

Abdul-Kareem—who, I realize, has disappeared into a crowd of male relatives—manages to find me briefly to tell me that the family's most beautiful house (and one that he covets for himself, for us) is nearby but is being rented by a foreign embassy. When I visit it, I see that the house has latticed, stained-glass windows, marble pillars in the living room, and a British-style library.

The house in which we will live is filled with people. They sit in a huge semicircle of liquid eyes. Abdul-Kareem must be related to all of Kabul, judging by the number of relatives who visit that first afternoon.

Holding my arm, Bebegul moves me around from one group of women to another. She is in a transport of joy and importance.

No conversations are private. This group is one body, one soul, one family, one clan. Whenever someone enters or leaves the room, everyone rises and chants, almost in unison: "*Salom aleikum, khoob hastain chitoor hastam . . . enshallah.*" (Greetings, peace be with you, are you well, are you good, as Allah wills it, so shall it be.) "*Bamanakhoodah, Hodahafez.*" (Good-bye, God be with you.)

My brothers- and sisters-in-law, many in their thirties, execute quick, cringing half-bows as they grab Ismail Mohammed's hand to kiss it. This strikes me as embarrassing and infantile.

How little I understand!

He is their patriarch, their leader, their father, their chieftain who provides sustenance and status. He can do no wrong. He can have them killed. Whatever opportunities they or their children have or will have, beginning with the relatively good lives they enjoy compared to 99.9 percent of the rest of the country, are all thanks to him and none other.

I am unprepared for my first-ever Muslim prayer service. Suddenly, effortlessly, all the men drop to the floor; they are down on all fours, prostrating themselves, placing their foreheads to the ground, facing Mecca, as they begin the midday prayer.

I have never seen Abdul-Kareem pray. He has never gone to a mosque. He does not have a prayer rug or *tasbeh* (prayer beads).

The unified prayer service in the living room is accomplished gracefully but in a masculine way. Their bodies, their minds, their voices, and their souls are all involved in this rather physical spiritual practice. I am so mesmerized, so taken over, that I do not really notice whether the women pray. I am later told that women do not go to the mosque. I learn that women pray at home, alone.

This religion seems very public. It assumes that everyone obeys the laws. Prayer takes place at the appointed hour at home, at work, at school, on the street—as well as in the mosque.

Somehow prayer in America seems more private, certainly for Jews who pray discreetly at home but mainly in synagogues. True, Christians in America begin meals with religious prayers and everyone swears on the Bible when they testify in a courtroom—but neither Abdul-Kareem nor I take religion very seriously. We do not know anyone who does. The major thinkers and artists whom we read and quote are atheists.

Hours pass. I do not see Abdul-Kareem anywhere.

I find myself surrounded by smiling, friendly women. The non-English speakers pat me in a warm and motherly way or simply hug me. This is nice. The French, English, and German speakers ask me what I think of Kabul (who knows? I have yet to see it), where we shopped in Europe, and whether I miss my family.

I grow drowsy. It is a hot afternoon. The room has no air in it. Massive velvet drapes shield us from sunlight. I can't remember anybody's name. I sit quietly, half asleep and half awake. This seems to be quite alright.

The room continues to hum with greetings and tea sipping and comings and goings. After all the small talk has been exhausted, the women yawn, stretch, and look equally dazed. Some women have gone to relax in Bebegul's quarters. They sit on their haunches, elbows on knees, smoking, spitting out nutshells, laughing, and gossiping.

I am only twenty years old, and I am now a member of this household, which consists of one patriarch, three wives, twenty-one children (who range in age from infancy to their thirties), two grandchildren, at least one son-in-law, one daughter-in-law, and an unknown number of servants and relatives.

Our first meal in Afghanistan is an unbelievable feast. As I will later learn, a special cook was hired for the occasion. It looks like every conceivable Afghan dish is on display. We eat on the floor, cross-legged, on lovely tablecloths placed over the carpets.

By now I am no stranger to this food. For two years, whenever Abdul-Kareem and his male countrymen would get homesick, they would cook traditional Afghan food for us. I have had my share of *pilaus* and *chilaus* (rice dishes) piled high, flavored with saffron or garlic, and eaten with yoghurt. From the moment we first met, Abdul-Kareem cooked for me, as did his friends, most of whom were unmarried or in New York City without their wives. They cooked hearty soups and turned simple vegetables, like cauliflower and eggplant, into dishes fit for a sultan.

The parade of platters is impressive and never ending. There is shish kebob, which, I learn, is rarely served at home but can be bought all over Kabul. There are maybe six *different* kinds of white and yellow and brown rice dishes. Hidden in one pilau one might find a whole boiled chicken, a roasted duck—even a goose. Some dishes are flavored with fried onions and topped with almonds and grapes. There are platters of fried eggplant served with rich gobs of sour cream; juicy fat stuffed cabbage; *kofte* (meatballs) served with spicy salads; stuffed dumplings.

For dessert we have the most delicious fruit I have ever tasted: luscious grapes, hybrid melons, lemon-oranges, all of which are accompanied by cups of sweet custard topped with floating rose petals. Baklava, French pastries, and soft, sweet, and sticky candies end the meal.

And still, after all this, fresh offerings of pistachios are served, more tea is called for. We are also offered cold fruit juices.

At the appointed hour my father-in-law rises, and when he does, everyone else rises, too. He again embraces me and Abdul-Kareem and leaves with his third wife and their infant son. Not once have I seen him talk to Bebegul.

Thereafter the second wife and her set of children depart as well.

Bebegul's own family remains: her sons, daughters, daughter-in-law, son-in-law, and grandchildren—all linger on. My new brothers- and sisters-in-law mimic Ismail Mohammed's roving eye and crafty ways. I am captivated by their comic inventiveness. They put me at my ease by laughing about the three wives.

Abdul-Kareem has been talking nonstop in Dari (Afghan Persian) for at least ten hours now. Other than a few hurried whispers, we have not really spoken to each other or sat near each other. He is in his element. He seems happy to be with his family, happy that they have given him such a grand reception.

Finally we are alone in our rooms. The night is dark and almost completely silent. We are standing on what Abdul-Kareem tells me is "the roof of the world." We are nearly 6,000 feet above sea level. The stars are clustered like golden grapes and literally seem within reach. We are too exhausted to speak. We fall asleep in our clothes.

When I awake the next morning, the sun is blazing into the room. I immediately look out the window—and there they still are: my white-peaked majestic mountains, part of the vast Himalayas.

Abdul-Kareem is gone. I am completely alone. I open the door and see that, hours ago, a servant left breakfast right outside the door. He is still sitting at the end of the hall, waiting for me to get up. I gesture: The tea is cold, and the bread is stiff. Can I have coffee? He smiles, rushes off, and returns bearing a new tray with warm flat bread (nan), coffee, a small pat of butter, and a selection of pastries from yesterday's feast.

Life is good.

TWO

The Imprisoned Bride

I have put off writing about what comes next for a very long time. Reluctantly I take out my old tattered diary with the brown plastic cover and look at what I wrote when I was twenty. More than half a century later, the writing embarrasses me. The contents are also heartbreaking. I am afraid that reading my diary, and writing about the events it briefly records, will force me to remember what I have spent years trying to forget. It happened, it's over, I survived, let's move on.

The psychotherapist in me knows that I am resisting. I do not want to be overwhelmed again by a clash of cultures, one that was unanticipated and for which I was totally unprepared. If only Abdul-Kareem had prepared me or acknowledged that the task before me would be difficult and frightening. He did not do so.

In 1920, when Saira Elizabeth Luiza MacKenzie Shah, aka Morag Murray Abdullah, and her Afghan husband, Sirdar Iqbal Ali Shah, were about to cross the border into the tribal no-man's land between India and Afghanistan, she wrote:

> I looked back at the last outpost of my own people and knew there would be no possibility of my return if the odds went against me. My husband I think sensed my feelings. "Welcome," he said, "to the land of my fathers."
>
> It broke the spell. It reassured me. "Syed [Sirdar]," I said, "I trust you. You realize I am friendless here and have only you."

Syed promised to protect her with his life. But then, as they "passed finally out of sight of the last British post," Syed said, "There is still time to go back if you regret your decision. Time for *us* to go back."

Abdul-Kareem made no such chivalrous proclamation. We never even discussed what my life might be like in Kabul, even on a temporary basis. I still had a semester of college to complete. I believed that the two of us would embark on adventures, like the explorers of a bygone era. Abdul-Kareem had allowed me to believe this.

But I had ignored each and every warning sign to the contrary: His distracted restlessness in Europe, his suddenly reduced budget, his obvious joy at being embraced by his family, his utter dependence upon his father and the government for money.

I expected to meet his family, but I also believed that we would travel across the entire country: forging rivers, crossing deserts, perhaps summiting mountains, memorizing Persian poetry beside campfires. Instead my time in Afghanistan was characterized by a lack of adventure and only a minimal exposure to the country.

This is how most Afghan women experience life—they don't. Few rural women venture beyond their own village or garden plot or courtyard. The same is true for most city women—except if they are allowed to accompany their fathers abroad when they are young. Their subsequent adjustment to purdah and life beneath the burqa is also traumatic.

It's not just what happened—or what didn't happen—that matters. It is that Abdul-Kareem treated living in the tenth century as completely normal, in fact as somehow superior to life in America. His refusal to discuss my situation was maddening. But how could he? A discussion would force him to acknowledge that his country, where he hoped to make his mark, was medieval and that our lives—my life in particular—would be very different from what they would have been in America.

The excitement of our arrival took at least three days to wear off. More relatives kept coming in a steady stream. Essentially we sat around as if it were a wake. I found this was the Afghan way of socializing: to sit silently, attentively, unselfconsciously, happily, for two or three hours, rising every time someone new comes in, at which time one repeats the standard greetings.

The warm and friendly family faces, the inescapable mountains, the hovering heavens filled with brightly polished stars, the unexpected luxury of my surroundings, even the food, all confirmed that my grand adventure had begun.

On my first morning (it would never happen again), Bebegul and Fawziya, Hassan's sweet and lovely wife, join me for breakfast. The immediate family has two, possibly three Fawziyas and multiple Mohammeds, much as an Italian family has many Johns.

In addition to the usual fare, the cook has prepared some eggs for me that Bebegul insists I eat. Fingering her prayer beads, she stares at me as I chew. She will often stare at me. It is disquieting. The eggs are a bow to the West. In Kabul women do not have eggs for breakfast. It is considered a European custom.

For two days I happily eat the leftovers from our feast. On the third day the household meals return to their normal fare. For me this is a disaster. The cook, like every Afghan cook, uses ghee, an evil-smelling, rancid clarified animal-fat butter that is left unrefrigerated. It is their cooking oil.

It is loved and considered to be a healthy local delicacy. No one would dream of using Crisco, which the specially hired chef had used for our first meal. Most foreigners, who have not grown up with ghee, abhor the taste of it, partly because ghee wreaks considerable havoc on soft foreign stomachs. The smell makes some foreigners nauseous; others throw up after a few mouthfuls. I literally could not eat anything cooked in ghee.

The daily routine is as follows: In the morning Abdul-Kareem and the men disappear and are gone all day. The women mainly stay at home. The servants clean and cook. Bebegul stays in her own quarters and sews and hums to herself. She orders her servants about, checks on their work, sits in the garden.

Every day I have lunch with Hassan's wife, Fawziya, and her children in their family quarters. Sometimes, but only rarely, Bebegul joins us. The meals never vary. They consist of a rice-based dish with a spicy tomato-based sauce studded with chunks of lamb or chicken. I drink cup after cup of tea and devour the flat bread (nan). I live on nuts, dried fruits, and yoghurt.

If I can remain on such a wholesome diet, I might easily live to a ripe old age, just like the Hunzas nearby, in Shangri-La.

Abdul-Kareem's older sister, also named Fawziya, is staying on for a while. She is fearfully elegant with a beehive hairdo and an aristocratically Semitic nose. She smokes cigarettes with an elaborate holder but "never in front of my father," she assures me.

Bebegul's daughter Fawziya can speak broken English and German. Hassan's wife, Fawziya, and I speak in French and a little bit in English. She has been appointed to keep me company.

Every day I pace the garden, back and forth, forth and back; I visit every tree: the apricot tree, plum tree, apple tree, cherry tree. I visit the flowers. I ask everyone—the servants, the children, the wives—to tell me the name of each tree and flower in Dari. "*Chee-as?*" (What is this?)

Next I visit Bebegul and watch her sew.

Then I sit outside on the second-story terrace and read and read and read.

Finally on the fourth day I tell Hassan's wife, Fawziya, that I have to go out.

And I get up to leave.

I am a young American girl used to getting out and doing things on my own. I have been taking public transportation by myself in New York City since I was ten years old. I am not used to having a driver. I am not used to staying at home. I am not used to being in the company of only women. But most of all I am not used to being without my constant companion and soul mate, who has become something of a husband missing in action.

"I must see the city, the people, the bazaar," I explain in French.

She replies happily, "Oh, then we must go to the tailor and have some clothes made for you."

She claps her hands, a servant appears—but no driver is available at the moment. Fawziya tells me that Abdul-Kareem will arrange everything for tomorrow.

"Why can't I just take a walk? Why don't you come with me? We'll go together."

Hassan's Fawziya, a mild and gentle soul, looks confused and then a bit terrified. Finally she says, "Why not talk to your husband? Ask *him* to take you on a tour of the city."

Thus I discover that upper-class Afghan women do not simply go out. Here "going out" means that a woman first dresses up and puts on a soft chiffon headscarf and a long but fashionable coat—she might even don gloves. Usually she does not spend time browsing in the bazaar the way foreign (*ferengi*) women do.

No matter how hot it is, she does not appear in public with her arms or legs bare. She makes a specific appointment, keeps it, the male driver waits for her, and then he returns her safely home. My female relatives never, ever do their own food shopping.

That is a job for male servants. Only poor and servantless women face shame and danger by having to wait in line amid rowdy and sexually aggressive male servants. As women they are often repeatedly kicked to the back of the line as new male servants arrive. To avoid prying male eyes and leering attention, these women often prefer to wear burqas.

An Afghan woman who walks or shops alone is seen as proclaiming either her sexual availability or her husband's and father's poverty. A male servant and a female relative are the minimum requirements for any proper Afghan woman who shops in the bazaar.

Although Afghan women were emancipated from their ghostly, full-length burqas in 1958–59 (and, before that, in 1929), social custom still demands that they wear headscarves and coats at all times. Those who eschew these garments are yelled at and followed.

Some women who go out alone also wear the burqa as a way of shielding themselves from the dust and dirt—although their shoes still take the brunt of it. I suppose that some women enter this airless, claustrophobic, moveable prison (or sensory deprivation chamber) for what they believe are religious reasons or simply out of habit.

In 1960, only a year before I arrived, the British mountaineers Joyce Dunsheath and Eleanor Baillie wrote, "In the cities [in Afghanistan], strangely enough, the veiled woman is still the rule rather than the exception; only the young girl is usually in modern dress. The Afghan chaudris . . . are in soft colourings, blues, greens, rust, wine, grey, for instance, usually of silk. . . . Less than six months before our expedition started little girls had been killed in Kandahar in riots over the [chaudri] question, we heard."

I heard that the government had to kill mullahs who were rioting over this issue in 1958–59. One hears things that cannot easily be substantiated.

To my Afghan relatives, so used to this way of life, I seem like an impatient, demanding, nervous, immoral, and potentially dangerous young woman. Why am I not content or at least resigned? From their point of view the women in their family are leading utterly enviable lives. They are never, ever hungry. In fact they are well nourished. They are not servants—they *have* servants. They do not have to labor in the fields or at the loom. They do not have to take care of farm animals from dawn to dusk. They can retain something of their youth for a longer period of time.

They have access to doctors—if absolutely necessary, even doctors and private clinics out of the country. They have the best midwifery and obstetrical care the country can provide. True, they do not have advanced educations or independent careers. True, as I quickly discover, their marriages have been arranged, and they married when they were still quite young. This in no way seems to offend them.

Why should it? None of Ismail Mohammed's daughters have been forced to marry illiterate or impoverished men. All their husbands are relatively well-to-do. No one's husband is a polygamist. Ismail Mohammed's sons have not taken second wives. My female relatives cannot imagine life without a husband and children. That would not be a life; that would be a living death.

One of Abdul-Kareem's sisters has no children, but her husband will not divorce her, nor will he take a second wife. The family is a bit scandalized by this. Clearly they must love each other. It is considered unseemly.

My female relatives are enviable ladies of leisure who lead prestigious and busy social lives. They visit other female relatives and receive visits from them all the time. They drink tea, spit out the shells of nuts, eat little squares of ghee-soaked cakes.

I keep to myself, spend time alone in my room, look unhappy, and want something that women cannot have in Afghanistan. I want my freedom. I want to do things on my own, alone, or at least with my husband.

Five days into my "sentence," I start visiting Bebegul regularly, twice a day. At least that's a short walk from the main house. Oddly I have never seen her talk to her husband. Whenever he visits our house, which isn't often, she keeps a reverent distance from him. Instead she embraces his third wife, Meena, and croons over Meena's infant son, clapping every five minutes for a servant. Bebegul has nothing else to say to her husband. For his part he never even looks at her.

It will be a while before I start hearing versions of what happened between my mother-in-law and her husband. Sometimes when we are alone, Bebegul points quite suddenly to Meena's house—which is some distance away. Dropping her prayer beads, Bebegul chants her husband's name over and over again: "Agha Jan, Agha Jan, Agha Jan." (Dear Father, Dear Father, Dear Father.)

I have no idea what she is trying to convey to me. Have her shame and humiliation driven her mad? Is she telling me that her husband is with another woman and that she absolutely cannot accept this? Is she laughing at him? Is she worshipping him?

I start trying to learn the language. I ask for a tutor. Until one arrives, Bebegul and Hassan's wife, Fawziya, teach me Dari phrases and names for things. We walk around the house, and I point to something, and they tell me the name for it in Dari. I make a list of all these words in phonetic English. I still have that list. A face is a *roose*. Eyes are *cheesm.* A chin is *zanak.* A cow is a *jow.* A village is a *kor.* "It's hot" is *"hawa garm ast."* We live in or on Hojamullah, and the bazaar is in Jadai Maiwand.

At night I try my Dari words out on Abdul-Kareem. This makes him laugh. It is clear that I need more formal instruction. He says that it will "all be arranged if only I am patient."

This waiting is hard for me. Words mean everything to me. I love to talk and to be understood. I love to understand what people are saying. Such exchanges are my lifeline. Here I am never alone—yet I feel like I am in isolation as well as under house arrest.

My situation: More than a week has passed, and I am still in purdah. My belly is bloated with tea, my tongue is shriveled from the delicious salted pistachio nuts.

I've watched the servants cook and clean, beat clothes and wash them in the garden stream, and make what will become the most wonderful yoghurt: They put the processed milky cheese into a pouch and hang it outside on a tree branch. It is delicious when eaten with pilau or chilau. Even now I usually ask for yoghurt to accompany the rice dishes in Turkish, Persian, Indian, and Afghan restaurants in America.

I've sat through hours of conversation among the women that I don't quite understand. I've listened to radio programs from India and China. One night I enjoyed a concert of classical Indian music—live—from New Delhi. I've already mastered the art of sitting politely for hours without understanding what people are saying. I've learned how to sit and not move. I am learning some Eastern-style patience, something that requires the practitioner to enter into a state of relaxed passivity and receptivity.

My true and only joy, reading, is seen as an act of despair or as a traitorous activity. Whenever I close my door and settle down with a book, I am invariably interrupted.

"Sister-in-law, are you unhappy? Do you want to play cards?" asks Rafi, one of my teenaged brothers-in-law, who is always home early from school.

Hassan's Fawziya gently trails into my bedroom suite with her two small children in tow, sits down on the carpet, and starts her routine of smiling and conversation in French.

I am trying to read *War and Peace* and do not wish to be disturbed. I explain that I am perfectly happy—*"Choob, choob,"* *"Je suis joyeux, cette est très jolie por moi"*—that everyone in college reads books all the time, that Abdul-Kareem and I used to sit side by side and do all our reading together, that even in high school—actually, since I was small—I have been reading books.

It is my delight and my salvation.

But here everything is done together: There is no such thing as privacy. This means that no one—absolutely no one—is shut out. Children and old people are all included in everything. But private activities—reading, wanting to spend time alone with one's husband—are seen as strange and suspicious acts. If someone chooses to stay alone, she must either be unhappy or untrustworthy. Who knows what she might be thinking or even plotting?

Night after night, sitting at the table (well, cross-legged on the floor), my nerves are worn thin with boredom and hunger. I say so. I say out loud for all to hear:

"I am really very hungry."

A few members of the family express sympathy for my plight, but no one does anything.

Two weeks into my captivity and I have gone out only twice. Both times it was with a small entourage that accompanied me to the tailor, who considered my choice of Afghan materials an insult to his European training. He carpets his shop for me with yards of British, German, and French fabrics.

I want sari-like materials for some long stay-at-home dresses, and I want a long soft tunic and Turkish "bo-peep" pants, but, other than Bebegul, the women in my family do not dress like that. The sari silks, which would probably fetch exorbitant prices in Bergdorf's or Bloomingdale's, are never worn. My female relatives wear only the most expensive English and German wool, French chiffon, lace, and satin, and the finest American mixed fibers. And, if I am to accompany Abdul-Kareem to embassy dinners, or to dinners at the palace, then I must be properly attired.

I am bored. I am *so* bored. I am puzzled. I do not understand why Abdul-Kareem does not take me along with him into the city. When I ask him to do so, he accuses me of wanting to ruin it for him; his position is perilous, and one false move from me can ruin it for him forever. As it turns out, he was right—but at the time I experienced being shut out as an insult and a rejection.

I did not yet understand that women have absolutely no place in the public, all-male environment. Had Abdul-Kareem brought me along, that would have proved that he had become a Westerner, rejected Afghan tradition—and could not control his wife.

It is still summer. It is quite hot. I decide to sunbathe on the terrace that adjoins our bedroom. I remember my bikini to this day. I bought it on East 57th Street in Manhattan. Abdul-Kareem loved it. It was very, very skimpy.

So, here I am, lying on a low chaise lounge, wearing sunglasses, drinking an iced fruit drink, and reading my damned book, when suddenly I hear a loud commotion inside. It sounds like men are yelling at each other. Then more men are yelling.

Suddenly, and totally unexpectedly, Abdul-Kareem (who is always at the bank or at the office or at some ministry appointment during the day) bursts through the doors.

"What do you think you're doing? You have managed to upset all of Kabul."

I am glad to see him so early in the day.

"What are you talking about?"

It seems that some workmen who are building a house about a quarter of a mile away caught sight of what they thought was a naked woman and could no longer concentrate on their work. A delegation had descended upon our house to demand that all women, especially the woman on the roof (me), be properly dressed.

I start laughing.

Abdul-Kareem is gentle. He must be desperate.

He says, "Please, please just come in and put something on. In fact stay off the terrace for today. These are illiterate, uneducated, religious men with a peasant mentality. Rumors spread here quickly. By tonight they'll be telling their friends that we are running a brothel."

Oh, Dorothy. You are no longer in Kansas.

What to do? Well, now that I've visited Bebegul steadily and exclusively for two weeks, I decide I can pay my respects to Tooba, the second wife. She lives far more modestly and goes to great lengths to serve me a European-style tea. She has two children, a son, Samir, and a daughter, Rabia.

I have been told that when she married Agha Jan, she lived with Bebegul at some point and that Bebegul treated her as badly as she treats her current crop of female servants. That means she cursed her, undoubtedly hit her, made nonstop demands, and then complained about her to my father-in-law.

The Scottish convert, Saira Shah, on her way to Mecca, describes a rather hellish Saudi Arabian harem, the rivalries between the fertile and infertile wives, the mothers of sons versus those with none: "If a woman has no sons or has been disagreeable to her [the mother of the firstborn], she will taunt her in the hundreds of ways the flowery elasticity of the Arabic language allows."

Why did Agha Jan marry a second time?

Bebegul and Ismail Mohammed (Agha Jan) are cousins. They are distant cousins, Abdul-Kareem tells me, but somehow I doubt this; I bet they are first or second cousins.

In any event Bebegul comes from a more well-to-do branch of the family. At one point her father had been the postmaster of Kabul. Abdul-Kareem told me that Bebegul would tell "stories about how they used to open letters [even in those days!] and censor the mail. She had seen her father and brothers do this."

At first the newlyweds lived in Kabul, then in Herat, a city they came to love and where Agha Jan served as the revenue officer. In other words he was in charge of the treasury. Just to understand what life was like in the late 1920s, Abdul-Kareem tells me what his mother has told him: "'There were no cars or trucks in those days. We had to travel on horse-back from Kabul to get to my husband in Herat. Along the way, my mother (Abdul-Kareem's maternal grandmother) died. We had to bury her by the roadside. Because we had children with us in our caravan, it took us thirty days to make the 1,200-mile journey.'"

After four years of marriage, during which two or three daughters had already been born, my father-in-law took a second wife. Many years after my time in Kabul, I ask Abdul-Kareem why his father remarried two more times.

First he says that he will not criticize his father.

Then he says that his father "felt sorry" for the second wife, who had fallen in love with him. She was a neighbor, and he was temporarily in Kabul but without his wife and children. Abdul-Kareem says that she tricked him into marriage.

"You must remember that at that time in Afghanistan it was very important for a man to have a son."

Perhaps because Bebegul had had only daughters, and Ismail Mohammed was in search of a son, he dallied with the neighbor; perhaps she indeed became pregnant. But Bebegul soon gave birth to a boy. In fact both wives probably gave birth to sons at about the same time.

Why my father-in-law took a third wife remains shrouded in mystery. Over the years I have heard rumors, half-truths, and suspected truths about his motives.

Bebegul had been disobedient in some important way, and he married again to punish and humble her; surely her sons would blame her for the rest of her life for all the additional co-brothers. Ismail Mohammed married the third wife because she fit into his economic or political plans. He married again because he needed a much younger and fertile wife—he wanted more children.

Ismail Mohammed is a religious man. There is not much night life in Kabul or Herat. Upstanding religious men have to marry the woman with whom they wish to sleep.

The day after I visited Tooba, the second wife, I make my way over to the third, currently reigning, and still fertile third wife, Meena. I find the visit shocking and inexplicable.

A duplicate high-ceilinged, ballroom-like living room exists there. This is where Agha Jan entertains, takes his meals, and reads his newspapers and business reports. It is carpeted richly in maroon and has thick velvet curtains at every window. Low wicker, wood, and brass tea tables stand near each of the plush European couches.

One of his daughters, fourteen-year-old Zohra, brings him all his meals. She bows in and out as if she is his personal servant. She is. Ismail Mohammed prefers to eat alone.

However, his children, whom I visit next, sleep on urine-soaked mattresses in rooms that used to be the servant quarters. The children wear clothes that are too baggy or too skimpy. Some have heads that are too big, others are too skinny. All have chronic colds or eye, ear, or leg infections. One fourteen-year-old is disabled with rheumatism.

They seem to be afraid of their father. But they also dote on him. Their mother, Meena, the daughter of an important conservative mullah, smilingly presides over this considerable chaos. She is a buxom, good-natured woman who sports flashy gold earrings, even when she is wearing her at-home costume of a cheap flowered acetate housedress and bedroom slippers.

The juxtaposition of the visible luxury enjoyed by Agha Jan and the destitution and servility of his children shocks me. Later my youngest brothers-in-law tell me the following: Laughingly, triumphantly, they say that Agha Jan wanted to save time and money with Meena's sons (their half-brothers), so he had four of his sons circumcised on the same day, when they were between the ages of eight and fourteen.

With contempt and giggles they tell me that these poor boys couldn't sleep the night before—and that they had such bowel movements the air practically turned green and the stink stayed for days. Why are they telling me this? To prove that Agha Jan loves them, the sons of the first wife, more than he loves the sons of his third wife? Are they saying that this love will translate into more of an inheritance for them or into better marriage matches?

Behind the walls of this family compound, what I view as cruelty is normalized and accepted. I tell Abdul-Kareem what I have witnessed.

He does not say that I'm imagining or exaggerating anything, but he will not discuss it. In fact he tells me only to keep my opinions to myself.

"How can your father treat his own children this way?" I ask. "And what about me: Can't you see that I am miserable and really hungry, starving? Why can't I cook for myself with Crisco? Why is the modern electric kitchen never used? Why can't we buy food that I can eat? I'll settle for tuna fish, Huntley and Palmer biscuits, anything in a can."

"You can't act differently. You have to fit in. They are watching us, waiting for us to make a mistake. Then it will be all over for me."

He says: "For me." He does not say: "For us."

"Abdul-Kareem, you cannot force me to eat what I can't eat. My adjustment to life in Kabul cannot be measured in digestive terms. It's not humanly possible."

He is quiet.

"Alright, tomorrow [this means I will have to wait until the evening, when he returns] I'll try to pick up some food for you. I think I know where there are good tinned cheeses and packaged cakes. But please keep it all out of sight, and don't eat it at meal times. It will only lead to a lot of talk."

"This is too crazy for me. So the high walls here are meant to shut everyone in and shut everyone out. No one is meant to see what goes on behind these walls, and no woman is supposed to see anything on the outside."

"Please don't ruin it for me," he says.

Again, he talks only about himself, as if *we* no longer exist, as if *he* means the two of us.

And now he sounds desperate.

"Look. This will all be changing. It has already begun to change. But, you, you are an American who has no patience and no perspective."

When did I become "the American"? When did he start fearing and mistrusting the very country and woman he had claimed to love? He continues.

"I have news that will cheer you up. The family wants us to have a 'real' wedding."

Well, I would love another feast cooked in Crisco. I would love a party. This time I will find foreigners who speak English to join us.

But what does a real wedding here mean? I will have no family and no Afghan ancestors or living relatives at my side. And who will perform this rite? A mullah? I am not a Muslim. Will I have to convert to Islam in order to obtain my next edible meal?

That's what's missing. There is no Jewish sense of humor here.

THREE

Burqas

When I was in Kabul, I had no idea that I was living at the center of the universe—at least that's what it was, back when the world was flat. I was at the crossroad where the East literally met the West. Traders traveled the Silk Road right through Afghanistan as they moved their precious gems, spices, skins, and silks back and forth between China, Russia, Persia, India, Turkey, and Europe.

Looking at the tattered diary that I began in Kabul, I am amazed by how much I understood at so young an age and by how carefully I observed everything around me. As a writer, I am also embarrassed by it. Sometimes I can't even understand what I am trying to say.

One thing is clear: I was writing about the punishment of free thought and free speech in Afghanistan—almost twenty years before Khomeini's Islamist revolution and more than forty years before critics of Islam—even Muslim critics, especially Muslim critics—would be demonized as Islamophobic, threatened with death, and censored. I used the word *patriarchal* long before feminism arose again in America. Now, fifty years later, I cannot imagine how or where I found this word. It certainly allowed me to accurately describe the treatment of women in Afghanistan.

Years later, back in America, I often wanted to say: "You think that *we* are oppressed by patriarchy here? Please allow me to describe the lives of Afghan women." For a long time I never said this publicly. I am saying it now.

But I also want to add something: American women are far more privileged and much safer than Afghan women, but that does not mean that we do not live in a patriarchal culture. We do.

There. Now I have offended everybody.

I continued my little diary for nearly a decade, trying to make sense of what had happened in Kabul. Here I am, uncensored, the day after my twenty-first birthday. The title page looks like this:

A Record of Unhappy Events
Or
My Afghan Sojourn
Or
Marriage is for One
Or
Notes for a cynical novel to be written by a thirtyish woman imperson-
ating a woman long since dead.

I am nearly seven thousand miles away from home and centuries back-
ward in time. Afghanistan is conservative on the outside, corrupt on
the inside. And Abdul-Kareem is drinking that cup of tea, the cup that
never ends but that weighs the stomach down so that it need not raise
itself up until tomorrow or the day after tomorrow (pas fardah) *or the*
day after that.

> *The fabled dirt and dust are real. So is the unexpected elegance.*
But I am surrounded by grinding, deadening apathy and passivity. I
do not think that anyone reads books. The servants are illiterate. My
mother-in-law and brothers-in-law are cruel to others. They are also
surprisingly vain and act as if they are superior to other living beings.

> *I have no freedom at all. No opportunity to meet anyone or go*
anywhere. His family watches me suspiciously. Am I getting paranoid?
No, they are afraid that if I am not brought to heel, tamed, that I will
ruin their family's reputation. I was a fool to believe that I could have a
cultural or intellectual life here. Maybe Abdul-Kareem, if he is allowed
to travel, will have such a life. Not me. I am an Afghan wife now.

> *My two sisters-in-law are warm and charming and dress like Eu-*
ropeans. They always kiss me on both cheeks each and every time we
see each other, even though we are living together.

> *But my mother-in-law, Bebegul, is very strange. Sometimes*
she just stares at me. It feels hostile, judgmental. Sometimes she
barges in when I'm undressing or changing, as if the sight of my

*nakedness helps her live over in her imagination my—or perhaps her
own—deflowering.*

*In our first real conversation (which we held partly in French,
partly in English, partly in Farsi/Dari, partly in German, partly in pan-
tomime, and with the help of an interpreter), Bebegul told me, over and
over again, about her long friendship with the Sharbans.*

Her point was that they are Jews and their leaving Afghanistan for
Israel and America made her very sad. She cried out: "Sharban," point-
ing at herself, then at me, smiling and mock-sighing to emphasize her
feeling of loss.

She immediately followed up this information with a request that I
convert to Islam. She told me:

"There is one God and Mohammed is his Prophet and Moses—
Moses is also his Prophet."

This last sentence she offered up with such hope, such sudden
mad friendship, that I impulsively told her I would think about it. She
kissed me, then went and dragged her prayer rugs out, demanding that
I choose one.

When I tell Abdul-Kareem that his mother has begun a conversion
campaign he says nothing. He pretends not to hear me. He leaves the
room.

It would be many decades before I would learn that a conversion to
Islam is pro forma for any infidel woman who marries a Muslim.

In the years immediately following the First World War, the Afghan
chieftain father of Sirdar Iqbal Ali Shah refused to bless his marriage to
the Scottish infidel Saira MacKenzie, unless she converted to Islam and
could also "hold the fort if called upon."

As the daughter of a Scottish Highlander, Saira knew how to use a
rifle. And she had already "embraced the Muslim faith with its simple
belief in the unity of God and the prophethood of Mohammed." In the
1920s Saira had no problem with wearing a burqa. She made it sound
like a regal, very princessy, thing to have to do.

When I was in Kabul, family members told me many times that
in the past certain foreign wives had voluntarily taken to wearing the
burqa. These wives were presented as great women: uncomplaining,
self-sacrificing, and wise in the ways of what would please their Afghan
families.

I will not even wear the lovely long chiffon headscarves discreetly
laid out for me. I do not like hats or scarves. They are too establishment,

too grown-up for me. My sisters-in-law wear fashionable European clothing. In terms of appearance I am also something of a disappointment to my brothers-in-law because I do not prize glamorous Western fashion.

I am judged only by my appearance. Next I will be judged on whether I can produce sons. As a dark-eyed, dark-haired Jew, I might have passed as exotic—in Sweden. Here, in the land of the thousand tribes, women (and men) have skins that range in color from brown to gold to olive to fair; hair that ranges in color from jet black to blonde and red; eyes that are green, gray, blue, and black liquid velvet.

Afghan faces are living testaments to the many immigrants and conquerors who have passed through the country. Here I am only a regular, nondescript, could-pass-for-Afghan woman.

Abdul-Kareem's second-oldest brother, Reza, who has studied in England, tells me quite dispassionately, "I've asked Abdul-Kareem many times why he brought you here. Doesn't he understand that a Western girl could never fit in?"

It is nearly two months without any freedom or privacy. My mother-in-law Bebegul is vicious towards her servants. My father-in-law treats his sons and daughters as servants. The sons all want their father's money and attention. They are married to him, they are his truest wives. Hassan does not seem to talk to his wife, at least not when anyone else is there.

I blame myself. I fear that I have managed to find another dangerous family. And they keep promising a wedding for us.

I have written "Promised wedding" in the margin of the diary. Clearly, this must have meant something to me. But why would I even want a wedding when it is so clear that I do not belong here?

It is difficult to know the date not only because everyone follows a Muslim, not a Gregorian, calendar but because today is like yesterday, the days melt into each other—no, "melt" is too soft a word. Rather, the days shatter into each other like large rocks, one after the other, along the road of time. Am I dreaming? Am I awake? I am alone. I am lost in a large, dark cave. I cannot find the exit.

I married someone else. I don't know who this husband is. But I do want to see the city, the camels, the nomads, the men on bicycles, the stalls, the tea-houses (choi chanas). *I want to hear the singing birds in the bazaar.*

And so I finally escape. Looking both ways, I walk out feeling like a criminal. I pass a kebob stand and a sweets seller. As I walk, the mountains fill me with awe, and the air is clear and fresh. I have no idea how to get to the bazaar so I take a bus that seems to be going in the right direction.

The buses are fancifully painted, riotously emblazoned with designs, sunrises, amulets, colors galore. I board one. The driver stares at me. I smile at him. He jerks his head in the direction of the back of the bus.

At first I think I see only a pile of clothing back there, but eerily the clothing, which is huddled together, is actually moving. Oh, my God! This is not clothing—these are women, all huddled together, wearing burqas, balancing babies and bundles in the female-only section. I am horrified, slightly hysterical.

Women literally have to sit at the back of the bus. This is before Rosa Parks, before the American civil rights movement begins in earnest. At dinner I can talk of nothing else. My relatives look away. Abdul-Kareem insists that I am "prone to exaggeration," and "overly dramatic." Then he hisses at me.

"If you are only patient and quiet, you will see changes around here that will surpass anything you've ever seen in America."

He honestly believes that the burqas and the gender segregation (or gender apartheid, as I call it), will, soon enough, disappear. He defends Afghanistan against my "American superiority."

"You Americans are so quick to criticize. But we are not savages. In many ways we are far more advanced than you are in America. Here we do not throw our elders away. Here we do not divorce our wives. Here we know things about life, about hospitality, that you Americans will never be able to emulate."

He has a point. But have I become an American so that Abdul-Kareem can again become an Afghan? Am I his necessary foil, his sacrifice, so that he can reenter the Middle Ages and rise?

I think that Abdul-Kareem is scared. He is a different person. What have they done to him?

Twenty years later Abdul-Kareem and I are talking in my Manhattan apartment. He insists that the moment I left Kabul—well, perhaps five years after my departure—a "goddam revolution" had taken place and naked-faced Afghan Muslim women walked the streets of Kabul just as women did in Paris or New York.

"C'mon, my second wife worked at an embassy and drove around Kabul in her own convertible. She was never veiled. There were women wearing miniskirts on the streets. The Russians ruined all that."

I say: "Abdul-Kareem, your second wife may have been born a Muslim, but she was not an Afghan woman. And the Russians were the ones who insisted on female literacy and education. They were the ones who'd indoctrinated Afghans with such beliefs. And, as for the miniskirts: I don't think of them as a sign of women's liberation."

Fifty years later I am sitting with a very knowledgeable woman who once lived in Kabul. She too insists that the late 1960s–1970s was a time of women's liberation. Maybe it's true, maybe for one bright and shining decade some social progress was made.

As proof she shows me a government publication from the early 1970s that has photos of women wearing only headscarves (hijab), or work-related headgear like nurses' caps, rather than burqas. I laugh. Then I say, "Most of these photos look carefully posed. They are meant to make Afghanistan look modern. The government was backing modernization at the time. But look how little spontaneity there is, especially in the street scenes."

She pressures me. I relent. "Okay," I laugh, "the rules regarding female dress codes were relaxed for educated city women in the late 1960s and 1970s, but that's it. Then the Soviets invaded, and the mujahideen and the Taliban returned women to the back of the bus and to their ghostly sheets."

Maybe I resist acknowledging this early and genuine Arab Spring (so to speak) because I regret having missed it. But with the knowledge of hindsight I also know how fragile and short-lived this progress was.

I am now looking at an online photograph taken in Kabul in 1972. It depicts women in burqas on Jadi Maiwand, one of the main streets of the city. Perhaps some women were indeed naked faced in Kabul. Others, like the women in this photo, were not.

In 1969 Kodansha published a book of photos taken in Afghanistan as part of its *Beautiful World* series. In 1967 the author, Masatoshi Konishi, and the Tokyo University Group spent two months in the country; they took 106 beautiful photos of mosques, ruins, and holy sites; 67 photos depict people—mainly Afghan men. The public space still seems rather womanless.

Only fifteen photos (22 percent) show female children, teenagers, and one elderly woman. Most, even the children, are wearing hijabs; many are wearing burqas. Konishi misidentifies what is clearly a child bride as a "seventeen year old" posed with her "twenty six year old husband." The child, who looks twelve, is smiling, wearing a headscarf, but she is sitting on a bench, perhaps to disguise their too-obvious height difference.

Perhaps there was a golden time, when some Afghan women wore short skirts and went out on dates and had boyfriends in Kabul. . . . Somehow, I still find this hard to believe, given my own experience and given what I now know about the history of Afghanistan.

In 1928 the Afghan king, Amanullah Khan, scandalized his own people when he urged Afghan women to uncover their faces. That same year Amanullah had his queen, Soraya, remove her light veil in public. According to the American journalist Rhea Talley Stewart, the king personally advocated the removal of the face veil and condoned the "shooting of interfering husbands." He said that "he would supply the weapons for this himself." He also promised that "no inquiries would be instituted against the women." Once, when he saw a woman wearing a burqa in Kabul, he personally tore it off and burned it.

Ah—a king after my own heart.

Religious Muslim scholars and other experts disagree about whether the Qur'an obliges women to wear burqas or face masks. Both men and women are advised to dress modestly; women are told to cover their bosom. As early as 1899, in his landmark book *The Liberation of Women,* the Egyptian intellectual Qasim Amin argued that the face veil was not commensurate with the tenets of Islam and called for its removal.

Historically, most Muslim-majority countries either abolished the face veil or refused to enforce the custom. Muslim feminists, especially in Egypt, North Africa, Turkey, Iran, and Lebanon, fought hard for—and won—this right.

In Afghanistan, King Amanullah discouraged the wearing of burqas but he did not prohibit women from veiling. Purdah, the seclusion of women, and polygamy were also officially discouraged but never prohibited by law or decree. And still Amanullah was forced to flee; he lived out his days in European exile.

My father-in-law, Ismail Mohammed, was one of King Amanullah's supporters. (God bless them both!) Ismail Mohammed was jailed and sentenced to be hanged for these political leanings. A mob of supporters freed him, and he fled to Iran.

Unlike Amanullah, Ismail Mohammed was eventually allowed to return. Those who had engineered Amanullah's departure then proceeded to plunge the country backward in time. Thereafter, for thirty years even the kings were cautious about the unveiling of Afghan women.

Many people assumed that King Amanullah had lost his throne because he proceeded to modernize or Westernize the country too quickly and that his unveiling of women had led to his utter ruin and almost immediate downfall. However, the diplomat and scholar Leon B. Poullada disagrees. He points out: "Decades earlier, Abdur Rahman, who never got beyond the talking stage of social reforms, nevertheless was faced with ten serious internal rebellions, four of which were so extensive he classified them as 'civil wars.'"

Afghans are known to riot. Afghans conduct blood feuds. Afghans overthrow their kings and leaders. Fathers kill sons, and brothers kill each other, as do nephews, uncles, and cousins, in pursuit of the throne.

*I*n the late 1960s I found Hunter's book about Afghanistan, *The Past Present*. I read it in one intense sitting. Then I went back, read it again, and underlined and typed up practically everything he wrote about women, the medieval-totalitarian nature of the government bureaucracy, the fanaticism of the mullahs, the existence of political prisoners, the tragedy of the burqa.

Had I read this before I left for Kabul—would I have gone?

I think not. But then I could not have written this book.

I have always wondered if Abdul-Kareem knew about Hunter's work. Abdul-Kareem certainly presented himself as having a vast knowledge of every book ever written about his country. However, over the years I have asked many experts on Afghanistan if they knew of this book. No one ever did.

Hunter's tone and concerns are so different from those of most travelers who have passed through—far different from my beloved Saira Shah's version of the country, too. Of course, as Sirdar Ali Shah's wife she might have been especially well treated, although she never quite acknowledges that this was the case. And she and her husband really lived outside Afghanistan and traveled widely. Every Western traveler has admired the humor of the generalized Afghans, their humility, and their ability to bear pain, cold, hunger, and illness with dignity and without complaint. Most of these travelers have essentially described Afghan *men* interacting with other men and with foreign travelers. The Afghans are all seen as enormously good-natured, somewhat shy, rather comic but warm, deeply religious, and famously hospitable. This is all true.

The Pushtuns are admired, and rightly so, as do-or-die warriors with extraordinary characteristics: deadly accurate as snipers; proficient at tracking, hunting, trapping, and mountaineering; tribally loyal but bred to lifelong blood feuds; unspoiled; fond of poetry; and close to both Nature and God.

The travelers, who wrote about nineteenth- and twentieth-century Afghanistan, were mainly writing about tribesmen from the hills or about poor people, peasants, farmers, shepherds, small shopkeepers, nomads, and house servants. They were not describing wealthy city dwellers or government or palace officials. They certainly did not describe Afghan men at home or in terms of how they treat their wives and children. How could they? Except for Saira Shah, who was both a woman and an Afghan wife, and the nineteenth-century Josiah Harlan, the first American who ever entered Afghanistan and who had lived among the egalitarian Kafirs in Nuristan, few travelers had ever been allowed to meet Afghan women. Many traveler-writers did not even realize that they had met only half of Afghanistan.

In the 1930s, Rosita Forbes described the hearty good-naturedness of the Afghan men with whom she traveled—but she also described the Afghan chowdry/burqa's narrow, grill-like opening for the eyes as constituting "a cruel mesh."

In the 1950s, the author and teacher Rosanne Klass described the Kabul bazaar as a "completely masculine world. The few women to be seen passed silently, shrouded in their chadris: disembodied phantoms."

In 1983, pre-Taliban, the American journalist Jere van Dyk wrote, "In over three weeks inside Afghanistan, I had not seen a woman up close. Those we had passed had turned away quickly, hiding their faces with the shawls that had covered their heads and shoulders. At a stream or beside a fire, I had tried to catch their eyes, although I had been told never to talk to or even look at them. The Afghans dedicate their poetry to women, but they seem to treat them like animals."

In *The Past Present* Hunter has riveting discussions about the Afghan burqa and purdah. I have since talked to many Muslim women and read many books written by them about the Afghan and Saudi-style burqa. Absolutely no Muslim woman has a kind word to say about it. (I am not talking about the headscarf known as hijab that does not prevent one from seeing, speaking, hearing, or being seen and heard.)

The chowdry, or burqa—the Saudi, North African, and Central Asian version of the head, face, and body shroud—is a sensory deprivation isolation chamber. It is claustrophobic, may lead to anxiety and depression, and reinforces a woman's already low self-esteem. It may also lead to vitamin D deficiency diseases such as osteoporosis and heart disease. Sensory deprivation officially constitutes torture and is practiced as such in the world's prisons.

Imagine the added shock if a Western woman—or an Afghan woman who has lived and been educated in the West—has to wear this odious garment. I never did—although once, in the early 1980s, I bought an Afghan burqa in New York City's Greenwich Village and offered some American feminists the opportunity to try it on, to see how it would make them feel.

Post-9/11 the Norwegian author Asne Seierstad lived with a polygamous Afghan family. She experimented with wearing a burqa in order to see what "it feels like to squeeze into the trunk of a taxi because a man is occupying the backseat." She writes, "How in time I started to hate it. How it pinches the head and causes headaches, how difficult it is to see anything through the grille. How enclosed it is, how little air gets in, how quickly you start to perspire, how all the time you have to be aware of where you are walking because you cannot see your feet, what a lot of dirt it picks up, how dirty it is, how much in the way. How liberated you feel when you get home and can take it off."

The Canadian author Sally Armstrong interviewed the Kabul psychiatrist Fatana Osman, who had never worn a burqa before the Taliban came to power. Osman described the experience as follows: "It was hot. Shrouded in this body bag I felt claustrophobic. It was smelly too. . . . It also felt like I was invisible. No one could see me. No one knew whether I was smiling or crying. . . . It was like wearing horse blinders. . . . [When I] tumbled to the ground, no one helped me."

Dear Edward Hunter names some formidable Afghan heroines whose stories match those of twentieth-century feminists in Persia, Turkey, and Egypt, all of whom fought tirelessly to end forced veiling. In Hunter's opinion no one in Afghanistan or in the world has ever heard about these heroines and about their resulting punishments because Afghanistan did not allow a free press to exist. Thus arrests were secret. The people knew things, but these things never became public.

Hunter introduces us to a heroine for the ages. Her name is Maga Rahmany, and she was the daughter of a Russian mother and an Afghan father. Maga had lived in France and in Turkey from the time she was seven until she turned fourteen. In 1938, when the family returned to Afghanistan, her father, suspected of reformist tendencies, was "soon thrown into the political prison in the King's own palace," where he would languish for many years.

(Abdul-Kareem was right to be cautious: He had to please all those in power who resented, envied, and despised his foreign education and his potentially reformist tendencies. At the time I had no way of knowing this.)

Hunter's description of Afghanistan in the late 1940s is very similar to a Taliban-dominated country. Women were not welcome in public. They could not attend the all-male cinema because they would have to remove their "tomb-like shrouds." They could not visit a male doctor or disrobe before one. They would describe their symptoms to their husbands, who in turn would inform the physician.

Women were not allowed out without a male relative as escort; even then they had to be fully veiled. A woman could not ask "another man to escort her, she would be breaking purdah laws" by doing so. Maga's father was in jail, her mother needed medicine, and Maga had no choice.

Thus: "Maga took fate into her own hands, put on her 'choudry' and walked out alone into the streets, an unprecedented act at that time." Worse: When her father was released from prison, Maga asked him to escort her to the cinema. He did so. Her presence caused a near riot. "Relatives stormed their home to protest. They warned that the two would be beaten up."

In 1950 Maga went too far; she dared to attend her all-female classes at Kabul University without wearing a burqa—and she visited female friends at night unveiled as well. For this Maga was placed under house arrest for three and a half years. Police arrived with instructions that Maga not leave her home unless she shrouded herself—and they mounted a permanent police and military patrol outside her house. Maga refused to wear the burqa, so she remained indoors.

This story reminds me of what happened to the first woman who unveiled herself in Beirut in the early 1920s. I heard the story from her daughter, Rhonda al-Fatal, who was at the time married to the Syrian ambassador to the United Nations. When Rhonda's English-educated mother taught her university class bare faced and without a screen, she was told she could never do this again. A police guard was mounted outside her home as well. And, like Maga, this early heroine refused to leave her home for more than a year.

Maga studied at home in 1950, but the government refused to allow her to qualify for a diploma—and refused to allow her to leave the country to continue her studies elsewhere. Three years later Prime Minister Mohammed Daoud Khan allowed Maga to work alongside her mother at the United Nations. According to Hunter, Maga may have "lost any hope of marriage. An Afghan man would require intellectual courage to marry an Afghan woman whose face was naked." Maga's bravery was meant to die with her.

Thus, Prime Minister Daoud freed Maga from house arrest a mere eight years before my arrival. Cultures and people do not change all that much in only eight years.

In 1958, three years before I arrived, Afghan women were unveiled for the second time in the twentieth century. I was told that bloody riots had broken out and government forces had reportedly killed hundreds of rioters. Remember: Unveiling was not mandatory and veiling was not prohibited. Women did as their families wished.

This brief but essential background may help readers understand what I was up against when, naked faced and bare headed, I went into town on my own, and took a bus—just as if I were riding down Fifth Avenue in Manhattan.

In 1961, that first time alone on a Kabul bus, I was so stunned by the burqas at the back of the bus that I failed to notice that I, not the burqas, was the object of every man's attention. Turbanned and baggy-trousered men, young men, old men, tall men, men with rifles nonchalantly slung over their shoulders—all had apparently stopped talking or dozing and were staring at me. The men were still staring when I hastily got off the bus. I was unprepared, though, for the small group of men who also got off and began following me. Years later I would write, "Suddenly, I found myself bumping into people, being moved along not at my own pace. Someone brushed by me, slowly. A man in brown yelled something at me. Two large moustaches whispered near my cheek. Coins jingled. Laughter. What had I done? What had I forgotten to do? I realized that they thought I was an Afghan woman without her burqa, without even her headscarf and coat."

I was lost. I was also dizzy with heat and fear. I kept walking. Eventually the crabbed street flared into a European-style square, and I found myself facing a war memorial for Afghans who died fighting the British, a battle in which only one Englishman survived.

I hailed a horse and carriage (*gaudi*) and gave the driver the address of the family business. Oh, what a brouhaha my little expedition caused.

"You could have been kidnapped or held for ransom," Abdul-Kareem raged and nearly wept. "You could have been murdered. You can't wander around as if you're some dumb American tourist."

Then Abdul-Kareem told me about an Afghan minister whose wife had indeed been kidnapped and held for ransom. The shame drove her husband to commit suicide when she was returned. Abdul-Kareem was genuinely concerned that I could have been raped and murdered—which might have meant he would have to kill himself. I could not believe the intensity of emotions that followed upon a simple bus ride in order to sightsee.

Abdul-Kareem must be mad to think that he can waltz back into this medieval country and start a literary and theatrical salon. Who exactly will attend his performances of Eugene O'Neill, August Strindberg, Tennessee Williams, and Arthur Miller? Is he going to direct plays only for the English-speaking foreign embassy personnel?

If he is planning on translating these plays into Dari and Pushto—what cultural context do these plays have in common with people who are 99 percent illiterate and whose ideas of entertainment include rough sports on horseback, wrestling, shooting, and swordplay? He is definitely a world-class dreamer.

How the hell am I going to get out of here?

FOUR

Harem Days

y trip into town and what *could* have happened is talked about for days. However, my so-called escape has led to one good thing. The family has begun to take me out on some carefully choreographed trips. The chauffeur drives us to each appointment. I am always chaperoned or accompanied by at least one, sometimes two, female relatives and often by one male relative, too.

> It is early morning. This is my first official look at downtown Kabul. Our car windows are tinted so no one can see in. I keep rolling the window down to take it all in.
>
> The road is mainly filled with—men. Barefoot men, men on bicycles, men driving other men in horse-drawn carriages, men holding hands, men driving flocks of fat-tailed sheep, men riding donkeys, men with rifles slung over their shoulders and a full clip of bullets across their chests, men leading a train of camels, men all talking loudly, affably.

The car finally stops somewhere in the center of the city. I get out, stand up, look up—and am awestruck. We are surrounded and embraced by majestic mountains. Kabul is a city in a valley, a city in a crater. For a moment it feels like the dawn of the world. Afterward, whenever I spend time in the American and Canadian Rockies, I will always be reminded of Kabul, with its wide open sky and thrilling mountains.

There are rows of flat-top adobe houses climbing up (or down) the mountainside. The houses are perched, oddly tilted. They have probably been here forever. But they also seem so precariously angled. What happens to them in a fierce rainstorm or a mud-slide?

Barefoot boys in long tunics and loose pants are selling yoghurt and fetching tea. There is an endless flow of human and animal traffic, both heavily laden with goods, fruits, vegetables. Fruit sellers are offering huge melons and gigantic grapes. Huge mounds of carpets are moving forward carried by men who are bent double.

My favorite British traveler, Rosita Forbes, was in Kabul in the late 1920s. She marvels at the "cacophony of sound" in which the "singing of birds predominates." She writes, "For in every cupboard shop, with the merchant tucked away on a shelf among his canes of sugar wrapped in brilliant paper, his furs, knives, striped rugs, long-necked bottles, fat stomached pots, his silver bracelets and gold-embroidered caps, there is a cage or half dozen cages full of the smallest imaginable birds. And they sing. They never stop singing."

Thirty years later Rosanne Klass describes Da Afghanan, a smaller bazaar, rather wonderfully. It is "an Old Curiosity Shop of the world": "These heaps of battered necessities were crowned with wild, gaudy jewels: a gilded French telephone or a sheaf of lacquered Uzbeck spoons; a volume of Sir Walter Scott, an exquisitely molded Greek coin turned up by some plow. . . . Once, I found an old mortarboard cap from Oxford University. It seemed as though, from the Universe of Objects, the crippled, the lame, the halt and the blind had all found their way here to await the day when someone might possibly look upon them again and find them good."

Klass lived in Kabul in the 1950s and again in the 1960s. Naked faced, she taught English to male students who ranged in age from twelve to twenty-five and who came to Kabul from small villages. Like other foreign women, and like the intrepid female travelers, Klass was always able to roam the bazaars freely.

Afghan men may stare at the foreign women or may occasionally harass, even kidnap, them, but mainly such women are valued as customers and as the wives of powerful foreign diplomats. Such women do not really count and are avoided. They come from another world. They are naked faced, naked armed, and naked from the knees down. These are wildly independent women. Perhaps they are seen as super or as less than human.

I occupy a place somewhere in between. I may appear naked faced but never alone, and I am not allowed to roam the bazaar freely, gathering up merchandise and memories. I am an Afghan wife, and what I see is limited by my inability to travel alone outdoors. I see what I am taken to see. I am never allowed to simply wander about. My every interaction is planned and monitored.

However, in a country where women are still kept hidden, and brides must be bought and arrive—sight unseen—on the wedding day, a naked face is almost the same as the fully bared breasts of a prostitute. The level of sexual tension and aggression that may ensue is far off the Western charts. Paradoxically the Islamic veil functions as an erotic advertisement; imaginations run riot about how the hidden woman looks when she is entirely naked.

Many travelers have commented upon the bare-faced, often bare-footed Kuchi, the nomad women of Afghanistan. They are dignified, almost imperious, clearly physically strong. I am delighted by their presence.

Kuchi means nomad in Dari. Seeing them is heart-stopping. The first time I did, I stood still, at attention, but I was trembling with excitement. Here were our ancient nomadic ancestors—alive and right before my eyes; yet I felt I was dreaming—a dream perhaps of awakened memory. Here too were the camels, men on horseback, droves of sheep and goats, bands of children, an entire tribe on the move—and here are the women, wearing every piece of jewelry they own and all their splendid colorful clothing. These women are naked-faced, indigenous Afghans.

The Kuchis, who are Pushtuns, follow the weather, seasons, and pasturage as they herd their animals clear across Afghanistan, down to India (now Pakistan), and back up to Russia—year after year. Some are semisedentary, some are traders, but the pure nomads have no fixed abode. Rather, they have fixed gender roles. The women are responsible for child rearing, preparing the food and water (no small task), weaving their tents, and sewing their clothes.

In the late 1930s Rosita Forbes admired the Kuchi women's "bold and active" steps, the way "they walked all in a piece without movement of hip or shoulder. . . . With their shoes upon their heads they trod sublimely, bare-footed over sand and rock." In the mid-1950s Edward Hunter depicted them as wearing "all the colors of the rainbow, on foot and on horseback, as they had done before the dawn of recorded history."

Today, on this outing, there are no Kuchis walking through Kabul on their way to someplace else.

I stand on the banks of the Kabul River. Today, it is not surging. It is stagnant and muddy. Some men are bathing in it. Some naked children are splashing away. There are very few women visible.

Nearby stands a row of shops: A man could choose a beautiful karakul lambskin in brown, gold, silver gray, or black, and have his hat ready by the next day. These shops are stalls which open directly onto the street. The vendors sit and work on the floor.

Kabul has more than one bazaar. This one is an open bazaar. It does not look like the Teheran bazaar. It smells of wood-smoke, kerosene, tobacco, perhaps hashish, fresh produce, spoiled produce, spices. I am enchanted. Thousands of birds are singing. Instinctively, I look for the trees. But the birds are all caged.

We are here to see a tailor. I've been told, "He can make anything." It is true. I show him a fashion magazine photo and watch him quickly create a sample by just looking at me. He does not have to take my measurements. The tailor is not obsequious. He is business-like, very polite, very shy, and clearly proud of his skills. A young boy serves us tea while we wait.

To this day I remember the smart gray wool suit he chose to make for me. It fit me like the proverbial glove. He whipped up some sleek Western-style party dresses for me as well.

Oh, how I wanted dresses that would sweep the floor and be made out of the gauzy, sari-like materials with embossed gold designs and shot through with gold threads (very fairy princess–like), but the tailor and my female relatives say that this is out of the question.

I beg to walk down the street a bit more, just a little more. Suddenly I am surrounded by little children. They tug at my elbow, pluck at my sleeve, my handbag, even the buttons on my blouse. They are part of a small and persistent band of child beggars in Kabul. They look like pathetic trick-or-treaters but also slightly hideous, wearing the cosmetics of trachoma and parasitic infections. It is a wretched sight. I am full of pity for these children but my sympathy is mocked. I am told that their mothers are thieves, hiding behind buildings and in doorways.

Other than in Teheran, I have never before seen a blind and bare-foot child—or one missing a limb and on crutches—actually begging for bread. In the streets they swarm after people they recognize as foreigners. I immediately give them money. I give them whatever I have. I have begun to carry small candies for just this purpose. Afterward, at home, Bebegul laughs at me and then says in a harsh tone: "They are fooling you—they are richer than we are, they are tricksters in disguise."

I am saddened and puzzled by her callousness.

I do not understand the intensity of Bebegul's suspicion and distrust—toward beggars, toward servants, and toward me. Does my independence insult and frighten her—does she secretly share my need for personal freedom? Will she be held accountable by the family and by "all Kabul" if I am not tamed? Or does she dislike me because I am an infidel, a Jew, a Westerner, an American? Is she perhaps jealous that I got to spend time with her long-absent son? Or is she worried that I might have influenced him to become Other as well?

No matter. I am being taken out more often.

We see a recital at Zarghuna [a school]. It was too long but it was a diversion nevertheless. One speech was given in English but it was fairly senseless. "Let us, as women, make ourselves really free so that we can be better mothers in our homes and God save the King and Queen and all the audience too." One skit pointed out that you cannot criticize arranged marriages just yet. If you must marry a boy just because he has money then resign yourself to it and try to educate him yourself.

Ah well, the music was good and we were treated to a brief comic-pantomime. Princess Maryam was there. Flowers were thrown onto the makeshift stage. It was dull and mindless. But by now, even I could probably write a sweet little piece about it: Signs of an Afghan Awakening.

The prisoner is so grateful for her afternoon out.

The family is going to the movies! Our group never includes Ismail Mohammed, who does not socialize with his first family at home but who does see his four oldest sons every day at either the bank or at the import-export company. Bebegul never comes out with us, either.

I can no longer remember what we saw. It was probably an American movie. The married men (this includes Abdul-Kareem) do not talk to their wives or fiancées in public. The men sit apart from the women.

This is disconcerting but I am thrilled to be out. Afterward two men race across the parking lot to start the cars. Two men gallantly, protectively, accompany the women outside and herd us like treasured cattle across the lot.

Do they expect brigands or crusaders to attack us?

There is no lingering—no ice cream sodas or coffees or alcoholic drinks—afterward. What am I thinking? Muslims are not allowed to drink alcohol. Many do—but they do so secretly, discreetly, both at home and abroad. Also, the town has only one hotel and one new restaurant. The kitchens probably shut down hours ago. But mainly dining out is simply not done. Afghans are not used to any cafe-based nightlife. They probably still view it as an immoral and Western custom.

When an Afghan invites a guest for a meal or a party—for some of that fabled Afghan hospitality—he would never think of charging you for the food or drink or lodging. He opens his home to you. All that he has in the way of food and comfort are yours.

That travelers have to pay for food and lodging in the West is, according to the Scottish Saira Shah, viewed as sad, cruel, and uncivilized.

At the time I had absolutely no historical perspective. I had no way of understanding how daring Abdul-Kareem's family was being—and all for my sake.

Forty years before I arrived, Afghanistan's ruler, Emir Habibullah, still had a large imperial-style harem. He had many wives and concubines. According to the American journalist Rhea Tally Stewart, Habibullah "had one of the East's last large harems; whenever a tribe wished to make him a gift, they knew that a girl would be welcome." He had four queens, but no one was sure exactly how many women lived in the harem. Habibullah had fifty-eight children.

The people resented his wives, whom he dressed in the British style, which he thought fashionable; Habibullah and "a clutch of wives" would go out riding together. They were all lightly veiled—but wore European hats.

I do not live in a large imperial harem. I live in a much smaller domestic harem which has only (!) three wives and twenty-one children. My father-in-law does not hop from bed to bed as people believed Habibullah did. My father-in-law now lives only with his third and youngest wife.

One might say that Abdul-Kareem is treating me well. He is taking me out, showing me off; I am not completely hidden behind purdah

walls. And yet an air of danger and risk is associated with all our out-
ings. I note that none of Ismail Mohammed's wives ever seem to leave
the compound except to visit the homes of relatives.

*Abdul-Kareem takes me to a diplomatic function of some kind. I am so
excited but he made me so nervous I could barely enjoy myself. I am
not supposed to say anything to the Americans that might get Abdul-
Kareem or Afghanistan (!) in trouble.*

*I do not like what one American diplomat has to say. He explains
that American diplomats are not willing—nor should they be—to
challenge Afghans on their treatment of women or on anything else.
He says: "If they don't like us, they will turn to the Russians. We
can't tell them how to run their country. They are a proud and touchy
bunch."*

*I think my father-in-law is secretly flirting with me. I can't be sure
but he does look at me very carefully and his eyes are kind and soft
when I meet his gaze.*

*He is a very attractive man. He does not seem "old" at all. He
maintains a ramrod-straight posture and he is always nattily dressed.*

* * *

*Abdul-Kareem closes our bedroom door in order to whisper. We are
going to a Western-style party in the home of a young progressive Afghan couple. Foreigners will be there. The event is hush-hush. Men and
women are going to be dancing together. By now, this feels forbidden,
dangerous, even to me.*

*There is liquor and popcorn. The lights are dimmed. There are
rock 'n' roll records playing. Abdul-Kareem grabs my arm and tells me
that I had better not act like the other Western "whores" there, women
who agree to dance with men who are not their husbands. He remains
at my side the entire evening.*

Has he always been this controlling, suspicious? Perhaps he has
been and I mistook it for love. Many years later a college mate writes me
a surprising note. He says:

I was always a loner, the professional "Frenchman" who had to work
hard on his English. I saw Abdul-Kareem as an English "bloke," his
accent was somehow British as were his clothes and manners. You were

pure New York. You were closer to Jack Lemmon and Shirley Mac-Laine. You were wild and funny, as talkative as he was a bit "tight."

I had a (quiet) crush on you but Abdul-Kareem was always behind you or close by. I remember laughing with you a lot. You said things . . . OUTRAGEOUS! I really felt at ease with you . . . except Abdul-Kareem was ALWAYS around and you seemed tight as a couple, "going steady." I was old enough to know when not to waste my time.

Ah well.

How can Abdul-Kareem resist the pull of his culture, since his family is demanding that he surrender to it as the price for being allowed back in—especially since he has a foreign bride?

I am a goner.

The entire family (Abdul-Kareem and his brothers and sisters and spouses) attended another, much larger party. A garden party: About sixty people sat listlessly in the heat, politely yawning and smiling between mouthfuls of kebab, pilau, and sweets. The company was, refreshingly, "mixed" but the men and women sat separately.

A German woman, Heidi, the wife of an Afghan engineer, rescued me. Heidi is twenty-two and has been living in Afghanistan for six months. We walked off together, through the garden and into an adjoining field, where we lay down, face-up, side-by-side. Heidi whispered, but then she bellowed.

"I am bored, bored, bored. I have no real life here. I cannot stand it."

As foreign wives, we talked quickly and easily. In Kabul, I used French, English, and my knowledge of Yiddish to understand some German. Heidi spoke English well enough. We whispered because we knew that our conversation would be considered conspiratorial. We knew we could be interrupted at any moment, separated, and silenced.

"Phyllis, remember always that no opportunity to act sanely, rather than traditionally, should be wasted."

She said this mischievously, but with a slightly mad and desperate grin. It was very hot. Heidi had brought two bathing suits to the party. There was a swimming pool at the other end of the garden where the men were planning on swimming later.

"Let's go now," she suddenly demanded, "before it's completely off-limits to us."

We undressed, put on the bathing suits, and laid back down in the grass to sunbathe, still hidden from the party. We dozed.

Abdul-Kareem and my sister-in-law found us. They were both shocked, angry, worried.

"Important people" are at the party, they hissed at me, people who would never accept my behavior or poor choice of companions. Heidi's reputation is that of a "whore," they said, and she was "ruining" her poor husband, who was the "laughingstock" of Kabul.

They physically pulled me away from Heidi. And they kept talking: "Her husband's family is not as important as ours is," I was not to compare myself with her. They ride a motorbike, they have no car. They are both going to return to Europe or certainly, she would. He would have to send her "packing."

Ah—what could Heidi's crimes have been? That she acted like a Westerner? That she believed women had the right to swim—or was it that she dared talk to men other than her husband? Afghan girls have been killed for far less, both in Afghanistan and among immigrants in the West. The standards for women are different here; the line a woman must walk is razor thin.

The British-born author Alison Legh-Jones fell in love with Khaled, a "North African Arab." She married him in an Islamic ceremony and lived with him in the late 1960s somewhere in North Africa. In her book, *English Woman, Arab Man,* she writes:

After finding an Arab in my address book he decides it's time to tell me what to do if a local man tries to pick me up. "Ignore him. He's wondering how soon he can make love to you. If he doesn't go away tell him you're not a tourist. Say you're married to an Arab and he mustn't talk to you. If he's a good man he'll say 'Excuse me, madam' and leave you. If not let him talk to himself until he's tired of looking silly.

"If I see you talking to another Arab without my permission I'll kill you. As soon as a girl is seen with an Arab everyone assumes they're making love. Whatever you do, I'll find out. I've got friends everywhere. There'll always be someone watching you. As soon as one of my friends sees you with another man he'll come and tell me 'Your wife is no good. She goes with other men.'

"Don't speak to my friends either," he adds. "They're just as bad."

My own parents had also watched me very closely. They assumed the worst if I came home a few minutes late. The "worst" always meant that I'd been with a boy and had done "something." Whatever it might have been could "ruin my life" and "wreck all their plans for me."

I have exchanged one jailor for another, one jailhouse culture for another, far more dangerous jailhouse culture.

Have all American wives regretted their decision to marry and live in the Muslim world? No.

In 1945 the tall blonde Californian Marianne Likowski Alireza married Saudi Ali Alireza, a member of the royal family. Once Ali was sure Marianne was not Jewish, neither he nor his family ever insisted that she convert from Christianity to Islam. She agreed that their children would be raised as Muslims. Marianne would enjoy a fairy-tale world of diplomatic parties, shopping extravaganzas, and extended vacations in the best hotels in Europe and Egypt.

However, Ali told her in advance what life would be like in the harem, in purdah: that she would have to be fully veiled and that, with some exceptions, she would mainly participate in gender-segregated gatherings. Marianne did not aspire to be more than a wife and mother and understood that she, not her Saudi family, would be obliged to adjust. The presence of black slaves did not bother her; on the contrary she adopted the Arab view that such slaves were better off. At times Marianne's frustration and rage kept her in bed all day, but essentially she fit in and developed loving, lifelong relationships with her male and female relatives. She gave birth to five children and flourished in an extended family in which everyone lived, dined, and traveled together. Her mother-in-law and sisters-in-law embraced her with unfailing and spontaneous warmth. They did not reject her as a Christian infidel or foreigner.

Alireza's book, *At the Drop of a Veil,* was originally published in 1971, a quarter-century after her marriage in California. It is a joy to read, and as I did so, I decided I would quote her at length as an example of how such marriages can work out. And then, in the book's *last ten pages,* Marianne drops quite a bombshell. After fifteen years of marriage Ali suddenly tells her that he has unilaterally divorced her, Muslim style—and is taking the children away from her. By then their oldest daughter, Hamida, had just been married to her first cousin. Ali married a Lebanese woman and shipped all four children off to boarding school, first in Egypt, then in Switzerland. Marianne no longer had her American passport—Ali had locked it up the moment they first arrived in Saudi Arabia. Like me, Marianne was forced to enter America on a foreign passport. But she was a cool-headed and determined mother with helpful friends.

On a vacation with her four children in Switzerland, Marianne planned and carried out a successful kidnapping and took them with her to California. At the time doing so was absolutely unheard of. I hereby salute her courage and resourcefulness. Marianne regrets nothing—and she still spends a few months every year in the kingdom visiting her relatives. She writes:

> I have fifteen grandchildren and two great-grandchildren. . . . People say it's remarkable that I made my peace with life in old Arabia, but I say no. What is truly remarkable is that those around me helped me to make my peace . . . it was in my worst moments that they helped me the most, and then we laughed together. So, this is a story of people who proved that even though we came from worlds apart, we could give respect, tolerance, understanding, sensitivity, and love to one another and make a human bond. If I had it to do over again, would I? You bet! I wouldn't have missed it for anything!

More recently, in the twenty-first century, G. Willow Wilson, a young Colorado native, converted to Islam; she subsequently fell in love with and married a moderate Egyptian. In her memoir, *The Butterfly Mosque*, she quite movingly conveys the sense of camaraderie and security that comes from living in a large, Egyptian Muslim family. Like Alireza, Willow sometimes becomes impatient and bored but expresses joy and excitement about performing everyday household tasks. I will not criticize these women for finding happiness in the Arab world; however, this type of restricted, protected, and utterly family-centered life did not work for me. Alireza and Wilson freely chose such lives; I did not.

> *I have been here for two months and have been allowed out only five or six times. Is this imprisonment meant to tame me, break me, teach me to accept my fate as an Afghan woman? I want to go home.*
>
> *We thrash things out for hours the other night. Abdul-Kareem was not in the least bit understanding or guilty or apologetic. I discover that all along he has been editorializing what I say to family members when he translates my words. He says it's "for your own good."*
>
> *I do not understand why we are not living by ourselves as we have already done for years. I point out that he still has no job, is still*

completely dependent on his father for everything. He is also in a bad temper all the time.

Why do I have to ask twenty times for even the smallest thing? I am desperate for a tin of Huntley and Palmer biscuits or for a can of tuna fish.

But my nagging hunger is not as awful as having lost the man I once knew and trusted. He really doesn't seem to care that I am miserable. He spends all his time with his brothers when he is home. Just as they do. His eldest brother never talks to his wife.

He is slipping away from me. I am a burden, a liability. He can't even be bothered to buy a contraceptive. He is putting me at great risk. He is hard, indifferent.

Abdul-Kareem is waiting to be told what he can do next. He is waiting for his father to fix it up with the King and the government for him to become Somebody Important. But first, they are watching him carefully.

I am an unhappy and complaining wife. It is the only thing that makes him uncomfortable enough to hit me, yell at me, stomp out of the room.

He has begun to hit me.

Had I known that something like this could ever happen, had I known that we would have to live with his mother and brothers, I would never have come here.

Dear Diary: Thank you. Had I not written some things down, I would never have remembered that I had been asking that he use contraceptives.

I have no memory of Abdul-Kareem's hitting me—yelling at me, yes, avoiding me, yes—hitting me, no. I would not have remembered this if I could not read it here. Worse than any slap or kick Abdul-Kareem might administer, worse, even, than refusing to use a condom, is that my very Western husband has confined me to a very Eastern harem. I am in purdah, however posh. And he acts as if this is all quite normal.

My female relatives drink tea; eat luscious fruit, nuts, sweet, sticky cakes; entertain their many, mainly female, relatives who come to call. They also sew, cuddle infants, prepare young children for school. Above all they supervise the servants. This alone can be made into a full-time occupation.

The servants and the daughters-in-law usually bear the brunt of the oldest woman's or highest-ranking wife's frustrations. And her frustrations are many. I had known something about female-female cruelty in the West, but I learned even more about it in Afghanistan. Forty years later I published a work titled *Woman's Inhumanity to Woman*. It has a global perspective.

I have been talking about living in a harem. Let me explain what that means.

A harem is not a brothel, as so many Westerners erroneously believe. It is merely the women's living quarters. Male relatives can join them—but no male nonrelatives may do so. It is hardly a den of eroticism.

Western men have never been able to visit a harem—it is forbidden to them because the women are sacred (property), which must be kept separate and apart in order to protect them from strange men. Because foreign men have not visited the women's quarters, their imaginations have run riot. True, like a brothel (or a women's prison) a domestic harem is an all-female and a female-dominated environment. But it is more like a celibate nunnery or a nursery and sewing room. It is not a place where seductions and orgies take place. Historically only Western women travelers, who were allowed to visit domestic and imperial harems, have been able to render a more accurate report.

Eventually, like prisoners everywhere, so-called protected women are blinded by the light; their eyes grow accustomed to the darkness. The outside world seems dangerous, certainly unfriendly to women. Hence understandably, women become claustrophobic and agoraphobic. Women may even become anxious when they are outdoors.

I have begun to internalize the unspoken rules: Wait, and watch what the other women do before acting. Even I feel a bit too daring when I make my escapes into the city. I am beginning to experience as taboo, dangerous, what would be perfectly acceptable behavior back in New York. I am also getting used to spending my days at home, reading and waiting for the men to return.

It is impossible for a Westerner to imagine the deadening torpor of a protected life under house arrest. Eventually, one is grateful for the smallest outing outdoors—a lovely picnic in a burqa, being allowed to watch the men and boys fly kites or swim.

I am looking at a photograph taken in 1865 that is titled "Sweet Waters of Asia." Four harem women and two female servants are having a picnic in a park on the eastern shores of the Bosphorus; the women are wearing full hijab and niqab—their faces are entirely covered except for their eyes. I hope they are smiling. They are sitting on the ground on a tablecloth with bags and baskets of provisions nearby. It is unclear whether these are paid models or simply ordinary harem women who have agreed to pose for the photographer, one Basil Kargopoulo.

I wonder: How do they eat all the food they've brought? Do they smuggle it up under the heavy material that covers their noses, mouths, and jaws? Or do they flip the mask up when no one is looking and take a hurried bite—as if it is too shameful for women to eat or to be seen enjoying themselves in public?

Some early nineteenth-century British female travelers to Egypt and Turkey noted ironically that harem-confined women did not have to wear restricting steel corsets as the British women did. The Brits envied and sometimes romanticized the loose Turkish clothing, which was not only comfortable but also never went out of fashion.

Look: I've admitted that I spend my writing days dressed in flowing caftans. And I wear ethnic jewelry, which in the last decade I have color-coordinated with my filmy blouses and my nail polish. Yes, I could pass for an Eastern woman in another era. I steer clear of exotic excess—no time for it, but I appreciate it in others. Despite my strongly negative view of the burqa, I rather like the colorful and often shimmering kerchiefs that some religious Muslim women wear to great advantage. They are stunning with their many earrings, bracelets, and necklaces.

Ironically the nineteenth-century harem dwellers could not believe how confined their female Western visitors were in their corset stays, hoops, and bustles, which the Eastern women insisted on examining in detail. However, the Western reports showed us the price exacted by imprisonment in the harem.

In 1837 on a visit to Istanbul, the British-born Julia Pardoe noted that the Turkish harem women were indolent, childlike, and uneducated, and could only "live in the moment."

How very Zen of them!

In 1846 the British-born author Harriet Martineau visited the Arab Middle East. She writes about the harems of Cairo:

> Everywhere they pitied us European women heartily, that we had to go about travelling, and appearing in the streets without being properly taken care of—that is, watched. They think us strangely neglected in being left so free, and boast of their spy system and imprisonment as tokens of the value in which they are held. The difficulty is to get away, when one is visiting a harem. The poor ladies cannot conceive of one's having anything to do. All the younger ones were dull, soulless,

brutish, or peevish. . . . There cannot be a woman of them all who is not dwarfed and withered in mind and soul.

In 1865 the British governess Emmeline Lott also described the confined Egyptian women as apathetic, leading lives of "irksome monotony," which they bear by "puffing on [opium-laced] cigarettes constantly . . . [these are] the caged beauties of the East."

If women are weakened both physically and intellectually, and if they also believe that they are worth less than men—they will certainly be grateful for male protection. A woman reared in a harem knows that a woman is not valued for her educated brain or fearlessness but rather for her obedience, chastity, marital fertility, her ability to birth sons, and her willingness to live with cowives without complaint. Many harem women were happy to have cowives, slaves, and daughters-in-law because they needed help with the household and child-rearing chores—and with their husbands' need for sexual pleasure and more sons. The harems that Martineau visited represented another world, another set of values.

Toward the end of the twentieth century, my colleague Fatima Mernissi published a rather enchanting book, *Dreams of Trespass: Tales of a Harem Girlhood.* She describes growing up in a large, wealthy, sunny, polygamous harem in Fez, Morocco, in the 1940s.

For her it was an active, busy quarter peopled by magically philosophical, loving, and high-spirited women who concocted elaborate homemade beauty treatments that they applied to themselves and to each other; they also visited the hammam (the public Turkish baths) and the occasional movie—and always en masse, all together. Mernissi also presents the harem as a refuge for female relatives "in trouble," such as abandoned wives and war widows. She describes a Berber horsewoman, Tamou, who could ride and shoot as well as any man and who, upon seeking refuge, was asked by all the cowives to please consider becoming a wife, too; they so loved her company! (She accepted their offer.)

Tamou was a war heroine from the Rif Mountains. She rode in on a "Spanish saddled horse" wearing a "man's white cape"; Tamou had a Spanish rifle, a dagger at her hip, and "heavy silver bracelets with points sticking out . . . the kind you could use to defend yourself." She had a green tattoo on her chin and a "long, copper-colored braid that hung over her left shoulder."

But Mernissi is clear that the women were confined: They had to ask husbands and fathers for permission to leave. Women were not allowed to do their own shopping; they had to describe the purchases they wanted to a male servant. As a child, Fatima was bothered by the separation of the sexes. One of the wise harem women explained it to her: "There are two kinds of creatures walking on Allah's earth, the powerful on one side, and the powerless on the other. I asked [Mina] how would I know on which side I stood: Her answer was quick, short, and very clear: 'If you can't get out, you are on the powerless side.'"

Both Fatima (as a child) and I (as an adult in Kabul) were definitely on the powerless side.

At least Mernissi grew up loving these harem women who in turn loved her. I have come here as a feared stranger, knowing only one person, unable to speak the language, cherishing opposite values.

Abdul-Kareem refuses to acknowledge that this is so and that our living conditions are wrong, unacceptable, intolerable—for me and probably for most Western women.

He will not—he cannot—free me.

FIVE

My Mother-in-Law

Some of the most daring adventurers to the Orient fainted in the bazaar, spent feverish days in bed retching and dragging themselves to whatever passed for a bathroom, endured vertigo, nausea, dysentery, tuberculosis, jaundice, and malaria.

The Arab Middle East and Central Asia implacably assault the Western traveler's gastrointestinal and nervous systems with germs and parasites to which those of native inhabitants are usually inured. A traveler knows that she is really in Afghanistan when she becomes deathly ill.

I am in awe of those nineteenth- and early twentieth-century Western travelers, especially the women, who crossed deserts without enough water or food; who rode horses and camels right into sandstorms; who faced danger with daggers and pistols at their sides; who survived the kind of heat and humidity that make breathing difficult and the kind of cold that leads to frostbite or death; who went without sleep, privacy, soap, or a change of clothing for weeks or months.

As for me, I am not that kind of hale-and-rugged traveler.

I was and still am a soft city-bred American who never learned to ride, shoot, hunt, navigate by the stars, or speak ten languages. My immune system and my gastrointestinal tract are simply not ready for Kabul.

The hygiene leaves everything to be desired.

Even though I have a picture-perfect modern bathroom, the city's sewage system consists of open irrigation ditches that run alongside the streets. These ditches are used as a public bathroom—they are also used for bathing, doing laundry, and washing fruits and vegetables.

Long after I leave Kabul, I speak to an old Afghan hand, an American who lived and worked in Kabul for a few years. He describes "getting desperately, violently ill" after ordering precooked sauced meat at the Khyber Restaurant. In fact he soon "passes out cold." He tells me:

> I had dysentery several times in my first six months in Kabul. You could eat kebobs right off the fire in the filthiest little village and be safe, but anything that grows low and near the ground is totally unsafe unless you cook the hell out of it. Corn and oranges are safe. Anything you peel is okay.
>
> If you are thirsty and you don't know if the water is safe, you can eat a watermelon or cucumbers or drink tea, which has to be boiled. Bread is okay only if you eat it right out of the oven; otherwise it's been sitting there, and the flies have been landing on it, the dust blowing on it and you don't know who's been touching it.

Why did Abdul-Kareem not prepare me for what would inevitably happen to my stomach? I would have packed antibiotics and medications for diarrhea and dysentery.

Like everyone else, I come down with "the Kabul trots," a terrible form of dysentery (either bacillary or amoebic, which is more serious) to which foreigners are prone. I have no advance warning and gain little sympathy once I am afflicted.

If anything, I am a source of some mild, perhaps good-natured, amusement. Maybe my family feels that I am beginning to become a real Afghan. To an extent Afghans view foreigners as weak because they succumb to germs so quickly—without even putting up a fight.

Afghans are more fatalistic about illness and are not used to interfering with God's will. With so few doctors, hospitals, and surgical supplies, including medicine, and with so little money, this attitude may be a rather dignified and psychologically sound way of submitting to a fate that one cannot change.

When my health worsens, I beg for a real doctor to diagnose and treat me. I have no idea what kind of hospital culture I am up against.

In the 1920s the Scottish Afghan traveler Saira Shah described Afghan nomadic (Kuchi) attitudes toward modern doctoring: "The doctor is not usually called until everybody's advice has been taken. . . . The doctor, they will tell you, is but a human being. Allah is above all.

Besides, why does he cost so much? And why, if he costs so much, does he work at hospitals where treatment is free?"

Before I became ill, I wanted to visit a hospital in Kabul. I specifically asked to see a maternity hospital. My visit shocked me. I write about it some years later:

> *The corridors and courtyards of this long, low series of wooden buildings remind me of nineteenth-century Russia—a kerchiefed woman slapping a sheet to wash, a samovar in the doctor's private waiting room. A man, wearing a turban and a long quilted coat, is pacing barefoot, back and forth.*
>
> *The doctor, educated in Germany, greets us first, then turns to the man and speaks brusquely, with annoyance.*
>
> *"You brought your wife here too late. The baby is already dead. Your wife, not long, maybe a few hours more."*
>
> *Turning back to us, his guests, he smiles and offers us tea.*
>
> *"These provincials always come when it's too late."*
>
> *The husband has resumed his pacing, the doctor is stirring sugar into his tea. Suddenly the husband is yelling, the doctor yelling back. Quietly Abdul-Kareem translates for me.*
>
> *The man is refusing to pay any hospital fees because not only will he have to pay to bury both his wife and child, he will need that money to buy another wife to cook for him and take care of his other children.*
>
> *And where in the name of Allah did the doctor think he'd be able to get this kind of money? He has already paid for a car to transport his wife all the way from their village, which clearly was a waste of money. Why should he have to pay the doctor for killing his wife and child?*
>
> *I left the hospital as quickly as I could. I didn't want to hear the screams of women as we sipped our tea. Now, on the way out, the smell of blood was unmistakable on some of the drying sheets.*

Afghanistan is not safe for wives—or for anyone who might need medical help.

Long after my several bouts with dysentery, I discover quite by accident that my mother-in-law, Bebegul, has instructed the servants to stop boiling my drinking water and to stop washing my fruits and vegetables in boiled water.

Perhaps she thinks I am already "Afghan enough" to withstand any and all germs. Perhaps she wants me dead.

No one tells me anything. One day I happen to observe what the cook is doing. I bring Fawziya over to question him and to translate for me. It seems that he stopped doing anything considered special for me some weeks ago.

I assume that Bebegul is behind this. Of course I could be wrong. The cook might simply have gone back to doing what he always does—and no one told him otherwise.

There are many things Abdul-Kareem has not told me. His father's polygamy is only one item on a growing list. He did not tell me that his mother is mentally ill—or has suffered so much that she now persecutes any woman who is in her power—or that the culture empowers her to do so. He did not explain that I would have to live with her and spend all my time with her, that I would be at her mercy, and that he would not be able to interfere.

In Kabul I am told very little about my mother-in-law, but what I am told is scandalous, hardly believable.

Apparently, after her husband had taken his second or third wife, Bebegul had been found in a compromising position with a male servant.

Were they merely alone? Did they simply seem too happy in each other's company? Were they holding hands, was he trying to comfort her—or were they actually embracing? I cannot imagine things could have gone any further than this—but I hope they did.

Had Bebegul once been a woman of rare spirit? Had she been crushed, driven mad?

In any event someone had witnessed the transgression and had run screaming from the women's quarters. Bebegul had committed a killing offense. If her husband had shot her or had given orders that she be stoned to death, he would have been praised, not arrested.

Maybe he really loved her.

Maybe he was bound to her through their common ancestors. After all she was a member of his extended family of origin. Perhaps he did not want to kill the mother of his five sons and three or four daughters.

Therefore Ismail Mohammed condemned Bebegul—but to life. He never lived with her again. He rarely visited. I never saw him speak to her.

And he had eight more children with his new young wife.

Worse: Bebegul's sons blame her for having to share their inheritance with their new half-brothers. They do not blame their father for anything.

Many years later I ask Abdul-Kareem about his father's death. He looks somber. He speaks slowly and sonorously. "My father died in a car accident in 1976. He was behind the wheel. It was not his fault. The whole country came out to mourn him. He had the biggest funeral. Half the country came to pay a condolence call."

He goes on in this fashion for quite some time.

"And what about your mother, when did she die?"

"Oh," he says, almost offhandedly, "she died, too."

And he changed the subject right back to that of his father's death.

My father-in-law has sons and daughters who range in age from infancy to men and women who are in their thirties. His first two wives are celibate and lead lives devoted to their children, lives devoid of sexual affection. Their husband remains sexually vital and active in his midsixties.

In 1918, when Edith Wharton visited Morocco, she was troubled by exactly this phenomenon, which she observed in an imperial harem in Rabat and in wealthy harems in Fez and Marrakesh.

Wharton meets many perfumed and fluttering concubines who are locked up for life. In Fez, in the home of a "chief dignitary" (a plump, middle-aged, much adored man), she observes how the youngest baby boy is cradled tenderly by his father—even as they all wait for the arrival of the "majestic bearded gentleman" who is the patriarch's first-born son. Here is Wharton on this harem: "The redeeming point in this stagnant domesticity is the tenderness of the parents for their children. . . . One would suppose children could be loved only by inert and ignorant parents . . . but the sentimentalist would do well to consider the lives of these much-petted children. Ignorance, unhealthiness, and a precocious sexual initiation prevail in all classes. At eight or nine the little girls are married, at twelve, the son of the house is 'given his first negress.'"

I applaud Wharton's clarity about slavery and women's rights. She too finds the existence of slavery—and the absence of any guilt about it—unsettling, abhorrent, especially among the educated Moroccans. Wharton knows that the Caid (an important dignitary) is "enlightened, cultivated, a friend of the arts, a scholar and diplomatist": "He seems, unlike many Orientals, to have selected the best in assimilating European influences. And yet when I looked at the tiny [African female slave] creature watching him with those anxious joyless eyes I felt once more the abyss that slavery and the seraglio put between the most Europeanized Mahometan and the Western conception of life. The Caid's little black slaves are well-known in Morocco, and behind the sad child leaning in the archway stood all the shadowy evils of the social system that hangs like a millstone about the neck of Islam."

By the time Wharton visits Morocco, the West—but not the East—has abolished slavery. In the nineteenth century the valiant and persistent William Wilberforce fought for more than a decade to end the British slave trade. He triumphed. And America fought a bloody civil war that lasted for nearly five years before President Abraham Lincoln was able to abolish slavery.

Slavery has always existed in the Islamic world. It still does. It is a taboo subject. Few scholars have dared study it. Today, in our presumably enlightened and antiracist times, neither Muslim nor secular Western scholars focus on antiblack racism or slavery among Muslims. Instead both groups focus on and condemn racism and colonialism—but only by Westerners.

To this day Abdul-Kareem still focuses only on racism in America—and it does exist. He seemingly has no idea about the role that African and Arab Muslims once played in the Atlantic slave trade.

Encountering gender apartheid and waged slavery shook me to my roots more than half a century ago in Afghanistan. Oh, the women of Afghanistan, the women of the Muslim world. I was no feminist—but now, thinking back, I see how much I learned there, how clearly their condition taught me to see gender discrimination anywhere and, above all, taught me to see how cruel oppressed women could be to each other. They taught me about women everywhere.

Poor Abdul-Kareem has been away from home for so long that he has no bond with any of his brothers. The oldest brother, Hassan, Bebegul's firstborn son, is arrogant, cold, and envious. He has not been allowed out to study abroad like his brothers, Reza and Abdul-Kareem.

Abdul-Kareem barely knows his two younger brothers, Sami and Rafi, who might have been five or six years old when he left for Europe and America.

Poor Abdul-Kareem—his father, his brothers, his entire society are probably testing him. Would he, could he, fit in? Is he still "one of them"? If so, how could he have made a love marriage with a foreign woman, a Jew, an American? Is he planning to lead a modern Western life in Kabul? Drinking, smoking, parties with foreigners? Has he forgotten where he came from?

At the time Abdul-Kareem does not discuss any of this with me. I come to understand all this only in retrospect, many years later, when I am no longer in such personal danger. Abdul-Kareem might be ashamed of his country, but he has been taught that he has to be proud of it and is obliged to defend it from all criticism. He probably cannot bear to acknowledge the truth, even to himself.

But it is more complicated than that.

Abdul-Kareem has the best chance of rapid advancement only in this country and nowhere else on Earth. He decides to deny the reality of how things are by focusing on the role he will play in changing things from how they are to how they could be. In this he is very much a Westerner.

When Flaubert visited Egypt in the mid-nineteenth century—or, rather, when he toured the brothels of Egypt—he was struck by the routine and public nature of cruelty. Men cursed at and beat their donkeys and horses. And they insulted, cursed, and beat each other. He writes, "You would scarcely believe the important role played by the cudgel in this part of the world; buffets are distributed with a sublime prodigality, always accompanied by loud cries; it's the most genuine kind of local color you can think of. . . . All the old comic business of the cudgeled slave, of the coarse trafficker in women, of the thieving merchant—it's all very fresh here, very genuine and charming."

In the harem where I live, I am horrified by the way in which our slave-like servants are treated. The way my mother-in-law treats her female servants is criminal, tragic, barbaric, unbelievable—but apparently entirely normal in Kabul, both among the elite and among the peasantry.

Bebegul takes all her frustrations out on her female servants—and they simply take it, often smiling gamely and shrugging their shoulders between their yelps and cries of pain. Bebegul curses them. She throws things at them. She beats them. The servants take it, they never quit; in fact, if anything, they are terrified of being fired.

Their pitiful wage—any wage at all—constitutes a fortune to these people from the provinces. They can both help their families and not burden them, which is all that matters to them. Married servant couples spend years living apart, working for different families in the city, hardly ever seeing each other, always at the beck and call of their overlords.

In the 1920s and 1930s the British traveler Rosita Forbes observed slave auctions, mainly of black African ("Abyssinian") slaves on their way to the harems of Saudi Arabia. The boys were castrated and, if they survived, could one day become men of wealth and influence. The girls entered harems as concubines and domestic slaves.

At auction the female slaves remain face veiled but are otherwise displayed naked from the neck down. Forbes observes that female slaves are routinely raped and beaten by their masters. She is shocked that they accept their fate so casually. And then she comes to understand that the slaves "are escaping the starvation of their hills or deserts for a land of plenty, where they will be able to eat as much as they like." Forbes, with the help of an interpreter, questions one slave girl: "'You didn't mind leaving your people?' I asked. I don't know if she understood. The Arab translated her reply as: 'She says she worked like a camel and was beaten like a dog. For her, slavery meant exchanging the mastership of a half-starving father, or husband, for that of a man who would give her food, clothing and a certainty of existence.'"

In our Kabul household the servants never starve or go to bed hungry. They eat the cold leftover food every day and consider themselves fortunate. They have all the tea, fruit, bread, rice, and yoghurt that their stomachs can hold.

The servants never complain that they have no days off. The one-room building where the servants sleep has no electricity or heat. They sleep on a packed mud floor. No one ever complains, not even when the winds howl and the freezing weather arrives. For them it is just like being at home.

No one, including Bebegul's Western-educated sons, dares interfere with her reign of tyranny. One elderly female servant is named Daw-Daw. She looks ancient, at least eighty years old, which means that she is probably in her forties or fifties. Her face is weathered and lined, and she is practically toothless. Daw-Daw herds and milks our cows. She is on call at all times, seven days a week, twenty-four hours a day. She is Bebegul's all-purpose errand girl, sweeper, body servant, and scapegoat.

Bebegul is cruel, without mercy, when it comes to beating Daw-Daw. Some years later I described their relationship as follows:

Bebegul would hit Daw-Daw hard with her fist or with a steel pot, a broom—with just about anything she could lay her hands on. Bebegul would curse Daw-Daw, too. Poor Daw-Daw would try to protect herself from the blows, but she also tried to make light of them. She had no other place to go, no family, no village. This was her only home, her fate. And Bebegul had promised to bury her.

Such daily cruelty is shocking. Its normalization is even worse. I have just turned twenty-one. I have never had a servant in my home. I have been reading books about freedom and equality my entire life.

Of course I complain to Abdul-Kareem about it and when I do, he shuts me right up. He tells me that I am in no position to judge his family or his people or their customs because I come from a country with a history of institutionalized slavery.

"Wait a minute," I would protest. "I am talking about the savage mistreatment of servants who are essentially indentured, very like slaves, right under your family's roof. Why are you changing the subject?"

This kind of exchange is typical and would continue between us for the next half-century.

I am grateful for such conversations because they have prepared me for similar exchanges with others who also deny or minimize the cruelty and misogyny in the Islamic world. Many of my conversations have been with other Westerners who, in the name of antiracism, have insisted on seeing things from the misogynist's point of view.

I do not know it, but Bebegul has another agenda in mind for me. She either means to kill me—or to convert me to Islam. She is carrying on both agendas at the same time.

Here the women pray at home. Bebegul incorporates everything into her prayers. It is like a noisy, friendly Indian theater where entire families bring their dinner and their children and talk throughout the performance. For Bebegul life does not end where her rituals begin. Between *kalimahs* (declarations of faith) she curses the servants, orders tea for her guests, mutters shopping lists to herself.

Wherever she goes, Bebegul counts her prayer beads (*tasbeh*); always, everywhere, her eyes search for some sign of the Prophet's mercy.

Day after day Bebegul walks with me arm in arm in the garden. Inexplicably she hugs me. She explains that Islam is similar to Judaism: Abraham and Moses are both important figures in the Qur'an. She takes me into her rooms and retrieves an illuminated Qur'an from atop her armoire. She cannot read Arabic but she chants the text for me, page after page.

The next day Bebegul delivers a prayer rug, thick and small, to my rooms. Another day she delivers prayer beads.

"I miss my Jewish friends, Sharban," she intones. Then she urges me to convert to Islam.

If I don't, will she continue her other campaign—the one to sicken and kill me?

The next day Bebegul storms into my bedroom, a female servant in tow, yelling and jeering and trying to find and confiscate my precious hoard of canned goods.

"Our food isn't good enough for her—she eats from cans," Bebegul would taunt.

I am sure that Bebegul considers herself my jailer and tutor in all things Afghan. My headstrong trip into town might have been considered her fault, her failure.

Bebegul also follows me about, from room to room, and mainly stares at me. Sometimes she will storm off. Other times she will suddenly laugh, turn friendly, and again suggest that I convert to Islam. She does this by unfolding her prayer rug, fingering her prayer beads, prostrating herself—then beckoning me to come and join her on my own rug.

Is she serious? Abdul-Kareem is not religious, but she is. She even made the pilgrimage to Mecca. Is this that important to her? If I say I will convert, even if I do not mean it, will it make my life here easier? Will she then allow the servants to boil my water and wash my fruits and vegetables in boiled water?

If I say I will convert, can I *really* do this without meaning it? Many Jews have chosen martyrdom over conversion. And many have converted in order to save their lives—and then returned to Judaism when it was safe to do so.

This is my situation: I am Bebegul's captive, her prisoner; she, my jailer, might treat me more decently if I find ways to please her. It might even save my life.

This is difficult for me to write about. It is harder to admit that I was this foolish, this frightened, this alone that I would actually jettison the religion of my ancestors for another religion about which I knew absolutely nothing.

But I did it. I repeated what Bebegul had me say, a single sentence in Arabic, not in Farsi, and that was it: *la illah-ha illah allah, Muhammed a-rasul Allah.* (There is one god, Allah, and Mohammed is his prophet.)

I am not expected to do anything further. No one hosts a welcome party. I attend no mosque and meet with no mullah.

I try to discuss this with Abdul-Kareem, my very secular husband. He turns away. He pretends I have not said anything.

This is not something I ever tell anyone. Nevertheless I have never forgiven myself.

Recently Maria, a divorced American woman, turned to me for help. She was trapped in Bahrain because, like Betty Mahmoody, who had been trapped in Iran, Maria was also a mother who would not leave without her daughter.

Maria had cleared customs and had gotten the girl on board a plane, but a young and extremely stupid American embassy official persuaded her to come back, just to answer a few questions.

The girl's Bahraini father had remarried. He and his new wife, as well as their respective families, had already embarked on a successful alienation campaign against the stranded, unemployed, and friendless American mother. As I was talking to her, I asked her some routine questions about her birth and American citizenship.

"Are you a Christian?"

She was silent for a long while.

"Did you convert to Islam?"

Finally, and so softly I could barely hear her, she said, "Maybe. I think so. Yes." She sounded ashamed, broken, as if she had sold her soul.

I could understand how she felt.

For a while Bebegul is pleased with me. She hugs me each time she sees me. She hums happy little tunes. She even stops beating Daw-Daw.

Then she begins to go out almost every day, perhaps to share the good news that she has converted her infidel Jewish daughter-in-law to Islam. I am one of them now, and her family has no reason to feel ashamed about a foreign bride or a love match. We are now all Muslims together.

And she, Bebegul, has accomplished this.

But it doesn't matter. A private conversion between two women in their rooms could not temper Bebegul's mad and permanent fury.

Within a week she begins screaming at me again. This time, and for the first time, she calls me Yahud (Jew) over and over again, and she spits at me.

So: She too does not believe that I have really converted. Still I am surprised. This is an unexpected insult that cuts me to the core. While she still misses her Afghan Jewish friends, the Sharbans, Bebegul really doesn't want a Jew to join her faith. Maybe she does not believe that a Jew could be trusted to actually convert.

She is right.

Or perhaps she is just plain mean and mad and nothing that anyone does can ever please or change her. Since she keeps taunting me as a Yahud, I finally call her the only curse word I know that she will understand.

I call her a whore (*conchonee*).

Now I feel endangered as a Jew, as a woman, as an American, and as a foreigner.

I call Abdul-Kareem at his brother's office and am crying incoherently: "Your mother keeps cursing and insulting me. If you don't come home and get me out of this house right away, I'm walking back to America. I'll join a band of nomads. I'll do anything to get away. Why didn't you tell me your mother was crazy? She follows me around everywhere, she never stops watching me. Do you know that she's been doing this? How can you expect me to sit home all day and do nothing?"

Abdul-Kareem and I thrash things out again. He is not in the least bit understanding. He says that he does not have it easy either, that I could ruin it for him (that fear again). He refuses to help me if I refuse to make the necessary efforts.

Nothing changes. Nothing is happening. I have read all the books that I brought in with me. Abdul-Kareem is at home only at night, when he talks mainly to his brothers and always in Dari. I am trying to figure out how to make a long-distance call. I think the American embassy is nearby. Maybe I just have to throw myself on their mercy and on their very doorstep.

Abdul-Kareem is not working. But he insists that all his meetings with ministers and government officials, drinking tea with them, is actually work. He meets people at his father's bank and at the family's import-export company. He is in the bosom of his family. A top place will be found for him. Then he will be able to enjoy himself and start attending diplomatic functions, parties, feasts.

How can an American like me ever understand how dependent, how interdependent, Afghans are? I was raised with the belief that individuals can succeed if they work hard. Success and security come only from one's own efforts. I am so naive. I do not understand that one's family and friends—plus luck—are everything, not only in Afghanistan but everywhere.

I am someone who left home as soon as she could. Abdul-Kareem—to my surprise—seems to have no problem living with his mother and brothers and their families. What can I do except continue to try to escape? And to make the most of the parties I am allowed to attend?

I go to the American embassy and ask them to get me out of here. The Marine guards do not even let me in. My case must already be known. They explain that I no longer have any rights as an American citizen—not unless I can produce my American passport. They escort me back home.

My British-educated brother-in-law, Reza, tries to impress or at least amuse me with a hair-raising tale about a man and a dog. It was told to him on his recent trip to Mazar-i-Sharif.

In the country Afghan hounds (hunters) are reared as sheep dogs. They are trained to attack everyone except the shepherd and his family. Some years ago a stranger bumped into a flock and was chased up a tree by the hound. The shepherd demanded that the man come down and fight the dog—otherwise the dog would become a coward and be of no further use. Understandably the man refused. The shepherd raised his rifle to shoot him down.

The stranger flung his quilted robe toward the shepherd, muffling the shot and confusing the dog, which promptly tore out his master's throat. The local mullahs jailed the stranger when he told them the story. They couldn't decide what to do with him. Undoubtedly he had violated some rule, some custom; they would figure it out over time at their council meetings.

"Now," Reza laughs, "five years later, the man is still in jail, and the mullahs are still debating what to do with him."

I am horrified by the story, mostly by his humorous telling of it. And he's the brother-in-law who once lived and studied in England. These customs do not amuse me. They frighten me.

I know that there are massive injustices in America. But the people I know back home are the ones who criticize such injustice. As Americans they do not laugh about tragic miscarriages of justice.

I know that my American understanding of due process has no place here. The mullahs and those who look up to them have the last say. I am definitely at the mercy of another kind of culture.

Bebegul does not fire old Daw-Daw, at least not when I am there. But she does fire Fawziya's young and heavily pregnant nursemaid and housekeeper. And she does so sadistically.

The nursemaid-housekeeper's name is Madar Kamar (Kamar's mother). She is a rural woman about my age, but she might be a year older than I am. We are about the same height. Her complexion is both ruddy and fair, but her hands are rough. She is up at dawn and retires only after everyone else is sleeping.

Madar Kamar is good natured; she has no malice in her—she laughs all the time and is kind. Madar Kamar is also bashful and shy; she covers her face with her long veils when she laughs. She claps her hands with pleasure when I tell her about America: about our tall buildings, elevators, fast-moving crowded trains, and roads that run from sea to shining sea.

Madar Kamar is usually barefoot, and she keeps her hair in a long black braid. Like most servants she is on duty 24/7 and does not seem to have any days off. She sleeps on the floor, either across the threshold of Fawziya and Hassan's quarters or on the floor right next to Fawziya's two young children. Madar Kamar's seven-year-old daughter (Kamar) sleeps right by her side.

This means that Madar Kamar was married when she was thirteen or fourteen and had become a mother at fifteen—when I was still in high school. Her husband is a servant in another family, and they see each other a few times every year. Madar Kamar has already suffered four miscarriages; she cries like a child each time she talks about this. But now, with Allah's help, she is six or seven months pregnant.

We spend many hours of every day together. Both she and Fawziya help me learn the Dari word for whatever I point to.

Madar Kamar's fate has weighed on my conscience and haunted me down the decades. I may have been responsible for her extreme humiliation and hardship. As I contemplate escape routes for myself, I imagine rescuing Madar Kamar at the same time. But even then I understood that she would have no place in my world and that she is firmly rooted in Afghanistan and in a particular family network that can never be replaced or replicated in America.

My mistake—my sin, my crime, is this: I lend Madar Kamar a heavy sweater. She is cold. I offer it to her. She refuses this kindness many times—and then gratefully accepts it. Bebegul routinely goes through all the servants' things; she finds the sweater and concludes that Madar Kamar has stolen it from me.

I explain exactly what I've done. I take full responsibility. It makes no difference. Bebegul's mind is made up. Some years later I wrote about what happened next:

> One afternoon, Fawziya and I were finishing lunch upstairs. The sun was brilliant and flooded the thick carpets in the room. I felt drugged by the food, the sun and the hot tea. Someone put the radio on and the hypnotic whining of an Afghan singer floated in on globes of sunlight.
>
> Madar Kamar brought fresh tea up. Cross-legged, she began to pour it for us. Her hand was shaking though, and soon hot tears splashed over the teapot.

"What is it? What's the matter?" There was no answer, only she didn't stop crying.

When she got up to return the dishes to the kitchen, we followed her out.

Bebegul was standing right outside the kitchen-house.

Seeing Madar Kamar, she laughed a malicious laugh and pointed her finger at her.

"Whore-daughter, bastard-carrier, I will tell your husband about the other men who visit you day and night. Yes, yes, I myself saw one creep out this morning. I will tell everyone. You are a thief. No one steals from Bebegul."

Shocked, Fawziya ordered Madar Kamar back into the house. For the first time since I'd come, I saw Fawziya, a thin submissive daughter-in-law, fighting with Bebegul.

At dinner the men discussed the matter, taking care to gently chide Fawziya for fighting with Bebegul.

"Well," Hassan concluded, "I told Madar Kamar's husband to come for her tonight."

And so he did. He looked old enough to be her father. Madar Kamar was crying when she left. She would be returning to her village to wait for the baby; this meant less food to eat and a cold winter in very primitive conditions.

We kissed goodbye. I urged her to return to the city and to the hospital to have her baby. Gently, I reminded her that her village midwife had already "delivered" a stillborn and that she'd had three miscarriages under her care.

A month later I heard she had prematurely delivered a healthy and very much longed for boy.

I cannot protect Madar Kamar, nor can Fawziya, who depends upon her. I cannot even protect myself.

Many years later, as lawsuits are successfully launched in America against wealthy couples from other countries who are, correctly, seen as enslaving their servants—I remember that in many parts of the world (Afghanistan, for instance) slave-like conditions for servants are the norm.

And I remember Madar Kamar and Daw-Daw and the family's hearty male cook and gentle male gardener, and wonder how they are and what ever happened to them.

SIX

Trapped

I had hoped that I could get in and out of Kabul in no more than a few chapters. But now that I'm here again, I can't seem to get out.

This time I am not trapped. I am choosing to linger. This will be my last time here—and writing about it is the only way I will be able to visit Afghanistan safely, especially the Afghanistan of the past. The Afghanistan I knew, the Afghanistan my husband and his family once knew, is now a vanished world.

My life there was indoors. My adventures were interpersonal. Although I gazed at the mountains every single day, I could only dream about walking or climbing them. I am now seeing the country as if for the first time. I peer at photographs and read old newspaper clippings. I read the works of those intrepid adventurers who hiked or rode into the Afghan mountains, into the pink, red, and beige deserts, to the edge of the sapphire-blue lakes. Many Western travelers cheerfully rode buses without brakes and trusted they would survive the thousand-foot drops on the incredibly narrow mountain roads.

These travelers, both men and women, crossed shaky bridges over roaring rivers, braved desert storms, walked enormous distances during frigid winters, and visited all the cities and provinces of the Silk Route. In 1960, the year before I arrived, two British mountain climbers, Joyce Dunsheath and Eleanor Baillie, set out to climb Mir Samir, a 19,882-foot mountain in the Hindu Kush. A snowstorm trapped them at 17,500 feet.

They write, "As far as our vision was concerned Mir Samir [the peak] was not there. . . . We made no plans—we sat back, trying to keep warm in our little tent, while the blizzard raged outside, and did crossword puzzles from the 7th *Daily Telegraph* book."

Only the British can remain so calm and so eccentrically cozy as their very death stares them down.

At great risk to themselves, an Afghan soldier and porter who accompanied Dunsheath and Baillie on their expedition rescue them. The men inform the women that they are in "considerable danger . . . that [they] would be swept away tent and all."

Oh, how I wish I could have climbed a mountain in Afghanistan! But although I have climbed mountains since, I am now only an armchair traveler who lives through Dunsheath and Baillie. Still, even the hardy Brits needed the Afghan equivalent of Everest's Sherpa guides to save them.

The country can be deadly cold and inhospitable. I have never known such cold as I experienced in Kabul in my first and only winter there. And I was in a grand house, not in a wooden or mud hut perched on a mountainside where icy storms are as common as . . . ice storms. Abdul-Kareem never mentioned how extreme the weather is in Afghanistan, and I never independently investigated the matter. From afar, looking at exquisite photographs, one might conclude that deep snowdrifts are dreamy and that deadly desert storms are beautiful.

From 1965 to 1979 Roland and Sabrina Michaud visited Afghanistan and published a brief essay and ninety-eight spellbinding photos of twelve cities or provinces, including Herat, Mazar-i-Sharif, Nimruz, Tashburghan, Balkh, the Wakhan Valley, Bamiyan, and Nuristan. These photos depict the Afghanistan I might have known had I been allowed to travel—a timeless, gracious, truly exotic, and, except for the Kuchis and female children, an almost womanless place but nevertheless a country alive with dervishes, blacksmiths, shepherds, camel drivers, shopkeepers, men in teahouses, armed Pushtuns—all the faces of humanity.

I visit these places now in photos and in books. I meet Afghanistan for the first time in precisely this way.

I am a child of the New World and am used to fast subway trains, supermarkets, and kitchen machines that make cooking an easy matter. Being in Afghanistan enables me to see how most people have lived for millennia—at a much slower pace, valuing that which is given, knowing that all outcomes are uncertain.

For years at college Abdul-Kareem talked to me about the glories of the Moghuls, the dazzling minarets, the Gandahara School of Art, the fields of red tulips, the exquisite gardens that each conqueror and every Afghan emperor, shah, emir, or king has tenderly created. I am eager to see it all.

"Let's visit the Baala Hissar" (the High Fort), I suggest. "It's right in town. Are there tour guides in Kabul?"

The Baala Hissar is the fortress and palace that has been the home of many Afghan kings, beginning with the Moghul emperor Akbar. Abdul-Kareem is annoyed.

"This is now your home. In time you will see everything. Please don't act like an American tourist."

I want to see Bamiyan, which has been visited by many millions of people for two thousand years. In her book *Valley of the Giant Buddhas,* the Scottish Saira Shah, writing under the name Morag Murray Abdullah, describes the statues of Buddha that reside there: "[There are three] standing Buddha figures, the two largest 35 [113 feet] and 53 metres [172 feet] high, are of such striking appearance that they far overshadow such sights as the Pyramids and Sphinx in Egypt, or the rose-red city of Petra in Jordan. Originally covered in red and gold . . . the draperies and ribbons, as well as the crowns and other decorations, point to a unique culture-mixing of Persian, Sassanid, and Greek."

Now I will never see them; no one will. Over the centuries Muslim Afghans mutilated, shot at, and destroyed the faces, hands, and legs of the despised infidel idols; six months before 9/11 the Taliban finally blew them up entirely.

People are amazed when I tell them that Islam is merely the newest religion in Afghanistan, that Zoroastrianism, Greco-Roman paganism, and Hinduism but especially Buddhism preceded Islam by ten to twelve centuries and continued to flourish there until the fourteenth century.

In the seventh century CE the Chinese Buddhist monk Hsuan-Tang documented the thriving Buddhist culture in Bamiyan. He found one hundred monasteries with several thousand monks in Bamiyan alone. In addition, Hsuan-Tang visited the Buddhist monasteries near Balkh, Kabul, and Jalalabad.

In 1269 that other merchant of Venice, Marco Polo, undertook an arduous journey to the courts of Kublai Khan, emperor of the world's largest land-based empire. Polo ventured eastward through Afghanistan and wrote about the Buddhist monks there. He found that they were soft-spoken, wore orange, shaved the crown of their heads, and spent their time studying, praying, and chanting. Two thousand monks might be sheltered in one monastery. Polo described the Buddhist monks in Afghanistan this way: "They live more decently than the others for they keep themselves from . . . sensuality and improprieties. . . . They live in communities, observe strict abstinence in regard to eating, drinking, and the intercourse of the sexes, and refrain from every kind of sensual indulgence, in order that they may not give offence to the idols whom they worship. They have several monasteries, in which certain superiors exercise the functions of our abbots, and by the mass of the people they are held in great reverence."

Had I stayed in Afghanistan, had I become Abdul-Kareem's Afghan wife, I might have seen the Buddhas of Bamiyan and everything else as well: the Great Mosque in Mazar-i-Sharif with its jeweled tile-work and arresting minarets, the mosque and tomb of Mirwais Baba in Kandahar. In photos the turquoise-blue domes of the mosques seem to melt into the sky. Instead, over the years I have read whatever has crossed my path about Afghanistan. I have spent hours looking at my worn copies of the *Afghanistan News,* a government magazine. I have twenty-nine of these magazines, which date from the mid-1950s to the early 1960s. These magazines are now of immense historical value.

The magazine's photos capture the country's breathtaking natural beauty. The majestic snow-capped purple and blue mountains, the verdant valleys (the Panjsher, the Wygal), the shimmering deep blue lakes (the Bandi-i-Amir), the massive medieval minarets in Herat and Ghor—all the brightly bejeweled blue, turquoise, and green tiled mosques.

In 1959 the Afghan government publicly announced in the *Afghanistan News* that the "wearing of the veil is not part of Islam, the religion followed devoutly by the entire Afghan nation. . . . The Chadari [burqa], or veil, worn by townswomen in Afghanistan has no religious basis." The government carefully notes that "it is not compulsory to go out with a chadari" and spells out the new clothing requirements. Women are required to wear "a scarf covering the head but leaving the face bare and a long-sleeved topcoat covering all the other garments, gloves, heavy stockings, and shoes."

Thereafter the government magazine has a number of carefully posed photos of female students being graduated at Kabul University; they are bare faced and wearing mortarboards and smiling. I see graduating nurses who are also bare faced and wearing nurses' caps. The mothers and sisters who have come to cheer them on are wearing long headscarves and coats. I see Afghan airline attendants in snappy Western uniforms.

The country *was* on its way to modernization when the Soviet invasion and the fundamentalist reaction to it stopped all progress and sent the country hurtling backward into misery.

When I was in Kabul, Abdul-Kareem minimized the burqas, saw them as "on their way out," became incensed if I criticized them. To this day Abdul-Kareem rails against the American choice of Hamid Karzai as Afghanistan's president—and why?—because, among other things, Karzai does not allow his wife to appear in public.

But, oddly enough, Abdul-Kareem does not praise King Amanullah for having unveiled the women in the late 1920s. On the contrary, over the years Abdul-Kareem has condemned Amanullah as a bumbler, a fool, and a murderer. He believes that Amanullah murdered his own father. According to the American journalist Rhea Tally Stewart, in her massive work, *Fire in Afghanistan 1914–1929*, Amanullah became king in 1919 after a dramatic power struggle with his uncle, Nasrullah, who had probably conspired to murder his brother, King Habibullah, who was Amanullah's father. Abdul-Kareem thinks that Amanullah and his mother, Ulya Hazrat, were behind the plot. Nasrullah immediately declared himself the rightful heir. According to Tally Stewart, "Nasrullah would have abolished all the existing aspects of modernity, which Amanullah ached to enlarge."

As we know, this is a time-honored pattern among Afghans. Uncles vie with nephews; brothers and half-brothers kill each other for the throne.

Amanullah had grown up as the son of Habibullah's most powerful wife—but he grew up in an imperial harem surrounded by many stepmothers (cowives) and step-siblings. Amanullah immediately liberated his father's many wives when he became king—and he shared his vision of modernization and coeducation with his people.

He delivered public speeches about the importance of educating daughters as well as sons. According to Tally Stewart, in 1928 Amanullah called it shameful that Afghan women were not educated and compared them unfavorably to European women who worked and were active. In Amanullah's opinion this was one of the main reasons Afghanistan was backward and Europe "more prosperous." In another speech, mainly to Afghan women, Amanullah said, "In no Moslim country other than Afghanistan, not even Turkey or Persia, are women 'buried alive.' Veiling has retarded your progress. . . . I want to see you disregard the wishes of your husbands in regard to veiling."

In the fall of 1928 King Amanullah spent five days publicly describing his proposals to end bribery, reform the military, provide old-age pensions, institute coeducation, improve trade—and unveil the women. The tribes rebelled, and by January 1929 the bandit tribal leader Bacha Saquo had driven Amanullah into exile.

Abdul-Kareem does not seem to like or trust his brothers. The brothers are all highly competitive, disdainful, and distrustful of each other.

> These are brothers who would kill each other if they had the opportunity, especially if there were something substantial to gain.
>
> Hassan, Agha Jan's eldest son, is a good-looking, petty despot: close-shaven, well-dressed, short, and, in his view, cheated of his inheritance because his father had too many other sons.
>
> He is furious that Abdul-Kareem and I have been given rooms in what he views as his home. Actually, this is Bebegul's home but she had a fight with Hassan and either moved out or was forced into the redecorated servants' quarters across the courtyard. Hassan is waiting impatiently to have a house of his own. One day, he explodes. He yells at me: "I've let you do whatever you do in my bathroom." He makes it sound as if I use his bathroom to commit filthy, unspeakable crimes.

Abdul-Kareem's two older brothers do not trust him at all. They don't seem to like or trust each other; perhaps they cannot afford to be affectionate toward one another.

In a way the only man in the family is their father. This household has more than three wives. Ismail Mohammed's *sons* are also married to their father. They talk about him incessantly. They watch his every move. They are starved for their father's attention and affection—and of course are fixated on their inheritances. But they act like his wives. He is their main subject of discussion.

My brothers-in-law frequently make self-conscious jokes about their father's virility and villainy. However, they still flush with pleasure when Ismail Mohammed openly favors or compliments one of them. They idealize, fear, and resent him. I believe that these sons long for their father's attention and power. No mere woman can provide what such father-starved sons want. Sometimes my brothers-in-law adopt a wildly humorous attitude toward their father's inability to show fatherly affection. They tell me, "Sometime after the war, our father used to listen to the American radio broadcasts about family life in America. He was very impressed by the fact that many fathers would go to their children's rooms and kiss them goodnight."

They pause and we all laugh. The sight of that proud patriarch making the rounds of some fifteen- or twenty-odd beds in the greatest of discomfort but in all seriousness must have been pretty funny.

"It was impossible to keep up, though," Reza concludes. "Father stopped and went back to accepting our kisses on his hand. The whole thing was rather silly anyway."

Are most Afghan patriarchs this distant toward their sons, this physically cold? Is this precisely the way to guarantee filial obedience and permanent rivalry among sons for their father's withheld affection?

In her book about the Shah of Iran, the author Margaret Laing quotes Empress Farah, the Shah's wife, who ascribes her husband's reluctance to hug and kiss his own children to his not having been hugged or kissed by his own father; such things were not done.

This kind of father-son relationship seems to characterize many of the relationships between polygamous Muslim fathers and their sons. Some sons become subservient grovelers—who will never overthrow their father's (or leader's) tyrannical regime. The system works. Such sons end up adoring as well as fearing their father. Some sons—like Osama bin Laden, who was one of fifty-seven children—take a different route.

Bebegul's second son, Reza, is much taller than Hassan. Reza has a British accent and a slow, wry wit. He is ironic about his return from England. He returned to Kabul for what he calls his "golden castles in Asia," leaving behind a heartbroken young mistress and an illegitimate son . . . or so I was told.

Like Abdul-Kareem, Reza was also kept on a rather short financial leash. This is a government decision. They do not want young Afghans to experience the kind of high life that might make them think twice about returning home. Hassan was never allowed to leave the country, at least not as a student. I am not sure why, but I am sure that Hassan resents this enormously. It doesn't matter that he is being groomed to one day take over his father's place at the bank.

For now both Hassan and Reza work for their father. Hassan works at the bank, Reza at the import-export company, each in positions analogous to their order of birth. They parade and enjoy these positions as much as they feel cheated by them. Their salaries are minimal; they make no decisions, only their father does. At first Reza could not or would not adjust to life back in Kabul. He wanted no part of his father's feudal and emasculating authority. Reza took to his rooms and brooded for almost a year. And then he emerged. Reza himself tells me, "I finally accepted it. I am working for my father, and I'm engaged to a girl whose mother is English. I've seen her once, and even though she doesn't speak English, she is presentable enough."

Aside from his minimal salary, which pays for cigarettes and snacks, Reza does not have enough money to live on his own. Reza visits his fiancée, Mahtab, and her parents every week. His is a modern engagement. Traditionally an Afghan bride and groom meet for the first time on the day of their wedding, which is essentially a ceremony conducted only by and for men. The bride and groom meet afterward, when they first see each other reflected in a mirror.

As I came to learn, the bride cannot express any emotion whatsoever on her wedding day. If she looks happy, it will insult her mother and father, whose home she will be leaving forever. If she looks sad, that would be seen as an insult to her husband's family, especially her mother-in-law, with whom she will be living.

Reza spends his spare time visiting the house his father is building for him. He does not like the house. "Nothing works, nothing is right. He did not hire an architect. He sketched the house in the margins of a newspaper himself."

Reza's only satisfaction resides in the still more inferior position at the office occupied by his older half-brother, Samir (the first son of Agha Jan's second wife, Tooba). And Reza patiently points this and other facts out to Samir, and suggests and encourages him to petition their father for redress, sympathizing with Samir when their various strategies fail, as always. In this way Reza both reaffirms his slight edge over Samir and gets to enjoy a vicarious confrontation with their father at Samir's expense. Thus victorious, Reza has genuine compassion for Samir, who is still unmarried.

Samir is an absurdly skinny, angular boy-man. A frayed black karakul (Persian lambskin) hat is perched on his small sad head. He looks frightened at all times. His father has never arranged a marriage for him. Rumor has it that once, when the women "went out for him," the designated girl's parents rejected the match.

One day Samir, on behalf of his mother, Tooba, and sister, Rabia, invites me for tea. He ushers me happily into his modest home with high shrill feminine giggles of greeting.

Tooba serves us a plate of English lemon cookies—a luxury they can scarcely afford. It is late afternoon and cold. The three of us, strangers in every way, happily drink our tea. A feeling of closeness passes between us in place of bright conversation.

Tooba shows me Samir's room. It is like stepping into a luxurious miniature engraving. Light silk curtains fall on either side of the window. The bed occupies an alcove and is covered with a brilliant electric turquoise spread. A small tapestry hangs over the bed, and a lovely prayer rug is rolled up nearby. His is a beautiful, really perfect, room. No pretentious East-West clutter here, no heavy Germanic fireplaces, no heavy velvet drapes.

Instead of the expensive Western-style leather bedroom slippers that most wealthy Afghan men wear, a pair of comfortable Persian-style slippers stands near Samir's bed. Some magazines are arranged on the floor near the window. They carry illustrated stories of some of Samir's favorite places: a hotel overlooking the Nile, a garden in Shiraz, a folk festival in Uzbekistan.

Samir rubs one hand in the other, embarrassed and pleased at my obvious pleasure. He offers me more tea and "perhaps some fruit"?

How he must suffer, I think!

I am going crazy with boredom and loneliness. My sister-in-law Fawziya, Hassan's wife, tells me: "Pretend you are an Afghan woman. Forget that you were ever American. It's the only way you'll survive."

In Edward Hunter's book about Afghan women in purdah, he describes a "pattern of depression, weeping spells, and cruelty" among *Afghan* women, who were not raised as Americans. He quotes an unnamed informant who describes women crying, sobbing, and slapping themselves: "These poor, pent-up creatures have nobody else whose face they can slap. Except the faces of other females who must submit to them, a daughter-in-law perhaps, or a daughter. Outsiders simply cannot conceive how dreadful the feeling of isolation from life can be in purdah."

At the time everyone, including Abdul-Kareem, treats what I view as my captivity as a spoiled American woman's overly dramatic reaction to how things simply . . . are.

Hassan barely speaks to Fawziya. Once, right in front of her, Hassan asks me what I think of his wife: "If ten is the rating for beauty, what number would you give her? A two?"

Fawziya keeps smiling brightly. I am sure she understands his question.

I hug her. I tell Hassan that I would rate her far beyond a ten.

"Maybe Fawziya is a twenty. What do you think you are, Hassan?"

I do not like this vain and arrogant brother-in-law, who is so heartless toward his gentle wife.

Everyone in Abdul-Kareem's family has submitted to an arranged marriage. Only Abdul-Kareem has married a woman without any Afghan ancestors. He has not expanded his family's social or economic reach. He has married selfishly, for love. It is a scandal. Given what I now understand, I believe that his family was as warm and welcoming to me as they could be. But they are starving me. I am always hungry. I cannot persuade Bebegul or Abdul-Kareem to allow the cook to use Crisco.

I still find this impossible to believe. In all the years I was with Abdul-Kareem in America, he cooked for me so tenderly. I love all his Afghan dishes. I considered myself lucky to have had such a brilliant personal chef. Yet here in Kabul he does not seem to care that I am hungry but unable to eat the food.

Years later, in 1978, Aziz, one of Abdul-Kareem's younger half-brothers, comes to visit me in Manhattan. Aziz reminds me that I used to slip across to the home of his mother, Meena (she is the third wife), and politely ask for some food. Their cook used Crisco. The food was always gone but Aziz, who was ten at the time, would promise me that "next time" he'd save something for me. He never managed it.

I hear that a new restaurant, an American-style cafeteria, has opened in town. I decide that this would be a perfect opportunity for me to get some much-needed nutrition and for Abdul-Kareem and me to have some time alone together.

I have meat loaf, mashed potatoes, string beans, and apple pie. I am thrilled. Abdul-Kareem looks miserable the entire time. His mouth is turned down; he does not eat with me. He steers me to a far corner of the room "where people won't be able to see us making fools of ourselves."

Who is this man? My life is in the hands of a stranger.

"Abdul-Kareem, let's just move out. Can't we live at the Kabul hotel? Or, better still, why don't we travel a bit, see the country? Or can we at least rent a furnished home?"

He sneers at me. "You are a child. Do you mean to ruin me before I've even begun? News of this little meal of yours is going to land on some minister's desk, and it will be used against me. When will you understand that Afghans do not dine out in restaurants? It is not done."

"Excuse me, Mr. Afghan," I respond. "I see men in *choi chanas* (teahouses) sitting on raised platforms and drinking, eating, and smoking all over town. Don't you mean that *women* are not supposed to eat out or be seen in public?"

"I will not dignify that with a response. I will not talk about this."

He continues more softly: "The problem, Phyllis dear, is that you do not know how to run a proper Afghan household. You do not speak the language; the servants will take advantage of you. They will steal everything. And you—you would ruin us with your parties and liquor and dancing and music—"

"Wait a minute. I am the one who reads books. I am not a party girl. You are the one who likes to party."

"Don't you understand that I am being closely watched?"

"Are we living in Soviet Russia? Is this a totalitarian regime?"

"Phyllis, I beg you. Please lower your voice. People are not used to an Afghan couple living alone. They would not understand it. It would be seen as disrespectful to my family. No one is used to having his wife run around town on her own to sightsee. People would talk."

"Abdul-Kareem, I can't remain locked up with your mother, who I believe hates me. Even Fawziya is afraid of her."

Pro forma, Abdul-Kareem denies that I am in purdah. He insists that the women in his family and in his country are far happier and far more fulfilled than neurotic American women are. But he also takes his other standard tack.

"Things are going to change here. We can be a part of this. But until then I will have to be very careful. One scandal, one slip, and it can all be over for me. If you don't ruin things, you will have many things to do by my side. You won't have time to be 'locked up,' as you put it. I am going to be an important man here. Please trust me. So far, no one else will."

The man is cunning. First he tries to cut me down to size, then he insults my country and my culture, then he dangles the carrot.

*E*veryone knows that I'm at a loose and desperate end.

Thus I am beginning to get out a bit more but only under carefully supervised conditions. I see the longed-for sites as we pass them by on our way to visit someone. I see the beautiful tomb of Emir Abdur Rahman (1880–1901) in Kabul—but from afar. It seems graceful, like something from a fairy tale, like the Taj Mahal. I see Amanullah's half-built palace, the Darul Aman (or Dar-al-Aman) palace, which commands an extraordinary view.

I see the old British fort. Whenever we pass it by, Abdul-Kareem and every other Afghan is sure to remind me that the Afghans drove the mighty British Empire out. In point of fact the British had agreed to withdraw, and the Afghans proceeded to massacre 4,500 mainly Indian soldiers commanded by British officers, as well as nearly 12,000 camp followers, which means women and children. Only one British man, Dr. William Brydon, managed to reach Jalalabad alive. He was the sole eyewitness to what is known as the First Anglo-Afghan War (1839–42).

I come to love the Blue Mosque of Kabul. It is a small mosque near the Kabul River in the center of town. Its dome is azure blue, sky blue, a heavenly color.

The family has homes and properties in Istalif, Paghman, Jalalabad, and Herat. Paghman is a summer resort just outside Kabul. After I suffer several bouts of truly wretched dysentery, Abdul-Kareem, his brothers, sisters, and their spouses take me on a visit to Paghman. It is an act of enormous kindness, an all-out effort to cheer me up and perhaps to impress me as well. I am duly impressed and grateful.

Shahs, emirs, and kings made this their summer home, and their courtiers quickly followed. At the start of the fifteenth century, when Babur the Great conquered Kabul, he found that exquisite gardens already existed in Paghman. In the late nineteenth century Emir Abdur Rahman established his summer court here.

In addition to the Bala-Bagh (upper garden) palace, an ornate Afghan version of a European Victorian-era gingerbread house, there are other villas, a vast Versailles-like garden, showy statuary, fountains, fountain geysers, gazebos, waterfalls, lakes, flowers, trees—so many trees, and more greenery than I have ever seen.

There is even an arch built by King Amanullah in imitation of the Arc de Triomphe. This one commemorates the Afghan victory over the British.

This is not an example of simple and overt Western colonialism. This is an example of the Eastern appropriation of Western architecture and landscaping. In a culturally Eurocentric world, everyone, including wealthy Afghans, wanted a little bit of European culture at home.

This is ironic, since so many Western travelers to the East want to go native—wear turbans, ride camels, dine and sleep in tents or at least on carpeted floors, drinking tea and coffee flavored with cardamom.

Rosanne Klass, in *Land of the High Flags: Afghanistan When the Going Was Good,* explains it this way: The Afghans were in isolation for so long that when they emerged, "they realized they had been left aside in a changing world . . . so they rushed to accumulate what the world had in the meantime stamped as accepted goods, in arts and elsewhere."

We visit Paghman sometime in mid- or late October. The family's European-style villa is not in use. The furniture is covered with white muslin sheets. It feels ghostly, uninhabited, but still grand. Does Ismail Mohammed travel there with his third wife, or does he use it only to entertain foreign business contacts? Does he come here at all?

We remove the sheets from the couches. What an attempt at good-will! My sisters-in-law and my brothers-in-law tell jokes to cheer me up—and Abdul-Kareem translates for me. They try so hard to please me. We had hoped to have a picnic but it is too cold, almost blustery. The way Afghans, Persians, and Turks organize picnics has been honed to a high art. The meal is meant to be unhurried, the conversations leisurely. One is expected to dine, doze, take a walk, fly kites. Being in nature is paramount. Abdul-Kareem and his Afghan friends took me on many such picnics in New York City, and the slow and courtly pace seemed to take place outside time.

On this precious day in Paghman we dine indoors but picnic style. (Actually every meal is picnic style since we always dine on the carpeted floor.)

The Afghans and Persians have a great reputation for both writing and reciting poetry aloud. Although the great Persian poet Firdausi, who wrote the *Shahnamah,* established himself in Ghazni, and the mystic poet Rumi once lived in Balkh, none of my well-meaning relatives recited any poetry that day in Paghman.

Afterward we tour Paghman. Slowly we walk through lush green gardens surrounded by emerald trees and rushing streams; the air is filled with the sweet songs of birds. I can still remember a young boy by a stream: such large beautiful eyes. I remember the smell of his skewered ready-to-eat kebobs and the taste of his sticky candies. We bought luscious melons from another young boy.

By then I thought nothing of child workers. They were everywhere. Families used their young children to help with cooking, shopping, gathering wood, babysitting, tending ailing grandparents. Children would feed the donkey or the chickens, herd the sheep, milk the cow, plant and harvest, and earn money in any way possible.

Businesses in Kabul routinely used young boys for errands and pouring tea. Fruit and vegetable vendors, butchers, tailors, kebob stands, bakeries all had boys as young as nine working with them full time, boys who were happy to be earning some money, perhaps learning a trade, or making lifelong contacts.

Afghanistan has been literally reduced to dust many times over. According to military historian Stephen Tanner, "In 1221 [many sources say 1219], the Mongol army descended on Afghanistan like a force of nature, or in [Louis] Dupree's words, 'the atom bomb of its day.' Many communities in Afghanistan never regained their former stature. . . . Towns and farms based on centuries-old cultivation techniques lay naked in the path of the Mongol hordes."

The people of Herat rebelled and murdered their Mongol governor. Mongol forces launched a siege against the city.

"Herat held out for six months," Tanner continues, "but in the end its walls were breached and the people were lined up for massacre—a process that took seven days. Afterward a Mongol detachment raced back to surprise anyone who had emerged from hiding. It found two thousand more victims to add to the stupefying piles of bodies. Balkh, too, rebelled. . . . This time the massacre was so complete that a Chinese visitor who passed by the city's ruins a few years later could only hear the sounds of dogs barking."

As Rhea Talley Stewart describes it, the Mongols destroyed, "along with the people, the irrigation systems they had created. . . . Irrigation means life. . . . It turned [to] salt. Of all the places destroyed . . . only Herat, because it is in a fertile valley, really rebuilt itself."

On the subject of what has been lost, in *Land of the High Flags*, Rosanne Klass writes, "Ghazni is now little more than a village, which was once a gorgeous court. Balkh, the Mother of Cities, is a heap of rubble. . . . The scholars are gone, the poets, the heroes, the kings were gone, the land was stripped of life, the fields were ruined and barren."

As for the gardens and villas of Paghman, now they too are no more—they are gone, all gone. In my lifetime the Soviets reduced them to dust, debris. Now Old Paghman exists only in old photographs and in living memory.

Last night I viewed a series of old photos online taken in Paghman. I became quite melancholy. One of the early photos is in black and white and is labeled Royal Hunting Party. The royal residence may be seen both in sepia and in black and white. One photo is of Emir (King) Amanullah mounted on a camel. There are photos of men having a meeting "between the trees" (there is no other way to describe it). There they sit, on chairs, with small tables nearby, Russian style perhaps, framed—no, hidden—by the great trees that surround them.

Our visit to Paghman is one of my happiest days in Afghanistan.

But such days are too few. Winter is here early. Already the nights are cold. I do not understand how Afghans without indoor heating can endure the howling blizzards, shoulder-high snowdrifts, the icy frozen winters—yet they do. They are made of sturdy stock. They are as implacable as Nature here. Otherwise they could not survive.

SEVEN

Escape

I am determined to escape. But how? At home I am watched constantly. I am not allowed out by myself. When we go out, Abdul-Kareem stands right next to me and either drives the conversation or monitors what I say. So far I have not socialized with a single other American.

I am absolutely alone, without a single sympathetic ally or confidante. I have no money. The phone barely works—but who would I call?

I have already gone secretly to the American embassy.

I return a second time. A nice man tells me that he cannot help me because I am now an Afghan citizen and the wife of an Afghan citizen. He asks one of the Marine guards to escort me home. I did not understand that by marrying Abdul-Kareem, I was divorcing my country and revoking my citizenship. I am still flabbergasted that the embassy refused to aid an American.

Even if I could make a run for the airport, I have no passport and no way of paying for my seat. Perhaps I could convince an American or British pilot to take me anyway, but how would I know when a foreign flight would be waiting on the tarmac—and how would I get past the Afghan bureaucrats?

I am heartsick and frightened and can trust no one, not even myself. After all I am the fool who came here of her own free will, the naive dreamer who believed that she could have a grand, fairy-tale-like adventure without paying some terrible, unknown price. I—the bookish one, the sexy one—believed that being a woman would protect me. Well, I learned a valuable lesson: Quite the opposite is true.

Abdul-Kareem and his family can keep me locked up *forever*. They can do whatever it takes to break my spirit, place me under house arrest until I turn pliant, grateful for any social life at all. If I misbehave—I will be back in solitary. And I am hungry all the time. Since no one cares about this but me, I fear that I will grow too weak to make an escape.

While I am angry at myself, I am also angry at Abdul-Kareem. He pretended he was someone he is not, and lured me here under false pretenses.

I constantly think to myself: Can I simply walk out of Kabul along with the nomads? How long would I last on foot on the muddy or dusty roads and mountain rocks? Can I trust them not to return me for money and not marry me off to one of their own?

Can I turn to one of the foreign wives to help me obtain a fake foreign passport? Will she also lend me the money for a ticket and trust that I'd repay her?

Or should I write to my parents, have them wire the money to whomever my foreign benefactor turns out to be, and proceed from there?

Should I approach my father-in-law? He has remained aloof but has been courtly, gentlemanly, friendly toward me. As a matter of fact I have never seen him treat any adult woman unkindly.

He does not speak to Bebegul; true, he has three wives; true, his children all cringe as they bow and kiss his hand each time they see him; true, his young daughter is only a servant to him—yet his manner is dignified, benevolent, authoritative, and always slightly amused.

I decide to approach a foreign wife who is married to an Afghan. No foreign diplomat will allow his wife to get involved, lest it compromise his career and his country's relationship to Afghanistan.

I suggest that we visit a former mayor of Kabul whom everyone calls Papa, and whose second wife is a friendly German woman and someone I have met before.

Papa is known for having strung lights all over the mountains and for having been one of the few Afghans who was educated in Europe in the 1920s. He speaks German and French as well as his native Dari/Farsi and Pushto.

A picture of the exiled "emancipator king," Amanullah, still hangs in Papa's small but cozy living-dining room. Papa is no longer in politics. He owns a small business, and his wife has a dress shop. He receives us in bedroom slippers—a sandy-haired, warm-eyed grandfather of a man. It is late afternoon and it is growing cold and dark.

A servant brings in wood and piles it into the pot-bellied stove. Soon the water begins bubbling, and the wood-paneled room is filled with warmth and shadows. A Swiss clock ticks on the wall; a collection of leather-bound books stands on the shelf beneath the window. White curtains frame the windows and cover the table. Two freshly baked cakes have been placed near the plates and glassware.

Abdul-Kareem and Papa drink dark beer in Bavarian mugs as we wait for Mutti. She comes in, her cheeks reddened from the cold air.

"Ach, sorry I am late. You have been here long? My friend at the Deutsch embassy had a birthday party today—do you know that my cousin Heidi is made manager of the new hotel! Yes, she leaves for Munich in a month to get the staff. And what a hotel it will be, with a band, a cocktail lounge, only European food."

While she is still talking, Mutti has removed her fur coat and started to pour tea. It is hard to get her alone, but I finally manage it. Quickly I ask her if she will help me get out. She says she will.

Now, so many years later, I wonder if she actually would have done so. And would she have been punished, divorced—even banished from the country? Would her husband have been imprisoned? This all could have happened. I also wonder why so many Germans seem to be living in Afghanistan. Did they flee the war? Or did they have to flee Germany *after* the war?

I decide to write to my parents and ask them to call Mutti and wire her money for my plane ticket. I write the letter but I never send it. I save it and I have it still. It documents a telephone call between me and my parents. (I have no memory of it.) I write, in part:

> I am sure that my ticket and traveling expenses will be provided for me and I am not particularly averse in having such expenses fall upon the shoulders of he-who-has-made-the-journey-desirable. . . . Also, I want to finish college now. . . . I am quite torn about leaving Abdul-Kareem but I can't live here. I suppose I can lose myself in academic pursuits but I seem to be involved in a much larger "study" here, larger than anything I might learn in school. . . . Also, my books and papers have been held up at the border and I hate to leave without them.

I am no longer talking to Abdul-Kareem. We are fighting. By now after ten weeks in Kabul, I am stir-crazy, angry, frightened, and willing to risk anything in order to get out. I still cannot eat the ghee-drenched food. Abdul-Kareem still refuses to do anything about this.

Fawziya gently explains to me, again and again, that Bebegul will not allow the cook to use Crisco for our meals and she will not allow the cook to prepare meals separately for me. Fawziya is sad but there is nothing she can do. Apparently Bebegul told them that I am now a proper Afghan wife, not an American.

Many years later I learn that I might have gotten sick anyway. It seems that many smiling Afghan fruit sellers are known to pierce their shrunken melons and dunk them in the drainage ditch overnight. By morning the melons will have swelled and will look most appetizing.

My parents have told absolutely no one that I have married a Muslim man and gone off with him to Afghanistan. In their Orthodox Jewish circles what words would they use without revealing the extent of my rebellion against their entire way of life? If they tell people and I return home, would people still accept me? They maintain a prudent silence.

Rereading the letter I've written, I wonder: Why do I write that "I am torn about leaving Abdul-Kareem"? I am utterly miserable. He has put me in harm's way. Why am I still loyal to him?

Well, this is 1961 and I have not yet become a feminist—no American has. I may fancy myself a bohemian, but I am also a little bit of a 1950s-style wife.

Do I still love him? I will never really know. I argue with Abdul-Kareem many times about why I think he should leave Kabul, that there is no way he will ever transform his country, that Afghanistan is not populated with people who will enjoy Ibsen, Strindberg, Tennessee Williams, and the operas of Verdi and Puccini.

"Abdul-Kareem," I would say, "why not trust in your talent? Let's return to America. Here you are a rich man's son, and that may pave your way to a government position. But whatever you do here will never be what you can do in America."

Ah, but Abdul-Kareem is an outsider in the West, just as I am an outsider here. He could pass in both worlds, but he belongs to neither the East nor the West. Abdul-Kareem is genuinely a man without a country no matter where he lives.

In a sense his American education has ruined him for life in Kabul, but, even if he could succeed in America, he would never feel that he was a real American. His roots in America are fragile, recent, in comparison to the countless centuries his ancestors have lived in Afghanistan.

Abdul-Kareem is an Afghan and a Muslim, and as such he needs to be part of a large Afghan family, without which he has no identity, no social world, no sure footing. His family does not live in the West, nor are they truly cosmopolitan. The women live in the past even when they dress to kill, Western style. The men keep them there, firmly in the "past present," which is the title of Edward Hunter's riveting book.

Perhaps Abdul-Kareem is afraid of having to compete against other theater and film directors without his well-connected family's backing. He may be a loner—but he has not been trained to go it alone.

I have—I am a post–World War II American from a family with no connections but who is from a country filled with books, museums, libraries, concert halls, and scholarships.

I have been asking for a language tutor every single day. So far no one has arrived. I have threatened to walk out again on my own to visit the museum in Kabul. To my surprise Bebegul decides to accompany me herself. Apparently one of her many relatives has arranged it all.

To my shock her relative has had the museum emptied of all other visitors so that we might visit it undisturbed. It is thrilling but spooky to be the only ones in an otherwise empty museum. Amanullah built this on Darul Aman Road; Darul Aman means place or abode of peace.

I vaguely remember seeing some Roman-era glass figurines and a large gold and silver coin collection. Some coins date to the sixth century BCE and are pre-Islamic. There are Greek-Bactrian coins from northern Afghanistan, but there are also Hindu and Buddhist sculptures from the early centuries of the Common Era and lovely Indian ivories.

The museum has no paintings of women, although it has some beautiful pre-Islamic goddess figurines and sculptures.

Bebegul is coy, even charming. She teases me a bit.

"Are you *sure* there are no elephants in America?"

When I had first arrived, she had asked me this question quite seriously. After many conversations in halting English, French, and Dari (always with an interpreter), she understands that neither elephants nor camels roam America's city streets. Bebegul may have seen elephants when she and Ismail Mohammed were on their way back from exile in Iran and passed through India. When my father-in-law had to flee his country, Bebegul accompanied him; they fled Herat together. Bebegul hid the family's jewels and gold bars under a baby in the baby carriage.

Bebegul cannot believe that Americans actually keep dogs as pets. Kabul's dogs are wild and wolfish and always starving. The children stone them or worse. Dogs are considered dirty, religiously unclean. At night you can hear them howling.

As I have mentioned, an Afghan shepherd's dog is quite another matter. These are large fierce dogs trained to kill anyone but the shepherd and his family; they keep the sheep from straying. Afghan dogs are also trained to fight each other unto death. In situ Afghan dogs vary widely in terms of appearance and are not necessarily friendly or gentle. They are not like those more familiar "Afghan hounds," which were shipped off to England and Scotland in the 1920s, bred with other breeds, and trained as show dogs.

I love dogs but not necessarily when they are wild and starving. I see how dangerous they can be when a pack of five such dogs attacks a crippled pet deer I have named Lara. These dogs have managed to climb the wall—or find an open door—and have cornered Lara in our garden.

They are eating her alive, gnawing frantically on one hind leg. I run down. The dogs draw back, their eyes gleaming in fear and hatred. Lara lies in a twisted heap, death filming her large eyes. One whole leg has been chewed to the bone, it lies exposed under the stars, a dull white. Lights flash on in the house. "*Chee-as?*" (What is it?) The dogs turn round and round, then spring into the darkness. I slit Lara's throat with a kitchen knife. A sleepy, frightened gate watchman begs pardon of everyone.

I wrote about this awful episode many years ago, closer in time to when I had been in Kabul. Now I can barely remember it. Was it an omen about what happens to living beings if they are vulnerable? Was it a warning to me that I had better stay strong and healthy?

It is too late. Before I can put any escape plan into motion, fate steps in to rescue me in a rather risky way.

One afternoon I faint in the garden. I have never fainted before.

I have a temperature of 105 degrees. No one but me seems perturbed. At home at the first hint of a cold a doctor would be consulted. Most Jewish mothers in New York would rush someone with such a high fever—be it an adult child or a husband—to the emergency room.

Abdul-Kareem does not seem too worried, even though we know that foreigners have been "falling like flies" with a virulent strain of hepatitis.

I ask to see a doctor. Hours pass. Darkness has fallen. I am burning up and physically weak. It is soon late at night. I do something that I've never done before, something that is quite beyond my physical capacity *to* do.

I creep over to my father-in-law's house, ask to see him—and then ask him to summon a doctor as soon as possible. He explains that "our doctors don't usually come out in the evening." But he promises to look in on me.

I am feeling worse (if that is possible). I beg Abdul-Kareem to bring a doctor in to see me. It seems that all the family cars are in use, none are available. At about 3 A.M. a car is reluctantly dispatched, and it returns with an annoyed eye, ear, nose, and throat specialist.

I am burning up. The man looks me over—and ventures that it is "only nerves." He says, "These foreigners, especially the women, have weak stomachs and very jumpy nerves."

I fall into a brief coma, another first. I turn muddy yellow. I start throwing up. I am nauseous. A day or two later another doctor arrives. First he is served tea and engaged in polite small talk. Then he looks me over and says that I have what the other foreigners have—hepatitis.

He says that there is really nothing he can do.

I fear that I will die and be buried in a Muslim cemetery somewhere out in the wild countryside. I have just turned twenty-one and am seriously contemplating my death. Even this is not as frightening as Abdul-Kareem's apparent indifference.

What should I do? Kabul has no good hospital. Wealthy Afghans travel to Europe and America for their serious medical needs. Hospitals in Kabul do not even serve food; a patient's family has to bring it in, together with clean towels, fresh sheets, and the prescribed pharmaceuticals.

I do not want to see any more Afghan doctors. I beg to see an American doctor. And so Bebegul's entire family accompanies me to an American doctor in town. Eight people in two cars accompany me. Their presence, however well meaning, does not allow the doctor to see me privately.

By now I am paranoid. It feels as if my family is openly spying on me. (In retrospect my paranoia was justified.) Their presence is meant to intimidate me into saying only positive things about my Afghan family to the foreign doctor.

The American doctor understands this and engineers a way to take me to the far corner of the room where we can whisper to each other.

He tells me that I might be the only foreigner who is still alive with this strain of the disease this winter and that I ought to get myself on a plane and go home. But he also tells me that he can "set up an intravenous line" for me at home for a week in order to stop my too-rapid weight loss and to get some nutrients into me.

He sends a nurse over who inserts the tubing. Suddenly, half-asleep, half-awake, as if I'm dreaming, I feel that someone is tugging on my IV line. It is Bebegul and she is trying to pull it out.

I am afraid she is trying to kill me.

I cry out. Fawziya, Hassan's wife, is just passing by. She hears me, comes in, and sees what is going on. She sees that I am terrified. That gentle soul offers to stay with me until Abdul-Kareem comes home. This is a bold thing for her to do.

Fawziya: Wherever you are now, thank you.

When Abdul-Kareem comes home, he does not believe that Bebegul has tried to hurt me. He says that I must have had a hallucination.

Abdul-Kareem knows that if I don't die, I am going to leave. But in Afghanistan wives are not allowed to leave husbands. Even husbands don't necessarily leave wives—they simply marry a younger woman or two if they can.

Abdul-Kareem may have made a love match and brought a Jewish American back as his bride. But he has no intention of allowing his wife to shame him before his entire family and country.

So Abdul-Kareem has contrived a way to keep me there against my will.

I am his wife; we both believe he has the right to have sex with me and that I do not have the right to say no. He is desperate that I stay and so—without words and in anger—Abdul-Kareem embarks on a campaign to impregnate me. He does not stop, even though he knows I am ill and weak.

I am too fatigued to even get out of bed. I can barely hold myself upright. I have to crawl down the hallway to go to the bathroom. What kind of pregnancy could I maintain?

But if I leave, how could Abdul-Kareem be trusted with an important position? An Afghan man must be able to control his own wife.

If I am carrying Abdul-Kareem's child, I will never be allowed to leave Afghanistan. I will have to go through with the pregnancy even if it kills me, even if this possible future child would be born disabled. The husband who presumably loves me is willing to risk my death and the possibility of a deformed child—rather than risk losing his power over me or his honor.

These are not things we ever discuss. These are my conclusions now, many years later.

I may have loved Abdul-Kareem but I am now in a life-or-death situation. I discover that I love my life more than I love my husband.

One never forgets such lessons, especially when one is privileged to learn them at a relatively young age.

Abdul-Kareem begins to stay away from our bedroom until late at night. As the systematic attacks continue, Abdul-Kareem's oldest sister, also named Fawziya, mercifully offers to sleep in our bedroom to help me during the night. She understands what is happening. I will never forget her simple act of kindness.

Fawziya: Wherever you are, thank you, thank you. Call me, please, come to me, anytime.

I am a hopeless invalid. I am muddy yellow. I am constantly nauseous. I dream of food—but I can't eat anything. When I crawl into the bathroom to throw up, I see that a new *National Geographic* has been added to my pile of magazines. This one has a cover story about the Hunzas, who live nearby and whose diet of yoghurt, nuts, tea, and apricots has led to long lives. The magazine features many photos of the region's mountains. I look out the bathroom window and see a similar view.

I laugh. Then I cry.

I must be getting better. I am strong enough to crawl down the stairs in search of something, anything, to eat. I think I am hysterical with hunger. The house is quiet, deserted, no one seems to be around. Suddenly Reza, my English-speaking brother-in-law, appears. He is wearing an overcoat and is on his way out to visit his fiancée and her family. I beg him for some edible food. A plain cooked potato or some bread?

Slowly Reza puts on his leather gloves.

"I have no time right now, I'm already late." Reza pauses. He says: "I don't understand how Abdul-Kareem could have brought you here. I've told him that many times."

And he walks out, leaving me in a huddled heap on the carpeted floor.

I have missed my period. True, I am ill. But I might be pregnant. This could be a death sentence for me in every way.

I have to get out and it has to be now. I have only one card to play: the royal card. I must appeal to the king, not King Zahir Shah but my father-in-law, Ismail Mohammed, who alone has the power to return me safely to my home.

Why would he want a dead American daughter-in-law on his hands—or even a permanently sickly one? Why would he want someone living under his roof who keeps trying to escape?

I do not know it at the time, but Abdul-Kareem is engaged in a monstrous power struggle with his father, who has not really approved of his son's love marriage. Ismail Mohammed's opinion has nothing to do with me personally. It has everything to do with his ambitions for his third son—the son whose education in Europe and America was part of a vow Ismail Mohammed had made to Allah.

When he was quite young, Abdul-Kareem had nearly died of spinal meningitis. He had endured a difficult and painful recovery; Abdul-Kareem had to learn how to walk all over again. At that time his father vowed that if this son managed to prevail against all odds, he would have a world-class education.

I send word through a servant that I want to see Ismail Mohammed. He comes almost immediately. Once the household knows that we are in my bedroom together, Bebegul and her servants barge right in. Someone sends for Abdul-Kareem.

It is time for the afternoon prayer. Ismail Mohammed prostrates himself on the bedroom floor; afterward he tells me that he has prayed to Allah for my recovery. Then he asks the servants, Fawziya, and Bebegul to leave. He totally surprises me when he takes out a hidden cup of milk custard and proceeds to tenderly spoon-feed me.

I do not even have to raise the issue. He knows exactly why I've asked for him. Softly he opens the conversation.

"I know about your little plan with the German woman. I think it will be best if you leave with our approval on an Afghan passport, which I have obtained for you. You have been granted a six-month visa for reasons of health."

And he gave it to me on the spot: passport #17384. I have it still. The Kingdom of Afghanistan passport has retained its bright orange color, just as the nargileh, the "hubble-bubble," or water pipe, that I brought out with me has retained its turquoise glaze.

Ismail Mohammed also handed me a plane ticket. "We will see you off. It is better this way."

Abdul-Kareem curses me. Then he orders me to stay—after which he makes wild operatic promises: We will live alone. We will move right into the only hotel in town. He will allow me to get a job—and if I want to live in the country, he will become a farmer and work from dawn to dusk to support us.

My mind is made up. I want to live. I want no more of his promises and lies. I want my own life back.

By now Kabul is buried in snow. I fall asleep every night with my feet under the *sandali*—a low bench covered by a thick blanket under which a brazier keeps you warm, often all night.

I have missed another period. I will take any flight out, going anywhere.

The next plane out is an Aeroflot—the Russian airline which is returning Russian engineers from Cairo to Moscow with a stop in Tashkent, the capital of the Uzbek Republic.

I weigh about ninety-five pounds and have to hide my jaundiced eyes with dark glasses. As weak as I am, I am excited about seeing Moscow. I have only one hundred dollars with me. I am obviously expected to return straight home on a flight from Moscow to Copenhagen and from Copenhagen to New York City. Clearly, I am expected to return to my parents who are, in turn, expected to support me.

Abdul-Kareem calls me a bitch and a whore. He hits me—and then he hits me again—but I calmly continue to pack my clothes. He orders me to return. He says that he will be held accountable if I do not return; I am an Afghan citizen, traveling on an Afghan passport.

"I demand that you return as soon as you are well. You may finish your damn last semester at college, but that's it. You have responsibilities here."

For the next three years Abdul-Kareem will continue to make this demand. I do not yet understand that his government will actually hold him liable for my escape and will expect him to return my actual physical passport to the authorities.

Afghan officials never return my American passport. I do not return my Afghan passport.

I am sorry if Abdul-Kareem's government held him accountable for my nonreturn—and for the nonreturn of my Afghan passport. But it was either my life or his way of life. I allowed my culture and my family to have their way, just as he allowed his culture and family to have their way. We both chose survival on our own culture's terms rather than a tragic Romeo and Juliet ending.

A ridiculously large crowd of relatives dutifully accompanies me to the Kabul airport. Abdul-Kareem behaves solicitously, but he is only acting. In reality he is furious. He has been defeated. He feels defeated by his father more than by me.

The plane takes off. At first my feelings are as frozen as the temperature, as cold as the mountain air and the frozen fields of ice over which we fly.

Then I am filled with more fierce joy than my body can contain. I feel incredibly light, I am free, I have a second chance, I am going to live, I will be able to start over.

I get out. And I never return.

SECTION TWO

In America

EIGHT

Home in America

Lord God, here I am—free at last 30,000 feet above the good green earth. I am pregnant, I am ill, I have no way to support myself, but here I am: joyful and unafraid.

In Tashkent two nurses board the plane to inoculate passengers against typhoid. When we land in Moscow, an Intourist guide escorts me to a room in a dark and shabby hotel that I share with a roommate. They give all tourists roommates. They are all probably spies.

A Soviet agent sits in the hallway day and night. I have several books with me, including Hannah Arendt's *The Origins of Totalitarianism*. I tell my roommate, who is an English-speaking Russian, to look at it while she can. She asks to keep it. I hope this does not get her into trouble.

I visit the Kremlin, Red Square, and the surrounding area with two German architects who were also on the flight from Kabul and who are staying in the same horrible hotel. We find a restaurant and order the most delicious borsht in the world. I am too weak to visit any museums. It is cold and still snowing. The architects invite me to join them for the New Year holidays in Germany. Luckily they insist on paying for everything.

En route to Copenhagen I talk with another German man, who tells me that he managed a hotel in Kabul. His life story spans two world wars, a youth spent in China, and a five-year stint in a Japanese prison camp. I am once again struck by what appears to be a strong German presence in Afghanistan.

I sit at a table in the brightly lit Copenhagen airport. I drink some good coffee. I buy a white cable-knit sweater with my dwindling cash.

Another man, a British diplomat who was also on the flight from Moscow, sits down, starts a conversation, and promptly asks me to join *him* for the New Year holidays.

If you are young, female, and even mildly attractive, men are all over you.

I have ten dollars in my pocket when the plane lands in New York. I literally kiss the ground at Idlewild, now John F. Kennedy International Airport. I call my parents and rather nonchalantly say, "Guess who is back?"

My parents tell me to wait—they are on their way to get me. Did they think they were never going to see me again? My mother is guarded, suspicious, unusually silent. My father just hugs me. He is glad to see me. I think my mother is relieved, even overjoyed, that her prodigal daughter, her "little girl," has been returned to her.

I feel as though I belong nowhere. I now weigh less than one hundred pounds. And I have to tell my parents that I am pregnant. Our family doctor tells me that nearly every organ in my body is infected and that my pregnancy should be terminated on medical grounds. I agonize over whether to have an abortion.

Should I have this Jewish Muslim child—the tragic fruit of a love affair gone wrong? Will this child really be mine? How will I be able to raise a child on my own while I work and attend graduate school?

Yes, this unborn child also has a father and an extended Afghan family who can help—but not if I remain in America, and I will not condemn my child to be raised without me in Afghanistan.

In the end my body makes the decision for me. I suffer a painful miscarriage.

I mourn my unborn child.

Then I rush past any anguish and throw myself into my work. I have to finish my final semester of college, find a job, and apply to graduate school.

I started reading Freud when I was fifteen years old. I loved his way of thinking. So I decide to become what I call a Viennese witch doctor, a psychoanalyst. This should allow me the ability to work at home and to write at least half of every day.

But for now I dive back into French literature. My half-written thesis is on the French author Stendhal. As usual I find great solace in literature.

Stendhal writes: "I do not know myself, whether I am good or bad, smart or stupid."

He is speaking directly to me, describing me. I no longer know who I am. I thought I was invulnerable, forever healthy. I see that I am all-too-vulnerable, and that I've already been touched, marked, changed.

I also turn to my professors for advice. The eminent philosopher Dr. Heinrich Bluecher, who is married to Hannah Arendt, tells me to have an affair. My thesis adviser, the ever-wry, kind, and wise Dr. Elizabeth Stambler, simply tells me to get on with my Stendhal project.

I try to tell some college friends what it was really like in Kabul. In response they ask me, "Aren't you some kind of a princess now?" "You had many servants, didn't you?" "Did you live in a palace?" "Did you meet the king?"

They seem to think that living in purdah, in a harem, is a bit naughty, like living in a brothel. They do not want to understand anything.

I tell people that I've seen women shunted to the back of the bus and forced to walk around wearing body bags. I say that I'd seen servants who were treated like slaves and that I'd lived under conditions of gender apartheid.

No one at college seems to understand what I am talking about.

Looking back, I realize that I was in Kabul before the struggles against Jim Crow in America and racial apartheid in South Africa got underway. How could my friends have understood? I suddenly feel much older than my peers.

My college mates and professors make me feel a bit like Peachy Carnehan, the main character in Rudyard Kipling's unforgettable novella, *The Man Who Would Be King*. Carnehan and his companion, Daniel Dravot, are "wanderers and vagabonds." They decide to leave British India and go to Kafiristan (which is now called Nuristan) in Afghanistan to become kings. The pagan Kafiris decide that Dravot is indeed a god and declare him their king.

The story does not end well. Ultimately the Kafiris drop Dravot from a great height and they crucify Carnehan—but because Carnehan is still alive after twenty-four hours, the Kafiris turn him loose. They give him a present: Dravot's head, still wearing its crown. Carnehan, physically broken and half mad, flees and returns to India in tatters. He tells his story to Kipling's narrator (a journalist and Kipling's alter ego) and then almost immediately dies of sunstroke in an asylum.

Reader: I do not die, nor do I go mad. But I feel as if part of me, my innocent, ignorant, trusting self, has partly died. Like poor old Peachy Carnehan, I also have a tale of Afghanistan to tell; unlike him I have no one who will listen to me.

For now I am grateful to be home again in the land of libraries and liberty. I have been given a second chance.

Immediately after I return, Abdul-Kareem begins a letter-writing campaign to win me back. He writes almost every week. He calls me his darling. He professes his undying love, which makes me feel monstrous because I do not want to see him or talk to him or even write to him.

Only days after I leave, Abdul-Kareem writes to tell me that "everyone misses you a great deal. . . . It is silly to assume that you are homesick for Kabul and your husband's shabby existence." He continues by promising that he will buy me expensive gold and lapis lazuli jewelry.

Does he honestly believe that jewels are more important to me than my freedom? The sweet girl he once married died in Afghanistan, and mere baubles will not persuade me to give up my reclaimed independence.

Abdul-Kareem chides me for giving up so quickly on our marriage and tries hard to make me feel guilty for having left him. He alternates between telling me I am irresponsible and childish and insisting that I am the only one who can rescue him, who understands him, who can inspire him to do "great work."

His tone is ironic, sarcastic, self-pitying, pompous, and utterly heartbreaking. He is also relentless.

In my diary I write:

My God! Do I still love Abdul-Kareem? Is that even possible? He is the only man with whom I have ever lived. I shared part of my youth with him. I am used to his kisses. But his love and insistence that I visit Afghanistan nearly killed me. His overly solicitous letters are completely out of touch with my reality.

In the next letter Abdul-Kareem writes that he has "paid too dear a price for this damned career. I have lost you. How can I want it now?"

These are fine false words because Abdul-Kareem also begins to steadily boast about his upcoming trips to India, Italy, and France and about how well his first play was received in Kabul.

1959–1960. And so it began,
Abdul-Kareem and I are two college
students, very much in love.

*1959–1960. Here is a rather romantic
photo of the two of us in the
American countryside.*

1959–1960. That same day, long ago.

1961. Abdul-Kareem photographed me aboard the ship Le Flandre *as we began our voyage to Europe.*

ROYAUME
D'AFGHANISTAN

PASSEPORT
DE
PREMIERECLASSE

This is the Afghan passport that allowed me to reenter the United States on a six-month visa. It has retained its bright orange cover.

IDENTITÉ

Nom: MRS PHYLLIS CHESLER ██████

Nom du père: CHESLER

Nationalité: **AFGHAN**

Lieu de naissance: U.S.A

Date de naissance: 1.3.19

Age: 21

Qualité ou profession: N.

Domicile: KHOJA MULLAH, KABUL

Destination: U.S.A.

But de voyage: VISITING PARENTS

No: de l'état civil: NONE

██████

دیلارنوم جبیلر

ملیت: افغان

دزیږیدوځای امریکا

دزیږیدنیمه ۱۳۱۹

عمر ۱۹ نزده ساله

رتبادکار نلدرد

خای خواجه ملا کابل

دتلورنای ۱ امریکا

دتلو مقصد دین اقارب

دناهیت دیاق لیی غاورن

*Here is my Afghan passport, given
to me after my American passport
was taken from me. Please note: My
nationality is listed here as "Afghan."*

1961. I purchased this photo as I stood looking at this lovely little mosque, known as the Blue Mosque, on the Kabul River.

This photo depicts musicians who were hired for a celebration in Kabul. The image was on a postcard, which caught my fancy in the bazaar. I have kept these genial gentlemen nearby ever since.

A young Kuchi girl—clearly one who posed for the photographer. "Kuchi" means "those who move" and refers to the Afghan nomads.

Two bare-faced Kuchi women and a girl posing on camels. Nomad women usually walk.

He does not once ask about my college thesis.

His campaign continues. In letter after letter Abdul-Kareem reminds me that I have a duty to our marriage and to his country. I am intended to be part of an effort to help it. He needs me—and apparently so does his country, which is still "young and growing."

Abdul-Kareem refers to Kabul as my "real home" and suggests that I bring my mother over for a visit when I return. Oh dear desperate madman! My mother is an Orthodox Jew. She would just as soon fly to the moon as go to Kabul.

Rereading Abdul-Kareem's letters fifty years later is painful, tragic, hilarious, and educational. In his next letter Abdul-Kareem writes: "You seem to have cut yourself off altogether from me, my life, and future, but I still consider you the dearest part of me, my life and my future."

Abdul-Kareem tells me that I have embarrassed him before his entire family. Nevertheless he denies that he wants me to return only so that he can save face. He admits that he deceived and wronged me but castigates me for refusing to forgive him.

"If you come back, you'll give me a new life; if you don't, you'll end the one I have."

Is he writing to me or is he writing a play?

My first letter to Abdul-Kareem illustrates the emergence of a different sort of woman than the one who left New York, a woman I can recognize as myself.

I shudder, and wonder at the same time, that you still cannot understand what a shock and insult, what an unbelievable horror and threat the entire marriage was to me. I was a virtual prisoner in Kabul, starving, lonely, cut off from all decent human contact, cut off from all escapes, without the possibility of any hope.

If you cannot understand this, then rejoice! Your conflict is over, for you are a true Afghan and have returned home. My life in Kabul nearly killed me. Whether or not we loved each other, our marriage was an irresponsible mistake. How can you write to me so righteously, so indignantly that "marriage cannot be treated lightly" and that you "do not believe in divorce"?

Well, do you believe in hitting your wife? Do you believe in . . . unwanted pregnancies? You really are a man of your country because you obviously expect that I sacrifice myself—no, annihilate myself—just because I am a woman.

He responds: "Your accusations are partly true and partly the obsessions of a troubled mind."

He insists, "I cannot be the artist I want to be without you by my side. Wouldn't it be much better if we wrote about how much we miss each other, love each other, and how we are preparing for our reunion in the near future?"

Does this man honestly believe that I would ever return to Kabul?

My experience has rendered me quite wary about traveling to Central Asia ever again.

In the 1970s I became friendly with a number of Muslim artists and political dissidents. One, Reza Baraheni, was the head of Students Against the Shah. Reza would describe in grisly detail how he was tortured by the Shah's men. We were together during the first great electrical blackout in New York City, and he clutched at my hand, terrified.

"Reza," I said, "it's going to be fixed. Calm down."

"But you don't understand," he said. "If I don't call a certain number by a certain time every day, it will be assumed that I've been kidnapped and the wheels will start turning."

Years later Ayatollah Khomeini arrested my dear friend Kate Millett right after she had delivered a speech in Teheran on International Women's Day 1980. Reza was the one who had invited her. The following year he invited me to speak in Teheran for the same occasion. He said, "Phyllis, you understand the Muslim soul. Come, be with us."

"Reza," I said, "the next time I visit Teheran or Kabul it will be with the Marines and with NATO forces. Even then I might not come."

At the time Reza had high hopes for an anticolonialist and democratic Islamic revolution in Iran. He soon fled Iran for Canada.

After a few months Abdul-Kareem takes a new tack. He insists that "Afghan society now allows a great deal of individualism." He promises to "provide the freedom in which you can grow intellectually."

This cannot be possible.

As I've already noted, King Amanullah tried that—he unveiled the women and ordered public education for both girls and boys—and the mullahs and tribal chieftains exiled him. According to Talley Stewart, in the late 1920s Amanullah addressed a crowd in Kandahar, telling them, "If you are not educated, try hard to make your children educated. An uneducated person can do nothing. This education is not only for your sons but also for your wives and daughters. If the prevailing views regarding purdah remain unchanged, then there is no possibility of any progress in the life of the Eastern people, particularly among Moslems."

As we have seen, Afghans excel at fighting Afghans.

This is what Afghans do, even when they are not being invaded by foreign powers: They fight each other, tribe against tribe, brother against brother, half-brother against half-brother, cousin against cousin, uncle against nephew, father against son.

In his beloved novel *The Kite Runner,* Khaled Hosseini writes about the *Shahnameh of Firdausi,* a collection of Persian stories written in Afghanistan: There is no Oedipal drama in Iran or Afghanistan; instead, here Oedipus, the son, dies; his father kills him. "In 'the tale of the great warrior Rostam and his fleet-footed horse, Rakhsh,' Rostam mortally wounds his valiant nemesis, Sohrab, in battle, only to discover that Sohrab is his long-lost son."

At the time I was in Kabul, I knew nothing about Afghanistan's long and bloody history of never-ending tribal warfare, the lengths to which cousins and brothers would go to dethrone a relative. How could I? Abdul-Kareem never mentioned it. He was my measure of Afghanistan, and he was a genteel, dapper, hopeful, soft-spoken fellow, convinced that he and a small group of other men would soon be able to Westernize and modernize the country.

But now that I've done a bit of reading, I better understand where I was and what Abdul-Kareem and all the other reformers were truly up against.

When the Afghan leader Mirwais died in 1715, his son, Mahmud Mir, assassinated his uncle and declared himself leader. In turn Mahmud, a sadistic ruler, was assassinated by his cousin Ashraf, who then paraded Mahmud's head through the streets of Isfahan. Nadir Shah, a Persian leader, blinded his favorite son—and was himself assassinated under mysterious conditions. In 1747 Ahmad Khan was accepted as the new Afghan leader; he called himself Ahmad Shah Durrani (Pearl of Pearls).

This Ahmad Shah is considered the first king of the modern Afghan state. In *The Wars of Afghanistan: Messianic Terrorism, Tribal Conflicts, and the Failures of Great Powers,* the diplomat and author Peter Tomsen writes, "Ahmad Shah did designate his second son, Timur Khan, to succeed him but that did not deter some of his other sons from declaring themselves king. Ahmad Shah's multiple wives each championed their child's right to the throne. . . . Succession struggles resumed with a vengeance among Timur's twenty-three sons after his death in 1793."

This pattern continued through the nineteenth and twentieth centuries, right up until the Soviet invasion. Tomsen writes that Emir Abdur Rahman (1880–1901) "spent most of his twenty-one-year rule at war with [his] Mohammadzai relatives seeking the throne." Abdur Rahman prepared his son, Habibullah (1901–1919), to become the next emir—which he did, but Habibullah was similarly assassinated under mysterious conditions. Most likely either his brother or one of his sons was behind Habibullah's assassination. His son, the next emir, Amanullah (1919–1929), was lucky—he was at least allowed to flee and live out his life in relative poverty and bitter exile in Italy.

But the pattern continued. Thereafter Nadir Shah and his Musahiben brothers ruled. Nadir was assassinated by a student (in a complicated revenge plot), and his brother, Hashim Khan, served as regent for Nadir's nineteen-year-old son, Zahir Shah. Sometime later Zahir's cousin Daoud Khan got rid of Zahir in a military coup and, with Soviet Russia's help, ruled in his place. Well, at least he did not assassinate Zahir.

With a history like this—how could Abdul-Kareem have succeeded? This is Afghan-on-Afghan history, and it concerns only the major historical power struggles. This brief summary does not include the endless wars between villages, tribes, and clans, and between family members in the isolated mountains whose internecine warfare has not made its way into history books.

So too this brief history does not concern the Great Game, that is, the colonial powers vying for Afghanistan as the buffer state between England (in India) and Russia. In a sense Afghanistan was defeated first by thousands of years of endless invasions that utterly destroyed the country and its people and, second, by never having been colonized. No central government, no national infrastructure or railway, no educational and hygiene programs such as those Britain imposed upon India were ever imposed upon Afghanistan. The country remained a series of isolated snowbound tribal units perpetually at war with each other and with anyone who would dare try to rule them.

Perhaps Abdul-Kareem is an even greater dreamer than I am.

On the other hand Abdul-Kareem is too realistic, cautious, political, and cynical to take dangerous personal risks for the sake of "the people." He is an enlightened elitist surrounded by medieval customs. Like me, he is an artiste—but in Afghanistan he must become a civil servant. Abdul-Kareem is well aware of his country's history in terms of its corruption, nepotism, infuriating incompetence, and rule by rumor. But he is unable to face the truth that, as the refined and foreign-educated son of one of Afghanistan's wealthiest families, he lacks the bloody barbarism that might be required to tackle any of these hard injustices.

Until now no one has succeeded who has tried to do so. He knows this.

From the last days of 1961 to the last days of 1964, Abdul-Kareem refuses to take no for an answer. I write, saying that I will never return and that we must divorce. He responds, "It is important to know your decision because I am going mad in this limbo."

It is as if I have not spoken or as if whatever I—or what any woman—might say can be overruled by persistence and force. Abdul-Kareem begins to experience my desire to divorce him as a form of persecution. He also believes that we are still one, that what he feels is what I feel, too.

Abdul-Kareem thinks to instruct me: "Marriage is sacred."

Six months later Abdul-Kareem writes to my college president (!) to inform him that I am expected "back home" in Kabul. He does so with the authority of an Afghan husband, as if I am his chattel.

I am apoplectic and a little afraid. What power does this man think he has over me? Does he believe it extends to America?

Abdul-Kareem tells me that I should use my American passport when I travel to Europe but that I should use my Afghan passport when I enter Afghanistan.

But I do not have an American passport. It was never returned to me. Why does he think I have it? Abdul-Kareem also orders me to cut off all contact with our Afghan friends in New York. They will gossip and it will be used against him. I write another letter to Abdul-Kareem:

Dear Abdul-Kareem:
My decision is final.

I am not interested in your philosophies of divorce. You could divorce me in an Afghan religious court in a matter of minutes, and you could take three other wives before that.

You write about love, love, love. Please try to think of me confined upstairs in bed, cold, lonely, hungry, sick, and frightened while you are hiding from me as I keep crying for orange juice. . . . Try to imagine me as I limp downstairs, doubled over, to find you, and find you giggling and tittering behind a door, hiding from me. . . . Do you remember the first night you attacked me, telling me bitter little nothings in my ear, and then how you cried, said you hated yourself and wanted to die, and then fell asleep—as I remained awake, and the dogs howled in hunger, and the stars were close enough to touch? The next morning, you acted as if nothing had happened.

Abdul-Kareem, don't evade the truth any longer. I will not return to Kabul, I will not return to you.

Nevertheless Abdul-Kareem continues to ask me to "give our marriage another chance." He views divorce as "an amputation of a limb." He believes that my parents have influenced my decision to terminate our marriage. He has the audacity to write to them, to call their attention to "their moral duties."

Meanwhile he implores me to make up your own mind and then stick to it, adding, "Please let me know how soon you can come home!"

Abdul-Kareem knows that I am struggling economically. Nevertheless, and rather heartlessly, he continues to boast about all his successes: His "institute is [becoming] a fine organization." He intends to translate and adapt the American musical *The King and I* for an Afghan audience. The government is pleased with his work and has asked him to organize a repertory theater troupe. He will be paid only a civil servant's salary but after a year his salary will be revisited.

He invites me to join him on vacation in France.

If I were an Afghan woman, I would never be able to withstand such pressure. Thank God I am an American and far away from Kabul.

Abdul-Kareem turns nasty and sarcastic about my first postcollege job as a secretary and go-fer at a television production company. He writes, "I am very happy to hear that you have found such an interesting and profitable occupation in New York. Well, it seems you have made it, after all. It must be worth a husband to you. You were magnanimous to wish to know what I am doing. Please feel assured that it is not as big or as important as what you are doing."

He writes that he is busy working with Bob Joffrey of the Robert Joffrey Ballet and Rebekka Harkness, the multimillionaire.

His boasts, meant to tempt me to return to him, continue for years.

He mentions Elia Kazan, Helen Hayes, and the Moscow Film Festival. He also invites me to France and Germany, where he plans to meet with major film directors.

Later: "I have completed 80% of my film. . . . I am a little behind schedule because I co-sponsored and managed a concert tour for Duke Ellington in Kabul."

*T*he wily Afghan means to trap me.

After six months my Afghan visa expires and the US State Department contacts me. They say that I have to leave. I threaten to chain myself to the Statue of Liberty or go on a hunger strike. I am *not* going back to Afghanistan.

Has Ismail Mohammed's gift of an Afghan passport with only a six-month visa been a Trojan horse, a way to ensure that I had to return?

My parents calmly hire a lawyer, who convinces the authorities that I am indeed an American citizen, born and bred here. The lawyer moves for a divorce. Abdul-Kareem insists that he will never agree to a divorce and that no New York divorce could ever cover "our situation." In his letters Abdul-Kareem sounds as if he really believes that I am an Afghan wife and, as such, am subject to his decisions.

When I was in Kabul, I had expected the American embassy to come to my aid, to offer me advice and shelter, and help me leave the country. That did not happen.

When I returned home, I certainly did not expect the *American* government to question my right to remain here. Even though I am an American citizen, I *had* entered my country on an Afghan passport with a six-month visa. The lawyers my parents hired did not quite understand what was going on, either. This was a Kafkaesque experience. It was also uncharted territory.

Please remember: My Afghan sojourn and my fight to have my American citizenship rights recognized took place between 1961 and 1964—long before people began to write about what routinely happens to foreign wives in countries like Saudi Arabia, Iran, and Pakistan. And I had not yet amassed my own library about life in Muslim-majority countries.

Twenty years later, when I was researching international custody battles for my 1986 book, *Mothers on Trial: The Battle for Children and Custody,* I learned that most (if not all) Muslim-majority countries do not allow Western mothers to leave their husbands' countries or to return to their countries of origin with their children—even if the children were born in the West and hold Western passports.

Such countries believe that children belong to their father and to their paternal relatives, and never to their European or North American mother. If a father is insane, violent, or completely absent, his children still belong to their paternal grandmother or paternal aunt.

Betty Mahmoody, the author of the acclaimed *Not Without My Daughter,* has written movingly about such custody cases in her second book, *For the Love of a Child.*

Nevertheless Western women continue to fall in love with and marry charming Westernized Muslim men. The women have absolutely no idea what they will face in terms of government bureaucracies and patriarchal customs.

For Abdul-Kareem, even though I've left him, nothing has changed; for me everything has changed.

I no longer feel married. The man I married put me in harm's way and left me there. He then behaved as if my illness and possible death were not important; they were annoying developments that interfered with his grand plan. That's how I felt after I left Kabul. I had been terrified. And that made me angry, and my anger made me strong.

I now have three lawyers: Aaron Maze, Max Schorr, and Charles Koozman. Abdul-Kareem hires a lawyer, too: M. M. Shafiq Kanawi, Esq.

No, it does not add up to a good Jewish-Muslim joke.

Abdul-Kareem now promises to divorce me in Afghanistan and have the US Embassy certify it. He forgets that we were married in America, not in Afghanistan. He writes, "You can be sure that we in this part of the world are more civilized as far as getting divorces are concerned—we do not have to fabricate lies here in order to get a divorce—the truth is good enough."

Oh, please. But he has a point. One must have cause for divorce in New York State. Adultery or cruelty or God knows what else.

I have no choice but to move for an annulment. Abdul-Kareem immediately threatens to come to America and fight it. The man refuses to let me go. He writes on: "Phyllis, dear, we cannot turn the clock backwards and pretend that our marriage did not happen because it has happened and legally we are still married and you are my wife. The Embassy has informed your lawyer that one cannot annul a marriage like ours. I believe we can make our marriage work. Therefore, I am quite against a divorce. I bet that *if your own lawyer heard my side of the story, I am sure he'd prefer to represent me rather than you."* Abdul-Kareem threatens to fight all and any legal actions I may bring.

He further says, "My first proposition is that you should give our marriage and me another chance. I feel confident that I can give you the love and opportunities you need in life. I do not believe in divorce. My second proposition is actually not a proposition; rather it is a warning. On the basis of the charges you or your parents have pressed against me, I am forced to contest your charges."

At the time I pay no attention to the grounds for the annulment. I want only to be free of this marriage that threatens my freedom and my life.

The lawyers question me closely. I tell them that Abdul-Kareem had presented himself in one way but then behaved in a radically different way. He is not Westernized, as I once believed him to be.

Only many years later do I understand why Abdul-Kareem might have felt quite endangered by the grounds my lawyers chose. The fraud he is alleged to have committed is as follows: "That prior to said marriage and in order to obtain the consent of plaintiff and induce her to enter into said marriage, defendant falsely and fraudulently stated and represented that he would convert to the Jewish Orthodox Faith and would apply for naturalization and become a citizen of the United States and establish his marital domicile in the United States."

I did not know it then, but I certainly know it now: Apostasy is a capital crime in Islam.

According to knowledgeable Muslim and ex-Muslim dissidents, apostasy is the most serious crime you can commit under Muslim religious (Sharia) law. The distinguished author Ibn Warraq is a pioneer in this area. In 2003 he edited the anthology *Leaving Islam: Apostates Speak Out.* The contributors are from Pakistan, Iran, Bangladesh, Turkey, the Far East, India, Tunisia—and the United States. They describe having to break with their families after being threatened with death, having to flee, adopt new identities—or having to keep their conversion, even their atheism, strictly secret.

I have submitted courtroom affidavits on behalf of a number of potential victims of honor killings. In these cases the families of girls and women who had converted to Christianity vowed to kill them for this perceived betrayal of faith.

In 2003 the courageous Egyptian-born Nonie Darwish, author of *Now They Call Me Infidel: Why I Renounced Jihad for America, Israel, and the War on Terror,* wrote and talked about having been rejected and demonized by her family, and the considerable danger and contempt she still faces because she converted away from Islam. She is a gracious and eloquent woman, and my heart breaks for her.

Back in the early 1960s no one—not I or my parents or my lawyers—understood anything about how some Muslims view apostates—that they view them as traitors to the faith who deserve to die.

I now believe that the grounds my parents chose for the annulment also represented a wishful fantasy on their part. Perhaps they needed to minimize my rejection of their way of life by arguing that Abdul-Kareem had at least promised to become an American and an Orthodox Jew.

But if this got out, if anyone—a jealous brother, a political rival—believed this was true, Abdul-Kareem could have been jailed, ostracized, impoverished, executed—exiled if he was lucky. The rumor that he had even *considered* becoming a Jew could ruin him.

If this is why he would not let me go, it makes no sense. If only he had agreed to a divorce, I would not have had to move for an annulment. What does he want with me? Does he really love me this much? If so, how could he have treated me so badly? If not, does he actually view me as his property? Is this possible—am I his runaway cow he must lure back home?

He is certainly persistent—but his persistence is cruel and deceptive. Has he always been like this? I don't think so. No. But living in Kabul has hardened him, changed him, perhaps returned him to the man he was supposed to become had he not gone to America.

Even after he knows I've hired lawyers and am actively seeking a divorce and an annulment, Abdul-Kareem continues to share the intimate details of his life with me—just as if I were still his wife. He idealizes our relationship in the same way he once idealized life in Afghanistan.

Abdul-Kareem writes to my lawyers explaining that he is still trying to convince me to give our marriage another chance because he loves me. To me he writes, "I'll be honest with you, Darling, if you do not love me anymore, there is not a single thing in the world that I can do to keep you and there is not a single thing in the world that I wouldn't do to make you come back to me."

How debonair he sounds. He is traveling and leading the glamorous life he always coveted. I am working and going to school and barely have time to sleep.

On and on he goes, sharing all the names of famous artists he is meeting and befriending. "Satyajit Ray of India, Stanley Kramer, Peter

Ustinov, Fellini, and many others. [Nothing but] parties, parties, and parties. I am invited to two or three different parties, every day. I feel I need a rest, but I am afraid I cannot get it.

"How are you, Phyllis? Happy? Content? Remember me? Good-night, my dear, I shall never stop loving you."

Two years pass. Toward the end of 1963 my lawyers advertise in a number of newspapers in New York City, a means of summoning Abdul-Kareem to appear in court in the matter of an annulment. He never appears. I am not sure if his lawyer even comes to the hearing. According to the legal documents, I am the sole witness. I do not remember testifying. In response to these legal events Abdul-Kareem writes, "I never expected us to come down to this—Oh, well—that is life—love must be answered with hate. . . . As your lawyer must have informed you, I cannot be served [with] a summons here and our case cannot be tried in a U.S. court. Legally, you are an Afghan citizen."

On March 20, 1964, two years and three months after I left Kabul, Judge Charles J. Beckinella grants me an annulment, which will be finalized in three months.

I am now free to ask the Department of State to help me retrieve some of my possessions left behind—mainly my college papers and some books. I am told that "the United States Government has no jurisdiction over an Afghan national residing in Afghanistan." However, Robert J. Carle, a State Department official, offers to approach the embassy in Kabul to see if an "informal approach" can be made.

In 1965, eight months after the annulment is finalized, I write directly to Lowell B. Laingen, who works at the Afghanistan Desk in the State Department, and explain that Abdul-Kareem has promised, again and again, to return my papers to me. Finally, later that year, I hear from the American embassy in Kabul, from Thomas J. Wajda, the vice consul. He writes:

> While in my office, Mr. M. [Abdul-Kareem] mentioned that he is now having some difficulties with various Afghan authorities over your failure to return to Afghanistan. You may recall that when you left this country it was necessary for Mr. M. to guarantee your return. I assume that you now have no intention of returning to Afghanistan. If this is the case, you would probably be doing Mr. M. a great favor by returning your Afghan passport, and with it, a notarized statement concerning the annulment of your marriage. He would then, perhaps, be able to straighten things out with the passport authorities.

What kind of tribal-totalitarian police state is this?

Now, more than fifty years later, I believe that Abdul-Kareem could indeed have been held accountable for a missing Afghan passport or, rather, for a missing piece of Afghan property: me. I believe that he could have been punished for having brought an American bride home in the first place—and for then having lost her. He once mentioned that he spent a year in the army. I wonder, only now, if this was his punishment.

The Afghan monarch and the country's bureaucracy—that excuse for not getting things done, that system for leading people on for months and years and exacting whatever gain the individual clerk can obtain—has imprisoned and executed people for lesser crimes.

Ten years after I left Kabul, I reread these letters. My conclusion then was that I was a pawn in the power struggle between Abdul-Kareem and his father. Abdul-Kareem wanted his foreign Jewish bride, his father did not think he had made a wise choice. Abdul-Kareem once wrote to say that he had broken with his father forever, that he had been disowned. Maybe his father would not give him the money with which to pursue me further. I believe that everything that happened in that country, from the king on down, was father controlled.

I took only three things out with me when I left Kabul. One was a song that I carefully learned and that I still sing. Another was the bright turquoise nargileh, or water-pipe, that came from Mazar-i-Sharif. Last was my bright orange Afghan passport, which I have also kept—a memento of happier times, a memento of tragic times.

Please allow me to apologize to Abdul-Kareem here and now—if indeed the nonreturn of my Afghan passport caused him any difficulties whatsoever.

Nearly three years after I left, toward the end of 1964, Abdul-Kareem writes again, "Upon my arrival in Kabul I found a court document granting you an annulment. I must admit I was hurt. . . . We were so involved and I loved you so much that it is very difficult for me to accept that it is all over. Even now it doesn't have to be! Well, I guess that is asking for too much. I'd like to help you in any way I can, so please don't hesitate to let me know if there is anything I can do for you."

At the end of April 1965, the American embassy in Kabul received a sealed package that contained my college papers.

It is over. I am legally free. I will never be free. Here I am, still writing about it all, trying to make sense of what happened and what it may mean to other people in the larger scheme of things.

My young self may not have been wise, but she proved as strong, as persistent, and as adamant as her Afghan husband was. I was physically trapped and I got out. I was legally trapped and I got out, too. We were an evenly matched pair. Neither of us veered from our chosen path.

My parents are no longer alive, but I owe them a profound debt of gratitude for standing by me—their rebel child.

Abdul-Kareem once wrote, "I'd always hoped you'd use your time here to write a great novel—I know you can. Michener's *Caravans* is not literature; I always expected that someday you would write the first novel about Afghanistan that deals with the life, people, etc., and you would do it here with love and great insight."

Ah, Abdul-Kareem, this is not a novel, but here I am, writing about us and about Afghanistan as best I can.

NINE

My Afghan Family
Arrives in America

*I*n the decade after I left Afghanistan, I finished college and worked
full time while attending graduate school. I was lucky. I returned
to America when it was possible for a serious young woman to
become truly independent. In less than a decade I received my doctorate
and obtained a position as a professor of psychology.

I was also privileged to have come of age when second-wave feminism was sweeping the country. I reported for duty in 1967, and by 1969
I was one of the many visible leaders of this extraordinary movement for
women's freedom.

My Afghan experience taught me to recognize variations of sexism
(or gender apartheid) everywhere, including in America.

The civil rights movement: the voter registration drives, sit-ins, and
marches in the South were noble and tempting, but I could not go to Ala-
bama or Mississippi and also finish school. Instead I joined the Northern
Student Movement and tutored students in Harlem and in my East Village apartment. Like others, I ran into unexpected sexism and thus had
many more illusions upended.

Although I joined some anti–Vietnam War marches, and was considered more leftist than rightist, sexism among leftist men was as alive

as it was among those who opposed such marches as unpatriotic and dangerous.

Unlike many of my contemporaries, I no longer romanticized the masses or the people of the Third World. I knew too much about the oppression of women and men in at least one poor, illiterate, tribal, and religiously fundamentalist country. Thus, although I was a critic of sexism in America, I could no longer mindlessly demonize my own country or culture. I knew, firsthand, that it was far better here than elsewhere.

I knew what could happen to a woman living in the developing world. It had nearly happened to me. I could not forget how close I had come to an imprisoned life and an early death. Thus I was always concerned with women everywhere, not only with women in America, most of whom at least had the right to battle for their rights without risking death at the hands of their families—or prison, torture, and death at the hands of the state.

Such views set me apart from many in my activist generation.

In 1969 I published an article in *Mademoiselle* about some of my experiences in Afghanistan. I had not forgotten about the country, but Afghanistan was not part of my work and was no longer on my mind.

Abdul-Kareem and I no longer corresponded. I had no idea what he was doing or how he was. Still, I religiously clipped articles about Afghanistan whenever they appeared and kept them safe. I have them now.

I may have left Abdul-Kareem, but I remained connected to other Muslims.

I befriended Egyptians, Syrians, Lebanese, Israeli Arabs, Palestinians, Saudis, Turks, Moroccans, Iranians, and Pakistanis. Many were interested in what I had experienced in Kabul and shared with me their own stories.

I met Jihan Sadat and Raymonda Hawa Tawil (who became Yasir Arafat's mother-in-law). I became friendly with the leading feminists of Egypt: Nawal El Saadawi and Laila Abou-Saif. In time I also met the academic Leila Ahmed.

I met Middle Eastern filmmakers, Iranian anti-Shah activists, a Turkish Japanese feminist, a number of brave Saudi Arabian feminists, and two exceptionally glamorous and defiant feminists: Fatima Mernissi of Morocco and Rhonda Al-Fatal of Syria.

I wonder: How are they now, where are they, are they alive and alright?

By the end of 1979 I had published four books that had been translated into many European and into some Middle Eastern and Asian languages. I was working on a fifth book—and I was also the new mother of a wonderful one-year-old son.

And then one day, toward the end of 1979, my phone rang.
It was Abdul-Kareem.
He wanted to meet.

Disguised as a peasant, he had escaped from Soviet-infiltrated and now Soviet-occupied Afghanistan. He knew it was time to get out "once the Soviets massacred their own hand-picked puppet-leader, Daoud Khan, together with Daoud's entire family, women, children and all."

Abdul-Kareem had been a deputy minister of culture and probably a member of Daoud's cabinet.

With only a toothbrush in his pocket he had crossed into Pakistan. After waiting in a one-room flat in Germany for five months, he, his wife, and their two young children flew to the West Coast; Boeing had promised him a job as a sales representative for Iran, Afghanistan, and Turkey. Ruefully, and with a characteristic touch of Afghan absurdist humor, Abdul-Kareem said, "It took many months to get the necessary visas. By the time I arrived in America, Iran had already been taken over by the mullahs, Afghanistan by the Russians, and Turkey had decided to buy from McDonnell Douglas instead. Boeing had no need for me."

Abdul-Kareem got out of Afghanistan before the Soviet invasion, but before he escaped he had lived through nearly two decades of increasing Soviet infiltration.

In his essay, "Soviet Military Involvement in Afghanistan" (which appears in Rosanne Klass's major anthology, *Afghanistan: The Great Game Revisited*), Yossef Bodansky writes, "Like their Tsarist predecessors, they [the Soviets] have always perceived their position in Central Asia in terms of global strategy. In August 1919 Leon Trotsky wrote to the Central Committee, ' . . . The road to Paris and London lies via the towns of Afghanistan, the Punjab and Bengal.'"

In another essay, "The Road to Crisis 1919–1980: American Failures, Afghan Errors, and Soviet Successes," in Klass's anthology, Leon Poullada, an American diplomat and author, writes, "It was not until Moscow began paying increasing attention to Third World countries in the 1950s that a more active and permanent Soviet role became manifest. . . . Moscow's influence in Kabul developed into a position of preeminence that was never threatened . . . by any outside powers."

During this time of post–World War II Soviet imperialism, America was unwilling to intervene or compete diplomatically, adopting instead a laissez-faire attitude toward Afghanistan. In her introduction to the anthology Klass documents America's mistakes in regard to Afghanistan: "In 1953, then Prime Minister [and prince] Mohammed Daoud asked for American aid to update an army which consisted of a few World War I biplanes and horse-drawn artillery." America rejected Daoud's request, and "Daoud turned to Moscow for arms, and the patient Russian pachyderm . . . began to edge its way into Kabul."

As a result of America's diplomatic miscalculations and Moscow's business savvy, the Soviets found an ally in Mohammed Daoud Khan, a cousin of the king and prime minister from 1953 to 1963. At that time Daoud had been asked to leave his post. He sat at home and brooded. Then Daoud and the Soviets got rid of King Zahir Shah.

Poor Abdul-Kareem! His adopted country, America, had let him—and America's own interests—down. I feel terrible for him.

Abdul-Kareem had dreamed of bringing his country into the twentieth century. Now the best he can hope for is to become a consultant on Afghanistan for the American government. Probably every other Afghan immigrant in town is looking for this kind of position. He gave a lecture at Freedom House about the five million Afghan refugees who had been displaced by the Soviet conflict and who were residing in Pakistan. He wanted to be of use, to undo the grievous harm to his country that was unfolding and continues to unfold.

Abdul-Kareem thought I might be able to help him become established in America by writing an article about him, his escape, and his views. He wanted a portrait in the major media. So I obtained a commission from the *New York Times Magazine* for a piece I subsequently decided not to write.

We talked for many hours and I taped our conversation. I wanted to help, but the material was overwhelming and, at the time, far too complicated for me to evaluate. (Klass's anthology had not yet been published and I was really unfamiliar with the histories of Afghanistan.) Also, Abdul-Kareem's emotions were too raw, even wild, and his political views seemed contradictory and confusing. I did not want to disappoint him—indeed I wanted him to understand that I did wield the power of the pen—yet I was afraid that publishing this interview would hurt rather than help him. He threatened to sue me if I did not go through with the project.

I reminded him that in America a writer cannot be sued for nonperformance. He never mentioned the article again.

Thirty-three years later, as I reread the transcription of this long interview, I find that it is historically priceless, a dramatic tale of how one man and his family experienced the gradual but heavy-handed Soviet takeover of their country.

Only now do I appreciate the importance of what he was saying. I regret that I did not publish his story sooner. Still, I admit it: I was happy to see him and to reconnect.

Until now, it was not easy for me to view him as a figure on the stage of history. Mainly I viewed him as my former husband—just as he viewed me as his former wife. I hereby want to acknowledge that Abdul-Kareem has always favored a modern constitutional democracy. He stands on record for individual liberty and even women's rights—so long as each husband can still limit the rights of his own wife. He is so proud that Afghanistan passed a constitution in 1964.

Abdul-Kareem is secular. The Bolsheviks were also secular—but their arrogant and heartless infiltration of his country—their essentially totalitarian nature—frightened and disgusted him. In retrospect, as I revisit this interview, I am again reminded of why the barefoot Afghan mujahideen (holy warriors) became so popular, not just in Afghanistan but around the world. They took on the Soviet giant with only their faith and their will to remain independent. They were the ultimate underdogs in a victim-worshipping era.

The Pakistani Inter-Services Intelligence spy and government leadership did not want to lose control of the border territory between Pakistan and Afghanistan; they found Afghan warlords who could be bought and were of like minds. The Afghan warlords did not want the Soviets to occupy and change their country. The Islamist Arabs viewed the battle against the Soviets as a religious jihad—and Afghanistan as a good place to train Muslim holy warriors for the future global jihad. At the time no one understood that the heroic holy warriors would one day become the savage Taliban or al-Qaeda.

Americans and Europeans did not understand that war was a permanent way of life for the Afghan tribes and that the Afghan warlords who subsequently arose would never stop trying to destroy each other at the expense of the Afghan civilian population.

In the mid-1980s the British American journalist and author Jan Goodwin visited Afghanistan twice and embedded herself among the mujahideen—the only woman among the brothers. In 1987 she published a dramatic book about the experience: *Caught in the Crossfire.*

The cover shows a turbaned Goodwin in male dress among the warriors, and the book is subtitled *The True Story of an American Woman's Secret and Perilous Journey with the Freedom Fighters Through War-torn Afghanistan.*

Although Goodwin is critical of the plight of Afghan women and expresses her loathing of the burqa, she is deeply sympathetic to the mujahideen and to their cause. To her they are freedom fighters, and one of her main goals in this book is to humanize them and to show how vulnerable and sentimental they can be.

The mujahideen's unexpected victory against the brutal, calculated, and better-equipped Soviet army was heroic, legendary, moving, and entirely unexpected. However, the victory was bittersweet because it led to the rise of the regressive Taliban, al-Qaeda, and other Islamist terrorist groups, as well as to prolonged civil war in Afghanistan. Many people blamed America for this never-ending debacle, but a lot of hands had stirred this putrid pot: the Soviets, Pakistanis, Americans, Islamist Arabs—and the Afghans themselves.

Pakistan had tricked America into backing the sadistic and anti-American warlord Gulbuddin Hekmatyar. Pakistan wanted to make sure that the Soviets did not incorporate any disputed areas of Pakistan, such as Pushtunistan and the tribal border areas. Hekmatyar was their man.

In her excellent book *Kabul in Winter,* the author and activist Ann Jones describes this particularly wicked warlord, who fought in (and arguably started) the Afghan civil war, which lasted from 1992 to 1996. Hekmatyar killed tens of thousands of his own people—mainly civilians, including those who were still trapped in Kabul. Jones describes what a professor from Kabul University told her: "Hekmatyar assaulted women students who appeared on campus in Western dress. Some report that he threw acid at their unveiled faces and at the legs of those who wore short skirts. The professor remembers that [Hekmatyar] more often beat women up. 'He's a psychopath. . . . He should have been locked up then.'"

The Soviets feared an increasing Islamification of their own Muslim republics and thus stepped up their indoctrination and infiltration of Afghanistan. Now, the Soviets moved their puppets into place more daringly.

Abdul-Kareem remembers it well. He tells me, "It was 1973 and I woke one morning, and a servant brought me coffee and told me that there had been a coup d'état. The king had been replaced by Daoud, who would remain president until 1978."

Abdul-Kareem realized that the Soviets could never succeed in a country like Afghanistan. He says, "Communism was designed for a country like Germany—that is to say, for a country that is highly industrialized. When you apply communism by force, rather than by harnessing it to the national will—when you are dealing with an underdeveloped country where there is no industry, where there are mainly peasant farmers, and no serious landowners—the result will be a disaster. On top of that, Afghanistan is a conservative and deeply religious Muslim society. The people will resist until there is nothing left of the country, and then the Russians will leave."

Oh, my. I wish he had described Afghanistan to me just like this way back when. I only wish he had said that returning to Afghanistan with him would mean real hardship and deprivation because the country was tribal and quite backward. On the other hand I had never intended to stay there. I really thought we would be meeting his family, traveling the country, and then leaving together.

Abdul-Kareem told me what it was like living in Afghanistan as the Soviets increasingly took over. What follows is an edited version of our original discussion in early 1980.

> *Phyllis:* How on earth did you get out of Afghanistan? But first tell me
>   what you did after I left.
> *Abdul-Kareem:* Oh, I was alright. Well, I never recovered. So I was
>   living alone until 1966. I had my career. Then I married again
>   and had two children. My wife, Kamile, had a career, and my
>   family scorned her for working outside the home.
>   I started an advertising agency in Kabul. Soon I had every
>   account that was worthwhile. I became the biggest advertising
>   agency in town. My clients included the International Hotel, the
>   national bank, the largest soap factory, the Castile Oil Company,
>   quite a few factories.

He is such a survivor, so ready to forge ahead no matter what, so admirably stoic, a noncomplainer, but someone who has been groomed for success.

> *Abdul-Kareem:* Then there was a change—someone I knew became
>   prime minister, and my other friend became the minister of
>   culture. They asked me to become the deputy minister of

culture and president of the national theater, which I began to reorganize.

As deputy minister of culture [1973–77], I was in charge of the national museums; the Departments of Archeology and Restoration of Monuments and Sites, International Cultural Relations, Fine Arts, Music, Folklore, and Films; the Historical Society; the Afghan National Theatre; and the UNESCO Desk.

I attended UNESCO [United Nations Educational, Scientific and Cultural Organization] conferences in Kenya, Japan, and Turkey and led study tours to Sweden, Britain, Russia, and Pakistan. I visited India and Pakistan many times.

I drafted and passed resolutions at the international meeting of UNESCO in Nairobi—I had Herat declared an international city, which meant the UN would contribute to the restoration of its monuments. I crafted the resolution that, when any country does archaeological research in a country, they must contribute to preserving and housing the objects they uncover.

Abdul-Kareem did become an important man in Afghanistan and also a player of sorts in the global village. But I bet he did most of his traveling alone, not with his wife. I would never have stayed back home in Kabul. He was lucky to be rid of me. I would have made this Afghan husband's life difficult.

Phyllis: What were the Soviets like?

Abdul-Kareem: They were bullies. Everyone was afraid of them. The king, the prime minister. If an official refused to do something the Russians wanted, he would be replaced. You should have seen how the officials would bow and scrape when dealing or socializing with the Russians. The Russians would come without appointments. They would demand to be seen.

The Russian embassy served the worst food and drink, and the official hospitality left a great deal to be desired, yet any official who was invited would never think of refusing to attend, as an anti-Russian attitude would get them fired.

I had no Russian friends—we never became friends because they were not allowed to mix with us.

This fear of the Russians was contagious. It was felt by the shopkeeper, the merchant, and the laborer. Fear and impotence led to hatred. All the Afghans hated the Russians with passion.

Phyllis: Did you know anybody in the various Afghan Marxist
   regimes?

Abdul-Kareem: Of course. They were very ordinary people: clerks,
   petty civil servants, men mainly from the provinces. They were
   jealous of everyone.

   When the Marxists took over, something very strange
   happened. The first thing these spokesmen for "the people"
   did was to move into the most deluxe houses in Kabul. Some
   moved into palaces. Nur Muhamad Taraki, the chairman of
   Afghanistan's Communist Party [1978–79], moved into the king's
   palace.

   All of them drove the latest Mercedes Benz, and their wives
   and children were given automobiles, too. These officials were
   supposedly the spokesmen for the peasants, and they had all the
   tailors in town working for them. They dressed only in the best
   clothes. They became so chic. They ate the best food. Meanwhile
   their peasants were displaced and lived terribly as refugees.

Phyllis: All the Soviet puppets ended up dead, assassinated by the next
   Soviet puppet. Daoud [1973–78] was assassinated by Soviet-led
   Afghan insurgents. Then Taraki [1978–79] was assassinated
   by his right-hand man, Hafizullah Amin. Then the Soviets
   assassinated Amin and installed Karmal Babrak at the end of
   1979. Who did you know?

Abdul-Kareem: I knew Taraki. He took his afternoon walks right in
   front of our house. He attended Teachers' College at Columbia.
   Hafizullah was also educated at Columbia University. He
   ordered Taraki's death; some say he killed him with his own
   hands. The Russians were pissed, but what could they do?
   They sent Amin a telegram saying, "Congratulations on your
   election."

   When the Russians invaded they used the opportunity to
   punish Amin, so they brought in Karmal [Babrak], who always
   did exactly what Moscow asked him to. I knew him, too. He
   was always invited to celebrate the anniversary of the October
   Revolution at the Soviet embassy. Karmal was obedient to Russia
   but to nobody else.

   Most of the people in the parliament were there to become
   rich, and each individual province was just helping each other to
   help themselves. In offices everyone would just sit around. If you
   tried to do anything, they would give you a rough time.

Phyllis: This is all Afghan politics as usual. What got the average
   Afghan so angry at the Russians—before the invasion?

Abdul-Kareem: First the Afghan Marxist state did nothing for
   them. They made empty promises about giving them land. The
   Russians tried to break the back of Afghan tribalism. They
   relocated people, breaking up tribes, in the hope that this would
   make it impossible for them to mount any resistance.

   In 1972 the Russians did nothing to help when people
   were dying from starvation as a result of a three-year drought.
   The government tried to hide news of the drought, but an
   independent newspaper finally printed stories of the famine. The
   newspaper encouraged its readers to adopt children who were
   being sold to wealthy families who could feed them.

   Then the Afghan-Russian communist government sent their
   armed forces to attack one particular village. A well-known
   religious leader lived there, and they wanted to arrest him.
   When they arrived, the people put up a fantastic resistance. They
   evacuated their mullah—the villagers carried him out on their
   backs. In retaliation the Soviet-led government ordered an air
   strike that completely demolished the village.

   To the people of Afghanistan the most sacred thing is their
   religion. And the Russians were taking their religion, their
   homes, and their land. The communists were trying to destroy all
   tradition in a country that is built on tradition.

God, I wish he had described Afghanistan to me in this way before
he took me there. But if he had, how, then, could he have imagined that
the American and European plays he started to direct would find an
audience in such a country? He is definitely my mad dreamer soul mate.

Phyllis: Why were so many Afghan leaders so vulnerable to being
   trapped by the Russians?

Abdul-Kareem: Russia found an ally in Daoud, who had ousted his
   first cousin, King Zahir Shah, from power. Daoud did not like
   Nixon. He [Daoud] was disenchanted with America because his
   request for arms was denied. So he asked Russia, which agreed to
   sell him armaments. Daoud became sympathetic toward Russia,
   having been a recipient of Soviet generosity. But he committed
   himself far too much to the Russians, and then he wanted out.

He did not understand that the arms deal was a quid pro quo situation.

Daoud thought that he was so smart. He thought he could use the Russians, without them using him. Daoud made the government something to be feared. Before he came into power, getting a passport in Afghanistan was an easy thing, but afterwards it was impossible to get a passport. He essentially created a police state, and he was directly involved in every minute detail of running the country. He spent hours a day selecting furniture for all the new embassies he was building. He wanted to choose the curtains himself.

He dares to talk about passports to me! Doesn't he remember what difficulties I—and possibly he too—had because of the missing Afghan and American passports? Has he forgotten how tightly the Afghan government controlled who would be allowed to study abroad, how much money they could be paid, and when they would have to return? Has he forgotten the pre-Soviet Afghan regime?

Phyllis: Did the Soviets force Daoud out of the country?

Abdul-Kareem: No, they just massacred him and his family: women, children, babies—Daoud, his wife, his brother, his sons, daughters-in-law, grandchildren. They were all killed. It was a massacre. They did the same thing to Tsar Nicholas II and his family. It was a coup d'état. The Russians attacked the palace.

The first attacks, which began at 12:30, were tank attacks, and that went on until about 4–4:30 in the afternoon. Then around 4:30 the air force took over, firing rockets at the palace. That went on for hours. It was all dark. It went on all night until about 8 in the morning.

Phyllis: Where were you?

Abdul-Kareem: When it started, I was in town. It was a Thursday. I was working at the Saudi Arabian embassy, and I had to drop the kids off at school in the afternoon because it was a half-day. I saw a man running. As he came near me, I recognized him and asked, "What's the matter?" He said, "There's a coup! They have taken over the radio station. Where are your kids?! Go home!" So I immediately went to pick up my son and then my daughter from their schools. Just as I got to my daughter's school, I heard gunfire. Machine guns were being fired, and the artillery bombardment had begun.

We were living in the huge house—you know which one— the one that used to be an embassy on Dar-Lamond Street, near the palace. Most of the fighting occurred right in front of our house.

That street was the residential Champs-Élysées of Kabul and I remember the house well. When I was there, his father had rented it to an embassy, and Abdul-Kareem always coveted it for himself. I am glad he finally got to live in it.

> *Abdul-Kareem:* That night was rough. We could not sleep. We stayed on the floor of one bedroom with the mattresses against the windows. In the morning it was announced that Daoud and his family had been eliminated.
>
> In April of 1978 every man, woman, and child feared for their life. Nobody was sure if they would still be alive the next morning. You were not allowed to get together with friends—all assemblies were forbidden. Some people living down the street had a swimming pool. It was Friday, and they had some cousins and other relatives visiting them. They were all swimming.
>
> By one o'clock all of the men had been arrested. They were imprisoned for two months. Daily seemingly random arrests were carried out by communist military men, most of whom were Afghans—militiamen who had been trained in the Soviet Union.

The Soviets are forbidding swimming! Once, in the late 1950s, the Afghan government completely freaked out when officials heard that Afghans and Americans, men and women, were swimming together in what was known as the Little America of the Helmand Valley Project. I remember when I was not allowed to swim with men present in Kabul in the early 1960s. Jan Goodwin, in *Caught in the Crossfire*, describes a hot day in the mid-1980s when she and her band of mujahideen brothers find a river. She writes, "Most of the men went down to the river to swim. As a woman, I was told, I couldn't join them, but I envied the men the chance to cool off."

Is everyone here irrational about women swimming? At least the Soviets do not forbid women to swim; they just don't believe in freedom of assembly, lest those assembled in the swimming pool engage in a conspiracy against Soviet tyranny.

Phyllis: Did the Soviets torture their prisoners?
Abdul-Kareem: Oh, yes. They wanted confessions. They kept files on everyone.
Phyllis: How did you get your wife and children out?
Abdul-Kareem: Slowly and carefully, through connections, and with many bribes, I was able to get passports for them and get them on a direct flight out. I stayed behind.

He is clearly reluctant to share any further details about this, and I do not press him.

Phyllis: What happened next?
Abdul-Kareem: I had to routinely pay off government officials. I sold my car. All of the money was gone. Meanwhile they arrested the minister of culture and expected his ten-year-old son to pay back the money the previous government had granted [the minister] to attend a conference in Jakarta. They did this systematically to anyone who was linked to Daoud. I was forced into hiding.

And now Abdul-Kareem faced *his* version of having to get out of Afghanistan. He was in dire danger and he knew it.

Phyllis: Who could you trust?
Abdul-Kareem: I trusted my brothers, but I wouldn't discuss my plans with them. They were frightened and felt that if I escaped, it would jeopardize their lives even further. They kept trying to persuade me not to leave, but I had no intention of staying.
Phyllis: Why were they not thinking of escaping?
Abdul-Kareem: It takes courage to plan an escape. You have to be brought to the brink. For me it was not enough to simply be alive. I needed more. I needed a purpose.
Phyllis: Ah, Abdul-Kareem, how I begged you not to stay—I saw that your dreams were doomed.
Abdul-Kareem: I was living alone. I would get up, make coffee, smoke cigarettes, and read all day. My American friends smuggled in books for me. A diplomat, the consul general of Bombay, lived

next door, and I would go and sit and chat with him and his wife. I really enjoyed their company.

As I listen, I wonder: What ever happened to my books—the books I had shipped for a semester's worth of reading, the books that were held up at the Khyber Pass because of a border dispute—the books that Kamile, Abdul-Kareem's wife, thanked me for again and again? Were they destroyed? Perhaps Abdul-Kareem had already read through them all.

> *Abdul-Kareem:* All this time I was looking for a smuggler who could take me across the border to Pakistan. No one wanted to take me—I was too high profile. I finally grew a beard and spoke to some Pushtun smugglers. They were experts. They smuggled all kinds of goods across the Pakistan border: tires, batteries, textiles, rice, wheat, sugar, everything. They were smugglers but savvy businessmen, too.
>
> In April of 1979 I was told by a friend that all the borders would be closed within two to three weeks. I had to get out. Finally a friend told me to go to his house, where he introduced me to a man who had a bus that took people across the Khyber Pass. I knew this was my chance. I cut my hair like a peasant, dressed in peasant clothes, and burned some letters I did not want the government to find. I told my friend that I would send the message "The goods have been delivered," when I arrived in Pakistan. He promised he would tell my brothers.
>
> It was time. I met the man with the bus at a shop in the city. He was a nomad. I took off my glasses, and I wrapped my shawl around my head and face. I saw many people I knew, but they didn't recognize or notice me. We got on the bus. It was a strange experience becoming invisible to others.
>
> *Phyllis:* That's how women must feel in the burqa.
>
> *Abdul-Kareem:* Well, I didn't notice. We sat way back in the bus. We went through five checkpoints on our way from Kabul to Jalalabad. My guide told me not to say anything, and he told all the officials that I was his son. I don't know how we got through. At one point some Communist Youths had me stand up and looked under my seat.
>
> *Phyllis:* What was the nomad's motivation for taking you?

Abdul-Kareem: I gave him some money, not a lot. He didn't mind taking me; he was going to Peshawar anyway. He also didn't know who I was. He thought I was going to Peshawar on a business trip. After we arrived in Jalalabad we discussed our plans. The most important checkpoint, the one I was most afraid of, was right before the Khyber Pass. We planned to go by truck to a village right before the checkpoint.

Then at midnight we would walk across the border to bypass the checkpoint. But when we got to Jalalabad, the curfew had already started. I stayed up all night. I smoked cigarette after cigarette. We left Jalalabad by bus at 10:30 in the morning. The bus went up to the Khyber Pass. It was crowded with chickens, bikes, and people. I was sitting on the floor in a crouched position. We came to the most dangerous checkpoint.

This was a military checkpoint. Russian military personnel got on the bus and searched it. They looked under the seats, everything. There was a collection of tents guarded by men with machine guns. The boy sitting right in front of me, no older than eighteen, was taken off the bus and asked where he was going and why. He said that he was going to Peshawar to work as a knife sharpener; he even showed them his knife sharpener. They took him into the tent. Twenty minutes later he came back. His whole body was trembling. Then we came to the military checkpoint. They searched the whole bus but didn't notice me.

The nomad left me, and a sixteen-year-old kid met me to take me across the border. The boy told me there had been an event the other day. Some people from Kabul had come—two men and two women. And they just crossed the border— they didn't stop, so the Russians fired at them with their Kalashnikovs. One man and one woman escaped. The other two were injured and captured. He told me, "So, whatever happens, don't ever run."

He handed me an empty kerosene can. He said, "We are going over there to bring kerosene back. They are used to people crossing over into Pakistan from Afghanistan to bring back kerosene." At the time there was a shortage of kerosene in Afghanistan. So we walked over to the kerosene tank. We came near a whole line of soldiers in uniforms with Kalashnikovs and pistols.

As we approached them, the boy started using his kerosene can as a drum. He pushed me, playing. He put my hat at an angle, and he danced right through the line, pushing me along with him. No one stopped us. When we were 50 meters away [about 50 feet], he said, "That's it. It is finished." Then we walked toward Pakistan.

I looked back at the checkpoint. Afghanistan was beautiful from the Pakistani side. Mostly it was all behind me. The boy changed my Afghanis for Pakistani rupees, and we got on the back of a minitruck leaving for Peshawar. I watched my country fade from the back window. I couldn't believe it—I just couldn't believe it. I was suddenly in a whole new world, with a whole new life. Afghanistan was the past. There was nothing, only myself, stripped of everything. The feeling of being free consumed me. I remember thinking, "Now I can breathe. I don't have to worry."

Phyllis: That's how I felt when I left—

But true to form Abdul-Kareem does not hear me.

Abdul-Kareem: I called my friend in Peshawar. Within five minutes he was there in his car. He didn't recognize me. He took me home and his mother started crying. My clothes were already there. It was a posh house. I had a beautiful bathroom. I took a shower and changed. I felt like a human being again. I sent a telegram saying that I had made it.

I ate for the first time in forty hours. I picked up the money that had been smuggled into Pakistan for me. I used my old passport, which had been given to me under the Daoud administration, and got a visa from my friend, David Block, who was a consul in the American embassy.

I flew to Karachi and then to Istanbul. Once I arrived safely and reconnected with my wife and kids, I began studying Ottoman history at the university.

He is an amazing survivor! He is hardy, hardworking, uncomplaining, ever hopeful. He is really so very Afghan.

Phyllis: Where did you stay?

Abdul-Kareem: My friends have a summer apartment by the sea that they never use.

Phyllis: That is extraordinary! To begin again at midlife cannot be easy. By the way, what was it really like for you after I left?

Abdul-Kareem: I was alone a long, long while. After I got remarried, I stayed away from my family. I would see my brothers maybe once a month, once every two months, until I completely divorced myself from the family.

Phyllis: Do you want to talk about us?

Abdul-Kareem: I have thought about us for eighteen years. Did you think about us?

Phyllis: Yes, no, not really, of course.

Abdul-Kareem: Well, I've thought a great deal about us. I have to carry the guilt. It's my fault. You know I loved you more than I had ever loved anyone. Did you know that?

Phyllis: Well, we were doomed from the moment you decided to take me to Afghanistan. The only thing you can blame yourself for was your need to return. You tried to have both me and a life in Afghanistan without realizing that you could never have both. That was an error of your youth, idealism, and your hubris. You thought you could do it.

Abdul-Kareem: Yes. There were bound to be certain losses.

There are awkward silences between us during this very long and rather formal interview. Whenever I bring up subjects such as polygamy, purdah, and the burqa, he absolutely refuses to discuss them. He says, flat out, "I will not talk about that," or "That is not a subject I will comment on."

Given his sophistication and worldliness, I am at a loss. Would commenting on these subjects in some way dishonor him or his father or his country? Is this stubborn misogyny the one cherished custom he has brought out with him into exile?

Or is he so understandably angry at the whole world and at his fate that he refuses to admit that Afghanistan—poor country!—is a primitive and barbarous region?

I understand why Afghans and other Muslims feel suspicious and shamed by the do-good projects undertaken by infidel outsiders.

But an international hands-off policy always dooms the women and the progressives. I wrestle with this conundrum constantly.

While my ex-husband is not an uneducated or impoverished man, he is now in exile. However, he does not have to start from scratch. He knows the language—he once lived here for a decade. He has friends and many acquaintances. The question is, Will he ever stop missing what might have been—and what once existed for him in Afghanistan?

*I*n the mid-1970s I spent months working on a book proposal about exile, which, I predicted, might be the largest new state created by the twentieth century and the psychology of the twenty-first century.

Many people are uprooted by war and poverty and by a desire to make a better life for themselves and their families. Some remain in refugee camps with absolutely no ability or incentive to make new lives; they just want their old lives back. Others happily emigrate but bring their customs and religious practices along with them. They keep to themselves. They live on the margins—or at the center but remain apart, different.

Like Jews.

Jews have prototypically lived in exile, but when necessary they have always moved, trading, selling, practicing medicine, and settling in ever-new locations. Jews have been forced to flee again and again and have learned to call many places home.

Now an untold number of impoverished and often illiterate refugees worldwide are similarly stateless. Most live in tents or in makeshift structures; they stand in hopelessly long lines, waiting for water, food, blankets, and medicine. Most do not move on; they cannot. They lack the necessary skills and resources. It is not their tradition.

Wealthy and educated refugees, like Abdul-Kareem, are usually alright, at least for a while. They have bank accounts, contacts, even relatives on many continents.

Abdul-Kareem has now joined the millions of immigrants who have come to America. His children will grow up as Americans. But he has become a biblical figure, a wanderer like a Jew, still dreaming of his golden castles elsewhere, of some past and future paradise that is now forever barred to him.

TEN

The Jews of Afghanistan

As a child I was affectionately referred to as the "smartest boy" in Hebrew school. At that time an Orthodox Jewish girl had no future as a rabbi, scholar, or cantor, so when I was twelve, I abandoned my beloved Torah study for other passions.

But the Torah was where I first read about Jews as an Eastern people. Our patriarch, Abraham, and matriarch, Sarah, both came from Haran and traveled to Ur Kasdim, which was in Mesopotamia, probably in contemporary Iraq. Thereafter Abraham and Sarah lived in Hebron, Jerusalem, and Bersheva, cities in Canaan, the Promised Land, and in Egypt.

Abraham and Sarah's son and grandsons, Yitzhak (Isaac), Esav, and Ya'akov/Israel (Jacob), married wives from Aram Naharayim, near Haran, and Nahor, which were in Mesopotamia between two rivers, probably the Tigris and the Euphrates. Ya'akov/Israel lived there with his two wives, Leah and Rachel; his two concubines, Bilhah and Zilpah; their eleven children; and his father-in-law, Laban. He did so for twenty years. Esav married Canaanite wives. Abraham and Hagar's son, Ishmael, lived in Paran, in the Sinai desert.

My ancestors once worshipped idols and were known as "wandering Aramaeans," Semites, Hebrews, Canaanites, inhabitants of ancient Israel: Arab Jews.

I remember that my notebook (or *machberes*) had a picture of the great scholar and philosopher Maimonides on the cover in a turban.

Perhaps I thought that Muslims and Jews were similar or at least different from Christians in the same way. Thus I took the long route to Jerusalem—by way of Kabul.

The story of my people is complicated. European Jews are known as Ashkenazi Jews—but some European Jews are known as Sephardic Jews; they are Jews who fled Christian or Muslim persecution in Spain and Portugal and were thereafter either persecuted elsewhere in Christian Europe or allowed to live comfortable-enough lives there for periods of time. And/or they then fled Europe for the Ottoman Empire (the Arab Middle East, North Africa, and Turkey), where they were welcomed. They also came to the United States.

Some Jews also lived continuously in Jerusalem and in the cities of ancient Israel.

I knew that Jewish and Muslim lives had been intertwined for millennia. I had no idea that historically Muslims had viewed themselves as superior to all infidels, but especially to Jews, whom they tolerated but also tithed, impoverished, humiliated, persecuted, exiled, and massacred.

Nevertheless I thought that the Jews of Islam (the phrase is Bernard Lewis's) got along rather well with Muslims. Despite my wild secular rebellion, the image of Jews as Torah-era figures remained imprinted on my heart.

Most Afghans still look as if they are living in a biblical era—they have long beards, wear turbans and veils, ride donkeys, and travel in camel caravans.

Afghanistan has been a fully Islamic country only since the fourteenth century. As I have noted, before that Afghanistan sheltered Zoroastrians, pagans, Buddhists, and Hindus—all of whom were either preceded by or existed simultaneously with Islam. Jews were also there.

After the Babylonian exile, some Jews found their way to Persia. In time, some "Persian" Jews returned to Jerusalem to rebuild the Second Temple; many remained in Persia, and some fled to Afghanistan. Legend also has it that the Afghan Pushtuns have always viewed themselves as "Bani Israel," the sons of a lost Jewish tribe.

Abdul-Kareem is a Pushtun.

According to the historian Vartan Gregorian in *The Emergence of Modern Afghanistan: Politics of Reform and Modernization, 1880–1946,* "The history of the Jewish community in Afghanistan is similar to that of the Hindus. The community, whose roots in Afghanistan were very old, was constantly rejuvenated by immigrations from Bukhara, Persia, and [Russian] Georgia."

Hebrew inscriptions that date to 750 CE appear on mountain rocks along the Silk Road between Herat and Kabul. In 1962, the year after I left, a group of Italian archeologists announced their discovery of one hundred Jewish gravestones in the Herat area that date to the eleventh century.

According to Gregorian, in 1736 "a large number of Jews were re-settled in Afghanistan by [the first] Nadir Shah, who sought thereby to encourage Indo-Persian trade."

The early history of Jews in Afghanistan is still being discovered and continues to make world headlines. In 2011–12 a treasure trove of Jewish written material from the eleventh century was found in a cave in northern Afghanistan. According to one scholar, some of the Torah scrolls contain Babylonian vocalization, which "seems to point to a ninth century CE dating." (Vocalization refers to how the Torah is chanted, the melodic style.)

Despite this rather long Jewish history in Afghanistan, when I was in Kabul, I did not meet a single Jew. At the time it did not strike me as odd.

Abdul-Kareem was the first Muslim I had ever known. When he courted me, he was tender, solicitous, and honorable. He seemed more adult than most college students, more responsible. Perhaps this was because he was four or five years older than other college students and had lived on his own for many years—as a stranger in a strange land. Perhaps Afghan men become serious at younger ages.

When Abdul-Kareem and I were a couple, I would have told you that the biblical Isaac and Ishmael were both Abraham's sons and were therefore half-brothers and that the persecution of Jews, first by the Roman Catholic Church, then by the genocidal Nazis in Europe, had been far more consequential expressions of Jew hatred than anything that might have happened in the Muslim world.

I believed that Jews had found refuge from the worst moments of the European Catholic Inquisition in Muslim lands; indeed many had.

When Abdul-Kareem and I were together, no books were available in English about Jews in Afghanistan, and few books were available about Jews in Muslim lands. My otherwise excellent college education did not include a single course about the religions, histories, and customs of the Islamic world or about religious minorities in Muslim countries.

Over the years I steadily amassed a small library of books by West-ern travelers to Islamic countries. I treasure this literature. It has allowed me to continue my travels. After 9/11, when I revisited these books, I was shocked and disheartened. Some of the most gallant Western adventurers glorified Arab Muslims and Christians but hated their Arab Jewish counterparts.

The great nineteenth-century British traveler Sir Richard Burton (*Personal Narrative of a Pilgrimage to Al-Madinah and Meccah*), romanticized Arabs (and other "natives") but was highly critical of Jews; he actually accused them of human sacrifice in his controversial book, *The Jew, the Gypsy and el-Islam.*

The French traveler Pierre Loti also glorified Arabs and, like Sir Richard, often dressed like one. In 1878, in a book titled *Jerusalem,* Loti described the indigenous Jewish worshippers of Jerusalem as having sinister eyes; he viewed their faces as having an "uncanny ugliness" given to "base, crafty, ignoble expressions . . . truly, the crucifixion of Jesus has left an indelible stigma."

Freya Stark is another dashing and well-known British traveler and author who traveled to Afghanistan. She also despised the Jews and condemned their attempts at post-Holocaust survival. In 1945, at the end of World War II, Stark published her book *East Is West,* in which she consistently equates "Fascist Rome" with "Zionist Jerusalem"; she describes Tel Aviv as having "ruthless vitality," and she views the "Arabs as David and the Jews as Goliath."

Much to my delight, I discovered that the great British traveler and author T. E. Lawrence (better known as Lawrence of Arabia) was *not* an anti-Semite. Lawrence, the author of *Seven Pillars of Wisdom,* was actually a Zionist. He viewed the Jewish national enterprise as a non-imperial endeavor and as potentially beneficial to the Arabs he so loved and whom he had assisted in their revolt against the Ottoman Empire.

However, many European Christian travelers to Muslim lands hated Jews. Perhaps life had indeed been safer for Jews among the Muslims—at least during certain periods when the Inquisition was at its height in Europe. Well, then, the Jews were right to have fled to Muslim lands. But the more I read, the more confused I became.

The Jewish *leaders* in Muslim countries—the upper-caste Jews, so to speak—were usually wealthy, educated, skilled, and cosmopolitan. Such Jews enjoyed almost fairy-tale lives in Cairo, Damascus, Baghdad, Istanbul, and Teheran, but most of the Jews of Islam were poor and led desperate wretched lives.

In 1918 Edith Wharton visited Morocco. Wharton documented the injustices suffered by the local Moroccan Jewish population at the hands of their Muslim compatriots: "North African Jews are still compelled to live in ghettos, [mellahs] into which they are locked at night, as in France and Germany in the Middle Ages, and until lately the men have been compelled to go unarmed . . . to take off their shoes when they passed near a mosque or a saint's tomb, and in various other ways to manifest their subjection to the ruling race."

Wharton notes that sun itself had been banished from the Jewish ghetto: "We were suddenly led under an arch over which should have been written 'All light abandon—' . . . into the Mellah of Sefrou [the sun] never comes, for the streets form a sort of subterranean rabbit-warren . . . [it is] a buried city lit even at midday by oil-lamps hanging in the goldsmiths' shops and under the archways of the black and reeking staircases."

What Wharton discovered about the lives of Jews in Morocco was also true for Jews throughout the Arab Middle East, Central Asia, and elsewhere in North Africa. Maimonides fled *Muslim* rule in Spain, only to discover that Muslim Morocco and Muslim Jerusalem both remained inhospitable to Jews and that Jews were being persecuted and forcibly converted throughout the Arab Muslim world. Maimonides, himself a skilled physician, was finally given asylum in Muslim Cairo.

According to scholars such as Rabbi Marc Angel (*Foundations of Sephardic Spirituality: The Inner Life of Jews of the Ottoman Empire*), Bat Ye'or (*The Dhimmi: Jews and Christians under Islam*), and Andrew G. Bostom (in his massive compendium of original sources, *The Legacy of Islamic Antisemitism*), while Maimonides was alive, the Jews of Yemen were required to remove feces and other waste matter from Muslim quarters. In Morocco, as late as the nineteenth century, Jews were required to salt the decapitated heads of executed rebels—even on the Jewish Sabbath—for public viewing.

According to Sharia law, Jews in the Ottoman Empire had to wear distinctive yellow badges, live apart in crowded ghettos, step off sidewalks when a Muslim approached or where a mosque stood, build houses that were lower than Muslim houses, and maintain a subordinate silence in the presence of Muslims. According to Rabbi Angel, "Jewish evidence was not accepted against the evidence of a Muslim. A Muslim could not be executed for murdering a Jew." Muslims also systematically taxed Jews and forced them to ransom Jewish hostages for exorbitant sums.

Although it remains controversial, even dangerous, to say so, the Qur'an views both Jews and Christians as infidels who must be forcibly converted, tithed, or killed. Luckily not every Muslim or Muslim leader obeyed the teachings of the seventh-century Qur'an. But many have, and periodic massacres and expulsions of Jews characterized Muslim, as well as European Christian, society.

As a child the Moroccan author and feminist Fatima Mernissi could not understand why the Jews left Morocco. In her romantic book, *Dreams of Trespass: Tales of a Harem Girlhood,* she writes, "The Jews had always hung around with the Arabs . . . since the beginning of time."

Mernissi seems to know nothing about the poverty or the forced conversions of Jews in her country or about the legendary nineteenth-century Jewish martyr, the Moroccan teenager Sol Hachuel, who was imprisoned, tortured, and beheaded because she refused to convert to Islam.

Mernissi reminds me of my Afghan mother-in-law who missed the Afghan Jews; they left for reasons that remained unclear to her.

The gravely beautiful book *Reading Lolita in Tehran,* by the Iranian American author Azar Nafisi, confirms that even before Khomeini Muslims viewed infidels, including Jews, as repulsive, beyond dirty. Iranians thought that Jews "drank innocent children's blood."

Nafisi understands that Jew hatred had been festering among Persians for a long time. She concludes that "we cannot blame everything on the Islamic Republic, because in some ways it simply brought into the open and magnified a preexisting bigotry."

The cyclical local Persian persecution of Jews forced one small group to flee to Afghanistan. According to the Afghan Israeli scholar Reuben Kashani, "In 1839, radical Shiite Muslims in Meshed [Persia] spread the libel that the Jews had insulted one of their saints, Imam Ali Reza. A mad Muslim mob pillaged Jewish homes, burned synagogues, murdered more than 30 Jews, and forcibly converted the rest. . . . Eventually [they] managed to escape to neighboring Afghanistan, particularly Herat."

However, Afghan ruler Abdur Rahman, who reigned from 1830 to 1844, ordered his forces to "slaughter 13 Torah scholars from prominent families in Maimanah [in Afghanistan's north]." Kashani notes that "in many Afghan *mahzorim* [High Holiday prayer books], it was the custom to mention the Maimanah 13 by name."

In 1856–57 the Jews of Herat were then expelled and many went back to Meshed, where they were promptly imprisoned, according to one personal account, "in animal pens."

One of King Habibullah's advisers was Mula Agajan Cohen, the president of the Afghan Jewish community. According to Kashani,

"Apparently Muslims resented the close ties that this Jewish leader had to King Habibullah, so they cut off his head and took all of his money." Nevertheless the Jews from Persia, Bokhara, and Georgia remained in Afghanistan, where they kept to themselves, wore distinctive clothing that set them apart (they were ordered to do so), fit in as best they could—and flourished. Afghanistan allowed them to practice their Judaism openly. These Jews remained in Afghanistan for nearly one hundred years.

When I lived in Kabul, I knew nothing about a Jewish history in Afghanistan, nor did I know anything about the intimate relationship between the sudden impoverishment of Jews and Hindus in Afghanistan in the late 1920s and early 1930s and my Afghan family's equally sudden wealth.

More than fifty years after I left Kabul, I discovered the hidden and somewhat explosive story.

Bebegul, my mother-in-law, kept telling me how close she had been to the Sharbans, or the Sharbanis, who were her Jewish friends. She kept asking me, rather wistfully, if I knew them.

"Why did they leave?" she would ask sadly, over and over again.

Rosanne Klass, the author of two books about Afghanistan, once celebrated a Jewish holiday in Kabul with Afghan Jews, sometime in the 1950s. She celebrated with a man named Sharban Ibrahim, who "for many years had been the doyen of the Jewish community in [Kabul] Afghanistan."

I wondered if this was the same Sharban Bebegul kept asking me about.

When Klass met him, Sharban was already on his way out of Afghanistan. His family had already left for Israel. However, Sharban escorted Klass to another Afghan Jewish family that was celebrating Sukkoth—a harvest festival when Jews take their meals in outdoor booths or huts. Klass was taken with the biblical beauty of the young hostess, of whom she writes, "[Her] face was the face of Rebecca at the well, it was Rachel, it was Sarah, it was Ruth gleaning the fields beneath the eyes of Boaz." The young woman wears a flowing headscarf. Her eyes are "enormous, shining, incredibly dark and liquid, utterly serene."

I wonder what the hostess's life was really like. Did she wear a burqa when she went out? *Did* she go out alone—or only in the company of a male relative or male servant? Could she read and write? Had she ever been out of Kabul or out of her own home and courtyard? Did her husband have more than one wife?

Klass does not tell us.

I knew Afghan Jews had settled in Queens, New York, as well as in Israel. I had to meet them. Klass connected me to Roy Abraham, the grandson of prominent Afghan Jews. He and I had an e-mail exchange for a year.

I finally suggested that we both attend a program about Afghan Jews that was to be held at the Center for Jewish History in New York City.

The evening turned out to be a book launch for Sara Y. Aharon's remarkable book, *From Kabul to Queens: The Jews of Afghanistan and Their Move to the United States*. Aharon is the granddaughter and great-granddaughter of Afghan Jews who once lived in Herat.

I recognize Roy the second he enters the building. He has an Israeli Jewish energy that is also somehow Afghan. He is wired, passionate, intense, fast talking but at the same time sweet, funny, easygoing. Roy is definitely a descendant of the biblical Joseph. He also seems to be related to everyone else who has gathered at the center.

Roy is warmly and repeatedly embraced. His many relatives are surprised but delighted to see him, and he introduces me to aunts, uncles, cousins, neighbors, and friends. All this happens before we begin to speak.

Roy confirms the obvious, namely, that the "Afghan Jewish community is small but tight-knit, everyone is related, we are very proud and do not want to assimilate." As he describes their customs, or at least the customs of his parents' and grandparents' generations, they sound . . . Muslim, Afghan, Arab, Sephardic. Roy explains, "Traditionally Jewish cousins often married each other in arranged marriages. The women were veiled and sequestered. They did not work or attend synagogue. Children lived with their parents after marriage or very nearby. The family is everything. It is your lifeline, your survival."

Afghan Jews prayed and wrote in Judeo-Persian and in Rashi script. Rashi, Rabbi Shlomo Yitzhaki, lived in the eleventh century in France and created a kind of shorthand for his brilliant Torah and Talmud commentaries.

Some Afghan Jews were polygamous, and Jewish girls did not attend school; they married at thirteen or fourteen. Boys married when they were eighteen or twenty. If they were wealthy, they could marry earlier.

Afghan Jews and Afghan Hindus exported and imported carpets, textiles, karakuls, furs, hides, machine parts, gold, silver, jewelry—and currency. They had offices and outposts in many places, including

Europe, India, all over Russia, in the Far East, and in all the northern Afghan cities along the Silk Road in Afghanistan. According to Roy, "My grandfather spoke Dari, Hebrew, Russian, Urdu, Japanese, and Thai. My grandfather and great-grandfather were in the import-export business. They bought and sold clothing, textiles, cigarettes, jewelry, diamonds, and money, currency."

The Jews and Hindus of Herat were the primary traders and bankers for the country. That changed in the late 1920s and early 1930s when King Nadir Shah decided that neither Afghan Jews nor Afghan Hindus would be allowed to continue their usual commercial ventures, including banking. This decision was partly influenced by the king's ties to Nazi Germany. Three scholars, Erich Brauer (in 1942), Reuben Kashani (in 1975), and Sara Aharon (in 2011), document what happened. According to Brauer, "In 1936, [Jews] were evacuated from Maimane, Shiburgan, Mazar, Tashkurgan and Ankhuy, by order of the powerful minister of finance, Mir Hashim Khan. . . . [By 1942] the Jewish population [was] virtually limited to the three towns of Herat, Kabul . . . and Balkh."

Government leaders claimed that Russian Jews in flight from the Russian Revolution were entering Afghanistan, and according to Brauer, to prevent this they decided to "exclude Jews from the area bordering on the Soviet Union. The true motive, however, was the regime's desire to take over the economic positions of the Jews in those towns."

It may be true that many Afghan Jews lost part of their fortune because of the Soviet revolution; the Jews had vast storehouses, trading posts, and cattle in Russia, all of which had been nationalized. However, as Brauer writes, "If anything more were needed to complete the process [of impoverishing Jews], it was supplied by the radical measures of the [Afghan] regime designed to concentrate the country's trade wholly in the hands of its rulers."

Sara Aharon's book carefully documents the almost overnight impoverishment of Afghan Jews and Afghan Hindus. King Nadir Shah might have been tolerant of non-Muslim "religious expression," but he prohibited non-Muslims from trading. Aharon writes, "In 1929, a Pashtun banker named Abdul Majid Zabuli described King Nadir Shah's emphatic belief that 'our own nationals' must exercise greater control over the country's trade. . . . He cited mercantile activities specifically dominated in Afghanistan by local Hindus and Jews. His urgent message to Zabuli in harsh, unequivocal terms to 'cut off the hands of the foreigner' thus suggests that he did not consider Hindus, Jews, and other non-Muslims as Afghan nationals."

As I read this, my heart stops. I recognize Abdul Majid's name. He brought my father-in-law in as one of the three founders of the country's modern banking system. I keep reading, but I am in a small state of shock. According to Aharon, by 1932 "a banking system, including Afghanistan's first joint-stock company was formed. . . . Despite religious concerns, it was dubbed the 'Bank-i-Milli,' or the Afghan National Bank."

I have to stop reading. My heart is racing. I get up and walk around the room.

This national bank became quite powerful. It had a virtual monopoly over commodities and the Afghan export-import trade. According to Aharon, "the Bank-i-Milli's monopoly would prove to be a main cause of the Jewish community's impoverishment."

Bank-i-Milli was my father-in-law's bank! This is where Abdul-Kareem's oldest brother, Hassan, worked. Without this kind of financial platform, Abdul-Kareem could never have come to study in America. We would never have met.

When I interviewed him in 1980, Abdul-Kareem told me how his father, Ismail Mohammed, rose from his position as an accountant in the civil service to become the keeper of the treasury in Herat. In 1929, when the people rose up against King Amanullah (whom Ismail Mohammed supported), rioting mobs demanded that Abdul-Kareem's father turn over the treasury. He refused to do so. Ismail Mohammed was immediately arrested, jailed, and scheduled to hang the next day.

And so this courtly polygamist and father-as-supreme-leader-at-home is also something of a hero on the world stage.

However, according to Abdul-Kareem, his father was so loved by the people of Herat "for his honesty" that they "helped him escape from prison and took him and his family to a holy sanctuary." From there he and his family fled across the border to Meshed, Iran. They hid their gold beneath the baby in a baby carriage. In Meshed, Ismail Mohammed began studying English and Russian. Abdul-Kareem told me, "A year later my father went on a trip to Germany via Russia by train. While in Berlin he had studied some aspects of banking. In 1930 he then returned to Meshed and his family. In 1930 my parents received word from Kabul that they could come back to Afghanistan. In 1931–32 they returned via Baluchistan and India."

Because Ismail Mohammed had remained faithful to King Amanullah, the new king, Nadir Shah, did not trust him. Abdul-Kareem explained, "Fortunately, a few business acquaintances asked my father

to assist them in founding a bank. Thus my father became one of the
founders of the Afghan National Bank. The founder appointed my father first as chief accountant and a year later as vice president of the
bank, a post he held until 1949."

*M*ost of my Jewish friends thought that my marriage to a Muslim was fashionable, exotic, politically correct, and desir-
able. Like me, no one had any clear understanding of the history of Jews
in Afghanistan or in Muslim countries.

But now I feel a little sick. I had lived in a country and with a family
whose fortune had been built on the systematic impoverishment of Jews
and Hindus. At the time I did not know this. Back then I was the kind
of Jew who believed that Jews could fit in everywhere, anywhere, as universal citizens. Since then my understanding of Muslim-Jewish history,
and of Judaism, has deepened.

Perhaps this chapter is a form of atonement, written with considerable anguish, by a Jew who was once forced to convert to Islam, and
who lived among Muslims in Afghanistan in captivity but also in splendor. It is for having coveted that splendor that I must atone.

Abdul-Kareem adored his father and his father's rise to power and
glory. He talked about it a lot. He told me, "Following the assassination
of King Nadir Shah in 1933 and the succession of his eighteen-year-old
son, King Zahir Shah, the Afghan National Bank was asked to serve as
the central bank. My father was sent to India to buy gold for the government treasury. Furthermore the bank was making necessary investments
and bringing industry to the country. In the 1930s and '40s they helped
build two textile, one sugar, and one nuclear factory."

Thus my Afghan family's considerable wealth, their palatial homes,
summer and winter chalets and villas, and properties in Herat, Jalalabad,
Paghman, and Kabul; their many servants, thick carpets, European furniture, and fashionable clothing; their ability to study and travel abroad
and to consult European and American doctors was at least indirectly
related to the impoverishment of the Afghan Jews and Hindus.

Making this connection stuns me.

I have to walk around the room a few times again.

I am certainly not saying that Abdul-Kareem's family stole their
wealth from the Jews (or from the Hindus), because that is not accurate.
What was stolen was the Jewish and Hindu ability to take their considerable banking and commercial skills to another level in Afghanistan.
The Afghan king Nadir Shah was the thief. His accomplices were Nazis.

The Abdul-Kareem I knew was never a Jew hater. He is not responsible for what an Afghan king did before he was born. A woman we both know described meeting Abdul-Kareem in Kabul in the mid-1960s: "He had a crew cut and was sitting quietly in the corner. All of a sudden, he began telling Jewish jokes. We hit it right off. He was then heading the Kabul theater, and we started knocking around Kabul together. He wanted to do a revision of *Our Town* set in Kabul. I remember that his family's living room was huge, maybe forty feet long. I remember marble floors and beautiful carpets. We listened to Ella Fitzgerald together."

Ah—that was the home in which I had been held captive. And there was Abdul-Kareem, missing Jewish New York, perhaps missing me.

When I ask Abdul-Kareem about Afghan Jews, he tells me that he still remembers with excitement his visits to Kabul's large covered bazaar: "The Hindus and the Jews were selling things. They had skins, furs, jewels, textiles. It was a wonderful place to visit. It was huge."

This must have been in the 1940s. Thus some Jews and Hindus were still conducting commerce.

"I remember visiting the synagogue in Herat. You had to bend to go through a small door. There were holes for shoes and a place where the Torah was stored."

The last time Abdul-Kareem visited Herat was in 1997. He remembers, "There was a young rabbi who dressed just like all Heratis do. And he had two pigeons under his long coat. He must have been about thirty-five years old."

I wonder who he was and where that rabbi is now.

The Afghan-German alliance actually began before the Nazi rise to power. I had no idea that after the first European tour of my hero, King Amanullah, Germany—not Britain (which crowded Afghanistan's border in India)—became the country Afghanistan would favor. In 1923, according to the *New York Times,* the German "Lens and Co. had obtained an option for installing all the proposed railroads in Afghanistan. . . . German engineers are already en route to Amanullah's country to make the necessary surveys."

In the 1930s Afghanistan began making deals with the Nazis. Understandings were reached, promises were made. Bank-i-Milli opened a branch in Berlin (!) that encouraged Afghan-German transactions. Trade increased between Nazi Germany and Afghanistan. Recall that initially the Soviets and the Nazis were allies; this meant that in accordance with their various trade agreements, all goods being transported overland to and from East and Central Asia would pass through Afghanistan.

According to Rajiv Chandrasekaran, author of *Little America: The War Within the War for Afghanistan,* "In the decade before the war, he [Zahir Shah] and his father [Nadir Shah] had sought development assistance from the Germans who had constructed a radio tower, a power plant, and a handful of small carpet factories and textile mills in Kabul, all of which were under a royal license."

In 1933 the Afghan authorities prohibited Jews from traveling without special permits and from engaging in any import-export businesses without a license. Such permits and licenses were of course withheld. According to Aharon, "Between the establishment of the Bank-i-Milli and the restrictions on trade, the Jews were hard-pressed to find sources of income."

In the late 1930s Afghanistan granted Germany the right to manage road construction in the country. Germany also began shipping equipment to be used in Afghan hydroelectric plants and textile mills; in return Afghanistan was sending Germany cotton and wool. According to Kashani, "Three hundred agents of the Third Reich assisted Afghanistan economically and also took part in overt incitement to anti-Semitism. . . . The Jews of Afghanistan had already in 1935 written to the Zionist authorities in Palestine about 'the inciters' who are Hitler's men."

I now recall that my Afghan family had only German cars— Mercedes Benzes. They also had many German appliances made by Siemens, such as radios. I remember meeting many Germans in Kabul. They were all quite warm to me. That wife of the former mayor of Kabul—the one who helped me with one of my escape plans—was German.

According to Aharon, from 1938 to 1945 Nazi Germany made payments to various Arab leaders—and to "Ghulham Siddique, the former Prime Minister of Afghanistan under King Amanullah."

The Jews of Afghanistan were quickly reduced to lives of squalor. They were also trapped. Some Jews, including the elderly chief rabbi, Mula Yakkov Simon-Tov, had already emigrated to Israel in 1922—he, poor soul, was murdered by rioting Arabs in 1936 in British Palestine. Mainly Jews were forbidden to leave the country until the late 1940s or early to mid-1950s.

One must wonder why. Why would a Muslim kingdom want to hold on to impoverished Jews—from whom they could borrow no money and levy few taxes? What kind of hostages were these Afghan Jews?

According to Aharon, in the 1940s Jewish men were drafted into the Afghan army but were not permitted to carry any weapons. Instead they were required to clean animal stalls and received no wages. Nevertheless Jews were required to pay a war tax (the *harbiyyeh*) because they "were 'exempted' from the military since they could not bear arms. What little money they had went to their military superiors in exchange for mercy."

Afghanistan was not a Nazi country—yet it not only impoverished its Jews, it also sheltered German Nazis after World War II.

In his charming book, *Afghan Interlude,* published in 1957 (four years before I arrived), the British traveler Oliver Rudston de Baer, who was there in the mid-1950s, confirms that many Nazis had indeed found a safe haven in Afghanistan.

He notes that the government underpaid the Germans as teachers, doctors, and engineers, because they "'might consider it unwise to return to their countries.' These people, of whom there were many, were completely in the power of the Afghan Government, for it was the Afghan Government, not their own, which protected them in return for their services."

De Baer once encountered a group of Germans who worked in a sugar factory in Baghlan. They were relaxing in a swimming pool. "Their unpleasantness on hearing that we were British convinced us that they were representatives of the many Nazis who, afraid to return to their own country, have settled in Afghanistan and are now busy doing innumerable technical jobs for the Government and who live in salutary fear that their residence permits may not be extended."

Photos of the Afghan army celebrating Afghan Independence Day in 1965 remind me of Hitler's army. The soldiers march stiffly, step high—they are almost goose-stepping. There is definitely a European and Nazi influence here.

The legendary warriors of Afghanistan do not look like European soldiers. I met some. They were tall, rugged, sweet, charming, low-key, turbaned men wearing loose-fitting clothing—who just happened to be deadly with a rifle and a knife.

But just as I am slightly and irrationally nostalgic for a country in which I was held against my will—so too many Afghan Jews of that era still miss Herat and Kabul, just as the exiled Iraqi and Egyptian Jews miss their homes and ways of life in the Arab world.

Many years later, safely perched in America, Afghan Jews insist that the Afghan *government* was helpful to its Jews.

Jack Abraham was born in Afghanistan and lived there until he was eleven. In 1964 his father built the only remaining synagogue in Kabul. Radio Free Europe quotes Abraham as saying, "We never had persecution in Afghanistan. And the government was very helpful to us. If there was any kind of a thing happening out on the street, they would inform the Jews, 'Take it easy, don't go to work' on these particular days because people were talking negative, and they would put police outside our doors for protection."

While the government may not have passed laws against practicing Judaism, why did the negativity in the streets require police guards at Jewish doors?

Sara Aharon ultimately concludes that the restrictions and expulsions were mainly because of "the Afghan regime's internal, insidious jealousy of the Jews and their supposed affluence." Thus, the Afghan government wanted to punish both the Jews and the Hindus in Afghanistan precisely because they had been successful entrepreneurs.

After 9/11 Afghanistan was in the news every day. It still is. Most newspapers carry at least one, usually two, articles on events taking place in Kabul or Kandahar or Mazar-i-Sharif.

After 9/11 journalists interviewed every Afghan they could find, anyone who knew anything about the country that had sheltered bin Laden. The media also interviewed Afghan Jews. Like many of the Jews of Islam, Afghanistan's Jews tended to remember their country fondly.

In 2001 Jacob Nasirov, who was born in Kabul and served as the rabbi of Congregation Anshei Shalom in Queens, told Felicia R. Lee of the *New York Times* that Afghan Jews are sad for "what was and what could have been in a once-beautiful country where Jews had lived for 2,000 years. The Jews were not insiders, but they were tolerated and allowed to establish their own businesses, to practice their faith."

Another member of the congregation, Michael Aharon, told Lee that the "Jews of Afghanistan had a very good life. When I see what has happened to this country in the last ten years, especially when I see kids without shoes, it really hurts me."

I am both puzzled and moved that these Jews still feel such fondness for Afghanistan, especially considering the nature of their impoverishment, followed by their captivity there, and eventual flight.

Perhaps I should not be surprised.

Jews have always yearned for Jerusalem, from which they'd been exiled many times, but they also yearned for each and every one of the countries where they had been persecuted and where their ancestors once lived and are still buried.

Biblical Jews wept bitter tears after leaving Egypt, where they had been the pharaoh's slaves. They missed what they were used to: the food, the smells—everything familiar, as opposed to the unknown wilderness and the fierce challenges that freedom imposes.

Andre Aciman in *Out of Egypt: A Memoir* and Jean Naggar in *Sipping from the Nile* write with love and nostalgia for the Egypt they had to flee. Like Lucette Lagnado, author of *The Man in the White Sharkskin Suit* and *The Arrogant Years: One Girl's Search for Her Lost Youth, from Cairo to Brooklyn,* these writers had charming and cultured extended families who had lived in the Ottoman Empire for many centuries.

According to Rabbi Angel, despite being impoverished and perennially endangered, the Jews of Islam still enjoyed a deep sense of community, continuity, religiosity, and dignity—and this is what these Jews find lacking in new and more modern places and times.

Abdul-Kareem had loved me, he had loved a Jew. I do not doubt this. I loved him, too—although everything changed after my first month in Kabul.

We were not Romeo and Juliet; we were not *Nino and Ali,* the beloved fictional creations of Kurban Said, aka Lev Nussimbaum. Nino is a blonde Circassian princess; Ali is a dashing Muslim warrior. They meet and live in Baku. As Kurban Said, Nussimbaum longed to unite the Muslim East and the Judeo-Christian West. His love story is set in the Caucasus just before the Russian Revolution.

Looking back, knowing what I now know, I must ask: How could Abdul-Kareem have been so foolish, so blithe, as to have brought a Jewish American bride back to a country that had impoverished its small population of Jews and granted safe haven to German Nazis? Did he think that the rules of history would never apply to us?

In 2011, Abdul-Kareem proudly told me that when he was the deputy minister of culture, he had negotiated treaties with UNESCO that would give "landmark status" to ancient sites in Afghanistan. Abdul-Kareem insisted that whatever foreign archeologists would discover should remain in Afghanistan and that the world body would fund both restoration and archiving. In this context he had restored the synagogues of Herat and Kabul. They are all empty now. One has been converted into an Islamic school for boys. I tell him this. He says nothing.

I ask Abdul-Kareem, "Why did the Jews leave Afghanistan?"

"Gee, I have no idea. Probably they up and left because they wanted to go to Israel anyway."

Like his mother before him, Abdul-Kareem claims to have no idea why Afghan Jews left Afghanistan. Is this sheer ignorance or deadly denial?

Ah, but who am I to condemn or mourn the plight of Jews in Muslim lands? What standing do I have? I am a Jew who quietly and privately converted to Islam while I was in captivity. I did so not at the edge of a sword but merely in the hope that doing so might make my miserable life more bearable in purdah.

No. I did so because I was terrified about what might happen to me if I refused to do so.

I was a secular antireligious rebel. One religion seemed as foolish and dangerous to me as the other. But obviously I was ashamed, embarrassed, by what I'd done. I never mentioned it to my parents or told any other living being. I did not take this conversion seriously. And I managed to forget all about it for many years.

I am writing about it here for the first time.

As I've said: I will never forgive myself.

However, the 9/11 attacks upon America forced me to confront my long-ago experience in a new and even more serious way.

ELEVEN

9/11

Where were you on 9/11?

There was a time when people asked where you were only about the day President John F. Kennedy was assassinated. Everyone remembered where they were and what they had been doing at that moment, as if time itself stopped when the fatal shots rang out in Dallas.

On November 22, 1963, I was at work. I left early. Later I bought my first-ever television set. I told the journalist Jack Newfield, my late friend and colleague, "I want to be able to watch the coming assassinations live, as they happen."

Our nation would bear witness to at least four more high-profile assassinations within the next half-decade.

President Kennedy's presumed killer, Lee Harvey Oswald, was himself killed two days later, on November 24, 1963—during a perp walk on live television. His killer, a Texas nightclub operator, Jack Ruby, was arrested, tried, and convicted; he died in jail in 1967.

These murders were like sordid wax museum exhibits, grisly horror shows, but they were history. They were played and replayed on national television. These events would forever haunt the memories and imagination of my generation.

A little more than a year after JFK's assassination, on February 21, 1965, Malcolm X, also known as el-Hajj Malik el-Shabazz, was gunned down by fellow Nation of Islam members in New York City due to his public condemnation of Elijah Muahammed.

On April 4, 1968, the Reverend Dr. Martin Luther King Jr. was shot to death in Memphis by the white supremacist James Earl Ray.

A mere two months later, on June 5, 1968, Senator Robert F. Kennedy was assassinated in Los Angeles by a Palestinian, Sirhan Bishara Sirhan, who still remains incarcerated in California. According to the Federal Bureau of Investigation, Sirhan's defense argued that he had been "psychologically scarred" by his exposure to the Israeli war for independence. An ad for a pro-Israel march had started "a fire burning inside him," and Sirhan became enraged when Senator Kennedy promised military support to Israel.

These immensely promising national figures, relatively young men (the oldest was JFK, who was forty-six), were all murdered. Our nation reeled, perpetually in shock. None of the killers showed any remorse.

This was the turbulent yet liberating decade in which I came of age after my captivity in Afghanistan.

*W*here were you on 9/11?

I was at home. I sat very still on my couch, transfixed before my television screen, afraid to move, afraid to miss anything, afraid to get up, knowing that when I got to my feet the old world would be forever gone, forever changed, and that we'd be facing a new and more dangerous world and time.

I was then living in Park Slope, in my hometown of Brooklyn, and my next-door neighbor, Anja Osang-Reich, was a German journalist who worked for *Der Spiegel*. By midafternoon we had both wandered out into our front yards. Anja remembers that I said, "Now we are all Israelis."

She wrote it down, and years later she interviewed me for a book she was writing about her experience of 9/11.

I knew in my bones that ordinary life would change for civilians everywhere: The world's airports would soon resemble Israeli consulates and embassies with metal detectors and elaborate screenings.

Like Israelis, American children have grown up knowing they are not automatically safe in their country or in their world. They understand the need for security at airports; they do not protest having to take off their little shoes and stand for a long while in a long line.

9/11 was also a turning point for American intellectuals and activists. Some blamed America and felt the jihadists were justified in mass-murdering civilians. Others, like myself, strongly disagreed.

One friend insisted that the people who worked in the World Trade Center could not possibly be innocent.

"How could they be," she said, "when so many people are starving to death and homeless, here and around the world?"

"Are you saying that we are all guilty because we live in America? Do you believe that America itself is somehow existentially guilty and deserves to be brought down?"

"Well," she said, laughing, "you've put it rather well."

Her heartlessness eerily paralleled the heartlessness of the 9/11 jihadists.

The Muslim warriors who carried out the attacks were young: Their average age was twenty-four. Their visas were mostly six-month "tourist/business" visas that were approved by the State Department regardless of red flags in their applications. Fifteen were Saudis, the others were from Egypt, the United Arab Emirates, and Lebanon.

These jihadists viewed the West and Western values as repulsive and dangerous. They despised the idea of human and individual rights, free speech, religious freedom, separation of state and religion, women's rights, gay rights, and a host of other rights and privileges, including the right to sex before marriage, the right not to marry, and the right to choose one's marital partner.

My heartless friend stands for all these values.

And therefore she was among all those who swiftly demonized anyone who dared say that Muslim Islamists had launched a war. Anyone who criticized Islamist terrorism was a "racist conservative" and an Islamophobe.

Ironically such a label was also applied to ex-Muslim dissidents like the Somali-born Ayaan Hirsi Ali, Indian-born Ibn Warraq, Egyptian-born Nonie Darwish, and the Syrian Americans Dr. Wafa Sultan and Dr. M. Zuhdi Jasser.

9/11 changed everything. It changed us all.

I will never forget what happened on 9/11. I can still smell the air: It was a sickening combination of industrial fuels, hate, and human suffering. Scorched souls, acrid and agonizing, burned my throat and my eyes and my mind.

9/11 was also a personal wake-up call. I felt as if Afghanistan had followed me back to America. Osama bin Laden, Khalid Sheikh Mohammed, Omar Abdel-Rahman, and Ayman al-Zawahiri had hatched this lethal scheme in their hideout in Afghanistan, where they were under the protection of the Afghan warlord Mullah Mohammed Omar.

Bin Laden called the 9/11 assault on America "blessed attacks" against the "infidel . . . the new Jewish-Christian crusade." He further explained that he had targeted the Pentagon and the Twin Towers because of American support for Israel.

I have a conversation with Pierre Rehov, an Algerian French Israeli filmmaker who has gone undercover to film terrorists on the West Bank and in Gaza.

"Look," he points out. "These guys are young and testosterone-laden men who are denied sex with women. They think they can only get that in paradise with seventy-two virgins. They are so sexually frustrated that they are willing to die to get laid."

"Yes, you have a point," I say, "but I have an additional observation. You know that bin Laden's father had fifty-seven children. My guess is that bin Laden was starved for paternal attention and approval—and he therefore became a charismatic 'father figure' to other, similarly father-deprived young men. Such deprivation in a savagely patriarchal culture may render young men particularly vulnerable to a bin Laden–like serial killer by proxy. In Afghanistan I had witnessed the competition between sons for a father's attention and favor. Abdul-Kareem and his brothers were constantly vying with one another in an attempt to secure positions within the family, which could be granted only by the patriarch, Ismail Mohammed."

Osama bin Laden's son Omar published a book with his mother, Najwa bin Laden, and the author Jean Sasson. The book is titled *Growing Up Bin Laden: Osama's Wife and Son Take Us Inside Their Secret World*. Najwa was Osama's first cousin as well as his first wife. They married when she was fifteen and he was seventeen.

Omar tells us that what enraged Osama and set the wheels of 9/11 in motion was that Saudi Arabia had allowed America to come to the defense of Kuwait in 1990.

The elder bin Laden was "offended by the sight of a mainly Christian western army defending their [Muslim] honor." Bin Laden coveted that honor for himself. His warriors had successfully fought the Soviets. Why not choose him and his men? Infidel male soldiers were bad enough, but, Omar writes, "At the first sight of a capable-looking female soldier my father became the most outspoken opponent of the royal decision to allow western armies into the kingdom, ranting, 'Women! Defending Saudi men!'"

Most Westerners utterly fail to understand the importance of woman's subordination in terms of Islamist male psychology.

According to Hillel Fradkin and Lewis Libby, the splinter Muslim Brotherhood group that assassinated Egyptian president Anwar Sadat "undertook their plot not only or even primarily because of the Israeli-Egyptian peace treaty. . . . Rather, they considered the work on women's rights championed by Sadat's wife, Jihan, an existential threat to true Muslim society."

There are men (and women) who view woman's freedom as so dangerous that they are ready to imprison, torture, and kill on a massive scale in order to stamp it out. Many Westerners refuse to believe that this is true or that what happens in Saudi Arabia, Iraq, Iran, Pakistan, or Afghanistan has anything to do with their lives in Europe or North America.

They are wrong.

The year 1979 was as much a turning point as 9/11 was.

On November 4, 1979, Khomeini's Islamists stormed the American embassy in Teheran and held fifty-two Americans hostage for 444 days.

Something else happened in 1979.

On November 20 five hundred transnational dissident Wahabi Islamists, led by a Saudi named Juhayman al-Otayei, stormed the Grand Mosque in Mecca and held it for two weeks. They took hundreds of hostages. The Saudi king bartered away his modernization initiatives in order to receive the religious permission necessary to launch a counter-military action at Islam's holiest site. This included having French soldiers supply poison gas and help craft the plan of attack.

When it was over, 127 Saudi soldiers were dead and 451 had been wounded. During the fighting 87 dissidents died at the scene and 27 in hospitals shortly thereafter. Of those who survived, 63 were beheaded in the public squares of eight Saudi cities.

The twenty-two-year-old bin Laden was outraged at how the Saudis handled this Wahabi takeover, which Khomeini promptly dubbed an "American-Zionist conspiracy."

Bin Laden was incensed by the treachery of *Muslims* who had called upon infidels for help. He would make it his mission to fund and train Muslim fighters against the infidels. And he did so in Afghanistan.

In the 1980s, while bin Laden was arming and fighting alongside the mujahideen, in separate incidents Iranian, Palestinian, and Libyan commandos bombed American embassies and Marine barracks, hijacked planes, blew up European synagogues and nightclubs, and exploded Pan Am flight 103 over Lockerbie, Scotland.

In the 1990s Iran's Hezbollah, al-Qaeda's Saudis, and Palestinians joined together and exploded a bomb-laden truck outside the Khobar Towers in Saudi Arabia, killing American soldiers and wounding hundreds of civilians; in 1998 al-Qaeda detonated two car bombs simultaneously, destroying the American embassies in Nairobi, Kenya, and Dar-es-Salaam, Tanzania, killing 224 and wounding thousands of civilians.

Islamists everywhere blew up hotels, ships, tourist buses, nightclubs, churches, synagogues, mosques, airports, trains, and shopping malls, and both Muslim and infidel civilians on every continent.

Something awful also happened in New York City.

In the early 1980s a blind Egyptian sheikh, Omar Abdel-Rahman, was implicated in the successful plot to assassinate Egyptian president Anwar Sadat. Abdel-Rahman was jailed, tortured, and eventually expelled from Egypt. Following his expulsion, Abdel-Rahman went to Afghanistan to work with Osama bin Laden, who was aiding the mujahideen in their resistance against Soviet occupation. Abdel-Rahman left Afghanistan to raise funds for international jihad.

Although Abdel-Rahman was on the State Department's terrorist watch list, he obtained a tourist visa and began delivering fiery Arabic sermons in New York City, calling for the death of Americans and Zionists and raising money for jihad.

In a fatwa Abdel-Rahman condemned Americans as the "descendants of apes and pigs who have been feeding from the dining tables of the Zionists, Communists, and colonialists." And he called on Muslims to assail the West, "cut the transportation of their countries, tear it apart, destroy their economy, burn their companies, eliminate their interests, sink their ships, shoot down their planes, kill them on the sea, air, or land."

Many good Americans believe that everyone has the right to say anything. Why would we prohibit anyone's free speech, especially if it takes place in a religious setting?

"In America, we have a First Amendment," a good friend pointed out. "Religion and state are separate. We can't just go into a mosque and censor speech or arrest someone for what they say or think or for actions they have yet to commit."

"You don't think these jihadists are crying 'Fire!' in a crowded theater?" I ask. "That they are not a clear and present danger?"

"That, my dear, must first be proven in a court of law."

He expressed the mind-set of many principled American law professors and judges.

But what if radical Islam/Islamism—as practiced by the likes of Osama bin Laden—is not exactly a religion but is, rather, a blend of fascism and totalitarianism, a political and military pseudo-religious ideology—a death cult bent on world domination? What if Abdel-Rahman's sermons consisted of illegal hate speech intended to legitimize bin Laden's war on infidels?

What if twenty-first-century Wahabi and Salafist Islamism is not what most Muslims wish to practice? What if such fiery sermonizers have hijacked the possibility of Islam's evolution and created a dangerous cult of their own? Who will stop these hijackers—if that's who they are? (Some say that they are not hijackers, that they are practicing the true Islam, that the Qur'an commands war against infidels.)

In 1993, under Abdel-Rahman's direction, jihadists exploded a car bomb in the parking garage beneath the World Trade Center in Manhattan. Evidence revealed that the sheikh and his gang planned to blow up the United Nations, the Lincoln and Holland tunnels, the George Washington Bridge, and the FBI building.

In 1995 Abdel-Rahman and his team were tried and convicted; they are all serving life sentences.

But Abdel-Rahman's followers remained active following his capture. In 1997 a jihadist group in Egypt shot and killed more than sixty tourists visiting the ancient temples of Luxor. The perpetrators were none other than Abdel-Rahman's own personal Egyptian theological gangsters, al-Gama'a al-Islamiyya. They mutilated some bodies and left leaflets at the scene demanding the release of Abdel-Rahman.

In late June 2012, in his first public speech, the Egyptian president-elect, Mohamed Morsi, of the Muslim Brotherhood, promised to work for the release of Abdel-Rahman—the blind sheikh—to have him extradited to Egypt on humanitarian grounds.

On September 11, 2012, at a sit-in protest a large group of Egyptian Salafists demanded the release of Abdel-Rahman. They yelled, "Death to Jews!" and insisted that the army of Islam would rise up under the leadership of Abdel-Rahman.

In January 2013 President Morsi again demanded Abdel-Rahman's release. Also in January 2013, al-Qaeda in North Africa commandeered an Algerian oil company and took many foreign hostages. The hostage takers also demanded the release of Abdel-Rahman. At least thirty-seven foreigners were murdered as the Algerian army ended the standoff.

Remember how the Saudis turned to the infidel French in 1979 when the Grand Mosque in Mecca was captured? Nearly twenty years later, in 1990, after having proved himself against the Soviets, bin Laden expected the Saudi royals to use him when Iraq invaded Kuwait. However, both the Saudis and the Kuwaitis spurned bin Laden's offers and again turned to infidels for military assistance.

By the time of the first Gulf War, bin Laden had made quite a name for himself. Between 1980 and 1989 (and with the blessing of the Saudi government), he became the chief financier of the Afghan resistance. He also trained, supplied, and funded Arab warriors to join the Afghan mujahideen and set up special Arab military bases in Afghanistan.

In 1988 bin Laden founded al-Qaeda for the purpose of waging a global jihad.

When Saddam Hussein invaded Kuwait in 1990, the Saudis rejected Osama's military services. Just as his Saudi father and older half-brothers had once spurned him, now the Saudi princes had also rejected him. Osama was furious and grew bitter.

In 1992 the Saudi king threw bin Laden out of the kingdom. Bin Laden found shelter in Sudan.

Between 1993 and 2000, and with the help of Dr. Ayman Muhammad al-Zawahiri and Omar Abdel-Rahman (the blind sheikh), bin Laden engineered a series of murderous attacks against American soldiers and embassies in the Middle East and Africa (Mogadishu, Riyadh, Dhahran, Kenya, Tanzania, Aden, and others).

In 1996 Sudan bowed to mounting international pressure and kicked bin Laden out.

That year bin Laden released his "Declaration of Jihad," and the Saudi kingdom revoked his citizenship. That's when bin Laden fled to Afghanistan, where the warlord Mullah Omar offered to protect him.

Bin Laden hatched his 9/11 plan in Afghanistan.

Once I was at the mercy of tribal law in Afghanistan. Now the entire world seemed at its mercy as well.

Ten long years passed, but bin Laden could not be found. Perhaps, like Saddam Hussein, he was living below ground in a rat hole. Or maybe he was living in an elite villa in Abbottabad, Pakistan, protected by America's presumed allies, the Pakistani generals and Inter-Services Intelligence. Indeed this is precisely where Navy SEAL Team Six found and assassinated him in May 2011.

But, as we saw in Benghazi on 9/11/12, al-Qaeda is not dead.

A long time ago, when feminists first raised the issue of rape, we were immediately accused of hating men. Eventually, wearily, I came to say: "All men are not rapists—but almost all rapists are men."

Similarly I am not saying that all Muslims or all Arabs are terrorists. I say: "Today most terrorists are Muslim Islamists."

I work with some of the Muslim and ex-Muslim dissidents and feminists whom I have named in this book. These brave souls have sounded the alarm against radical Islamic fundamentalism and terrorism. The lucky ones have fled to the West. Some live under armed guard or in hiding and write under pseudonyms. Many have been forced to defend their writings and teachings in courts of law in both Europe and North America. The unlucky dissidents have been jailed, tortured, or murdered.

Good people in the West have often failed to distinguish between Islam and Islamism; academics and journalists have been reluctant to accuse any Muslim of doing anything bad (like blowing up a hotel or ethnically cleansing black Africans, Jews, Hindus, and Christians), lest they be accused of profiling and Islamophobia.

I understand that racism is a valid concern, a burning issue. I am also an antiracist. But 9/11 had nothing to do with race. It was part of an aggressive political, military, and religious crusade.

America was attacked by ideologues who want infidels (of every race and ethnicity) to get out of Muslim holy lands. They also want Muslim women covered and subordinate. These ideologues are also at war with other branches of Islam, with promodern Muslim governments, and with individual Muslim freethinkers.

Such ideologues live on every continent; their complexions are all the colors of the human race. African-born and Caucasian converts to Islam, including women and former prisoners, are becoming more numerous in the West. The subject deserves a separate book. Some are sincerely religious or for psychological reasons require a strong and regimented structure. Others are highly politicized Islamists.

In the name of freedom they demand the right to renounce freedom. In the language of tolerance they demand that intolerance be granted a dignified place at the table.

I once debated a British convert to Islam, Yvonne Ridley, on Al-hurra TV. On September 28, 2001, Ridley was kidnapped in Afghanistan and held by the Taliban in solitary confinement for seven days. They tried to convert her, and she promised to read the Qur'an when she was free.

Afterward Ridley converted to Islam—no, she became a true believer: a hater of Israel, America, and the godless West. Ridley's instant rage level in a public debate was unsettling, even as political theater.

Persecuting and scapegoating infidels is a time-honored way of diverting attention from some real villains. The truth is that Muslim-on-Muslim violence is far greater than infidel-on-Muslim violence.

What Islamists accuse their enemies of doing (engaging in conspiracies, telling lies, controlling the media, brainwashing, lusting for a new colonial empire) is precisely what they themselves are doing.

In 1996 a stateless bin Laden published an 11,831-word fatwa entitled "Declaration of War against the Americans Occupying the Lands of the Two Holy Places." It also appeared in English in a London newspaper. It is quite a toxic read. He writes, "The people of Islam had suffered from aggression, iniquity, and injustice imposed upon them by the Zionist-Crusader alliance and their collaborators. [Muslims] are the main target for the aggression."

He attributes all Muslim suffering to this alliance—and concludes that "fighting [waging jihad] against the Kuffar [infidel] in every part of the world is absolutely essential."

Bin Laden defines *jihad* as a strictly military operation, not as an inner spiritual struggle. He writes, "There is no more important duty than pushing the American enemy out of the holy land," which includes or is symbolized by the Grand Mosque in Mecca and the Al Aqsa Mosque in Jerusalem.

The Al Aqsa Mosque was established in 705 CE—it stands right above the site of the pre-existing first and second Jewish Temples which were established in 957 BCE and 515 BCE, respectively—well over a millennia earlier.

Over and over again bin Laden condemns the Saudi regime, which he does not explicitly name, for having suspended "Islamic Shari'ah law and exchanging it with man-made civil law"; for its "inability to protect the country"; and for "allowing the enemy of the Ummah [the Muslim people]—the American crusader forces—to occupy the land."

He is really angry at the Saudis, his father's people, for having rejected and expelled him, for not rewarding his greatness. Although he mentions them repeatedly, he dares not focus on attacking them. He targets only the approved scapegoats.

He hates and despises America, Israel, and infidels everywhere.

He becomes the loving Father of Death to all the surrogate sons he sends to kill and die. Bin Laden promises his young jihadists paradise and the usual seventy-two virgins. Addressing the American secretary of defense, bin Laden writes, "[Our] youths love death as you love life. . . . Our youth believe in paradise after death. . . . If death is a predetermined must, then it is a shame to die cowardly. . . . Your problem will be how to convince your troops to fight, while our problem will be how to restrain our youths to wait for their turn in fighting and in operations."

What if bin Laden is right? What if our love of life and our own ethical standards turn out to be our undoing? How should the West fight against terrorists—by patiently infiltrating their groups, through targeted assassinations and drone attacks? Traditional military approaches cannot win in urban guerrilla warfare as terrorists happily hide behind Muslim civilians—including women and children.

My Israeli colleague says, "Now the world will understand what Israel has been facing. We have been attacked every day, both on the ground and in the world media. The Palestinians are still lobbing rockets into southern Israel and terrifying our civilians. The false propaganda against us has grown in quantum leaps."

"I know," I say. "In 2004 I estimated that the number of Israeli civilians who had, by then, died in a Palestinian Islamist terrorist attack was, in American demographic terms, the equivalent of 30,000–40,000 American deaths and approximately 300,000 Americans wounded."

"Well, then, just think about it. America invaded Afghanistan after only 3,000 American deaths," my Israeli friend notes.

It is true: 9/11- and Boston marathon–style terrorism might be new to America, but it was a daily reality for Israelis, who were shot down or blown up in their beds, cafes, nightclubs, hotels, hospitals, schools, and on buses for the last seventy years of the twentieth century. Matters worsened considerably with a new Palestinian intifada (uprising), which began a year before 9/11.

This jihad against the Jews went global. The genie had again escaped from the bottle, and the world inherited the whirlwind.

What had been happening to Muslim, Christian, Jewish, Hindu, Zoroastrian, and Bahai civilians (at the hands of Islamist terrorists) in the Middle East, India, South and Central Asia, the Far East, and the Muslim parts of Africa was now happening to civilians in North and South America and in Europe.

Over the years Abdul-Kareem has condemned the way in which the world first turned its back on Afghanistan and then jumped in for its own gains.

"Why don't they all just get the hell out and allow us to develop our mineral wealth, our gas and oil? Why did America use us to fight their Cold War against the Russians? Why did America abandon us to the Arabs and the Pakistanis once the Cold War ended?"

These are fair questions.

I acknowledge that American oil interests and American Cold War realities dictated our foreign policies. America did support the worst tyrants, the most dangerous reactionaries, to contain communism and protect the oil trade. These tyrants also held back the Islamist tide.

Many Westerners condemn imperialism, colonialism, and racism and believe that only the West is guilty of such crimes. This is not true. The West has behaved very badly—but so has the East. The West has changed, even repented somewhat; the East has yet to do so. We have abolished slavery and fought for human and women's rights; the East has yet to do so.

According to Ibn Warraq, most recently in his book *Why the West Is Best: A Muslim Apostate's Defense of Liberal Democracy,* Islamic culture is historically characterized by imperialism, colonialism, infidel hatred, militant jihad, massacres, genocide, conversion by the sword, antiblack racism, slavery, and gender and religious apartheid. These facts are poorly understood and often denied.

Many antiracists believe that American white supremacists, including police officers, have targeted, falsely charged, and even murdered African American boys and men. While racism definitely plays a role in who gets imprisoned and sentenced to death—it is also true that American law enforcement is facing an epidemic of black-on-black violence. Because feelings run hot and high on these issues and the matter remains unresolved, many antiracists project their negative feelings toward legal authority onto American military and counterterrorist intelligence forces. They view them as analogous to white supremacist police—and they view the most violent jihadists as being targeted for racial reasons, and not because they are enemy combatants and transnational soldiers in a military–religious war against the West.

What was the father of 9/11, Osama bin Laden, like as a human being, as a son, a husband, and a father?

After divorcing and banishing Osama's Syrian mother, Allia, Osama's own father, Mohammed bin Awad bin Laden, had little time for him; in his mother's absence Osama was mocked as the son of the slave by his fathers' other wives, and by Osama's half-brothers and half-sisters. He had fifty-six siblings. According to his son Omar, "There was something odd that I had noticed from my youth. Never once did I hear my father call his father, 'my father.' Instead, he always referred to him as 'your grandfather.' I have no explanation for this, other than it seemed to pain him to use the words 'my father.'"

In the days following 9/11, I was struck by how angry Osama was because President Bush had not immediately interrupted his reading of a story to a little girl to respond to the great—and greatly spurned—Osama. I remember wondering whether Osama was still vying for paternal or for male presidential attention.

According to his son Omar, al-Qaeda's Osama was an exceptionally cruel father who verbally and physically abused, tormented, and endangered his biological sons. According to Omar, Osama routinely beat his sons with his wooden cane "for the slightest infraction."

"There were times he became so excited when hitting [us] that his heavy cane broke into two pieces. . . . It was not unusual for the sons of Osama bin Laden to be covered with raised red welts on our backs and legs."

Bin Laden subjected his sons to long forced marches in the desert but allowed them little water. Although his sons suffered from asthma attacks, he had banned the use of Ventolin, an asthma treatment, because it was a Western medication.

In addition, according to Omar, Osama condemned his sons to "inferior schooling" by teachers who were exceptionally cruel to them, and the other students, who envied and hated the bin Laden sons, constantly threatened each boy with gang rape.

Nevertheless, his son Omar writes that he "still desperately loved his father [. . .] despite his cruelty." Eventually Omar and his older brothers realized that life was far more agreeable when their revered father was far, far away.

Many Muslim sons seem programmed to dote upon fathers who are both sadistic and absent and to subsequently gravitate toward similar kinds of male leaders.

Thus, when they were in Afghanistan, Omar was thrilled that his father had allowed him to serve "as his personal tea boy."

Omar was seventeen when bin Laden took his family to Afghanistan. Omar was eighteen or nineteen when his father stopped him from "washing" the senior bin Laden's feet. This devastated Omar, who displays a classic ambivalence toward the man who had tormented him. He writes, "Although I hated what he did, what his actions brought to his family, he was still my father. As such, I would never have betrayed him."

For psychological reasons alone, the overthrow of sadistic tyrants might prove exceptionally difficult among people with histories like Omar's. On the other hand Omar does ultimately leave his father and, together with his mother, writes a book about him.

Why did he do so? I would guess that the family may have needed to publicly disassociate themselves from the mastermind of 9/11. But I believe Omar wrote this book because he had finally concluded that his love for his father was unrequited. He had nothing left to lose or hope for. Omar writes, "My father hated his enemies more than he loved his sons. That's the moment that I felt myself the fool for wasting my life one moment longer."

Nevertheless, after bin Laden's 2011 execution by American Navy SEALs, his family published a letter in the *New York Times* condemning America for not having arrested Osama and given him a fair trial with a "presumption of innocence until proven guilty by a court of law," something that had been accorded Iraqi president Saddam Hussein and Serbian president Slobodan Milošević.

In their letter Osama's sons note that one son, Omar, had always condemned their father for his violence but that they all now "condemn the president of the United States for ordering the execution of unarmed men and women." The bin Laden sons view their father's execution as a "violation of international law" and have vowed to pursue the matter at the International Criminal Court and International Court of Justice.

How did bin Laden treat his wives?

Osama permitted himself the most powerful Western cars, planes, and weaponry, but he did not permit his five wives and children to use "refrigerators, electrical stoves, or the cooling or heating systems." His wives were forced to cook on "portable gas burners." His family was condemned to suffer the heat of Saudi Arabia and Sudan without air-conditioning—just as Mohammed the Prophet once did.

In the heat of summer in my own Manhattan neighborhood, I have seen religious Muslim men walking by in white lightweight Western-style summer clothing, followed by women wearing dark-colored and heavy head and body coverings. Increasingly their faces are shrouded as well.

These are the kind of men who permit themselves the best of both worlds while insisting that their women fly the flag of reactionary Islam on their bodies.

Was Osama cruel to women? Well—yes and no. According to his son Omar, like so many sons of Islamic polygamy, Osama loved his mother, Allia, "more than he loved his sons, his wives or his siblings." And, from his point of view, he was kind to his five wives—at least so long as they remained sexually available, fertile, modest, friendly toward each other, and religious; followed his relentlessly ascetic set of rules without complaint; and were obedient in all ways.

Polygamous husbands are not necessarily cruel to their wives—beyond the pain that polygamy itself inflicts. In Kabul I never saw my father-in-law, Ismail Mohammed, berate, mock, or physically abuse his wives, daughters, or daughters-in-law. He treated me with great tenderness. We were women and as such were viewed as naturally, biologically, inferior. Women are not worthy opponents; there is no honor in defeating us.

This makes the savage mistreatment of so many Muslim women at the hands of their male and female relatives something of a paradox as well as a tragedy.

According to Najwa bin Laden and Omar bin Laden, Osama allowed his wives to have little furniture. The wives had "no decorations, not even one picture hanging on the walls." Osama kept them locked up and isolated. Even when they were alone, just with each other, his wives swam in their dresses in their own private swimming pool.

When Osama relocated to Afghanistan, he expected the wives who accompanied him to endure freezing weather without any heat, to live in squalid huts and cave-like dwellings, to live without access to medical care or a social life of any kind.

According to Omar, Osama viewed the younger jihadists in Afghanistan as eager to kill—but "the quality of their characters appeared questionable." They had run away from "problems in their home countries. Some had fled to avoid being punished for violent crimes. . . . Others lived in such severe poverty that they had only eaten meat a few times in their lives. Most could not afford to marry."

Omar describes how such young men were shown doctored videotapes of "Israeli soldiers gleefully stomping on Palestinian women; Israeli tanks purposely destroying Palestinian homes; Israeli soldiers viciously kicking young Palestinian boys."

It is a known fact that Palestinians celebrated 9/11 in the streets. The women trilled and gave out candies. The men shot rifles into the air; everyone literally danced for joy.

In the late 1980s or early 1990s the author and filmmaker Saira Shah (yes, the granddaughter of Saira Elizabeth Luiza Shah), noted anti-Israel graffiti on the Afghan border. In her riveting book, *The Storyteller's Daughter,* she writes, "We passed a gigantic military installation. . . . Daubed on its flat surface, a patch of graffiti said, in English, 'Down with Israel.' I laughed aloud. What had Israel to do with this conflict? We were witnessing the birthplace of a worldwide Islamic movement. We had just passed one of the military installations sponsored by the CIA, funded by Saudi Arabia and engineered by an idealistic young Islamist firebrand. His name was Osama bin Laden. The volunteers were known to the Afghans as Arabs, although they were actually Islamic radicals from all over the Muslim world."

*W*hen I was in Kabul, I was laughed at for wanting to befriend a dog and for adopting a gentle deer that had been wounded.

"Dogs are dirty, filthy, unclean," my mother-in-law insisted.

Years later I encountered a Muslim taxi driver in New York City who became dangerously and righteously incensed when a passenger wanted to board with a small dog in tow.

Osama bin Laden was cruel to animals, including pigeons but especially dogs. Omar and his brothers had a pet monkey they doted on. Yet one of their father's men chased their pet down and then ran over it with a water tanker. Apparently Osama had convinced this follower that the baby monkey was really a "Jewish person."

I will never forget bin Laden and 9/11. It abruptly brought me back to my time in Afghanistan and reminded me of what I had learned about the difference between freedom and tyranny. It set my feet upon a new path.

TWELVE

9/11/11

Abdul-Kareem's wife, Kamile, is ill and has been asking to see me. My first free day happens to be the tenth anniversary of 9/11. So I agree to spend the afternoon, ironically or appropriately, with my Afghan relatives.

Kamile can no longer travel, so I make the trip to the suburbs. I have been visiting them in their home for more than a quarter-century.

When I arrive, Kamile and I embrace. Having shared the same husband makes us feel like sisters. We hug, we kiss—these are gestures I do not repeat with Abdul-Kareem.

No one mentions that it is the tenth anniversary of the September 11 attacks—the day that tore a hole through history. It is as though this event did not happen. It has nothing to do with them. Perhaps, they will not discuss it with *me*.

Perhaps it is shameful to them that Muslims attacked America and that the plan was hatched in Afghanistan; as with all things shameful, silence reigns. Or maybe Kamile is too ill and Abdul-Kareem too worn down with worry to focus on anything larger than themselves.

Kamile and I first met in the early 1980s when, unannounced, she rang the bell to my apartment in the midst of a blizzard. I laughed—because, unlike me, Kamile has blond hair and blue eyes, something Abdul-Kareem's brothers had valued. I liked her straight off. We talked for hours.

"I did not get along with his family. I think they hated me," she says. "Probably because I worked and remained independent."

"I don't think they hated me," I say. "I was not there long enough to be able to work, but I was a foreigner who could not be tamed. To them I was a liability."

"His mother was so mean to me." We say this at the same time. Softly I say, "She was a poor soul, driven mad by her life, but no daughter-in-law should have had to live with her."

I ask Kamile, "Why have you come alone and on such a dark and stormy night?"

Kamile wants me to stand by her side "for the sake of sisterhood" at an upcoming family gathering.

"We two are independent women, strong in spirit. Please come."

I arrive at their home. She is used to glamorous parties as a way of life. Abdul-Kareem is her protector, her life. As a mid-life immigrant, who has endured exile from two countries, she has no job, no money of her own, and her English could stand some improvement.

They are having a party that afternoon, and relatives are coming and going. Ismail Mohammed's third wife, Meena, and some of her children are present. They all hug and greet me with considerable affection. I am touched by their earnest welcome and return their warmth.

We all share having been in Kabul at a more hopeful time, when it was not at war, when the aroma of flowers and the songs of birds filled the air, and servants poured our tea. Even though I was unhappy there, this bond of sorts is unbreakable.

The shop where I get my photos framed is run by an Afghan family. Always, always, the elderly father insists on bringing me the expertly framed works himself. He can count on my greeting him in his native Dari: "*Choob astain? Chitoor astain?*" (Are you well? How are you?)

I offer him tea, he sits, he reminisces, he cannot believe I was actually in Kabul when he was a young man. He is the quintessential Afghan: courteous, courtly, gracious, and sweet. He has chosen to take care of me personally.

At Abdul-Kareem's family parties everyone gets up and dances—all together. I love this custom. The gathering that Kamile has asked me to attend is so crowded there is no room for all of us to dance. Finally, reluctantly, I leave the people with the warm and shining eyes, each of whom formally embraces me to say good-bye as they continue to drink tea and coffee and munch on nuts and little cakes.

In all the years that I've known her, Kamile has smoked nonstop—but in such an elegant way. She is known to take more than a drink or two. No matter. For years Kamile always managed to dress the part of a fashionable woman-about-town—yet as time went by, she left her home less and less and took to wearing the kind of caftans long associated with at-home harem life.

Well, as I've noted, I also wear a caftan when I write, and I write at home even though I have a writing studio.

Ma sœur, mon semblable. My sister, myself.

Despite everything, Kamile has two children who adore her and take care of her, just as they take care of their father. Abdul-Kareem now takes care of her, too, and very tenderly.

The three of us sit together in a room overlooking their swimming pool, which is surrounded by plants. Nearby Abdul-Kareem has a small library strewn with newspapers and a computer. They are both tired and worn down today. I actually have to ask for tea. This minor failing is uncharacteristic, unthinkable.

I am here this 9/11/11 on an errand of mercy, not to cross swords, but the heavy purposeful silence about 9/11 is deafening and painful. I should not be surprised—but actually I am stunned and a bit frightened.

"Phyllisjan," Kamile says, "my daughter was so glad that you introduced her to Seyran Ates."

Seyran is a Turkish German feminist who was shot and nearly killed for her work on behalf of battered Turkish female immigrants. Her latest book is titled *Islam Needs a Sexual Revolution.* Right after it came out the Berlin police suggested she take a vacation, and she came and stayed with me in New York.

Kamile speaks in heavily accented English. She continues but in a whisper.

"Talk to me about Seyran. Tell *him*"—and here she glances darkly at Abdul-Kareem—"that there are Muslim women in the world who want their freedom."

Kamile always comes brightly to life whenever I talk about the bravery and charm of Muslim feminists. She leans forward, smiles, and starts to speak—but Abdul-Kareem usually interrupts her and changes the subject. He is not that interested in what his wife might have to say, nor is he interested in what interests her—at least, not when I am there.

She expects me to mount a spirited defense of women's rights. I do what I can. Reluctantly I begin to tell Abdul-Kareem about some of the work I have done with or in support of Muslim and ex-Muslim feminists and dissidents. I express how horrified I am by the state of Afghan women. He responds by attacking American culture and American women.

"Phyllis, my dear," he begins. "Do you think that American women are happy? Look at them, half-naked, running after men, having to hunt down a husband on their own, they can't even keep him, they all get divorced. The grandparents live too far away to help with the grandchildren. Why should they bother? Americans throw their old parents out in the cold, just like the Eskimos do."

He goes on. His family indulges him. No one dares interrupt him. He is the patriarch, and Afghan family rules still apply, even in exile in America.

"Abdul-Kareem," Kamile ventures, "I want to hear about Phyllis's work."

"But I am talking," he explains.

Kamile tries again.

"Phyllis knows Muslim feminists, from Egypt, Syria, and Turkey."

Abdul-Kareem continues talking.

Kamile keeps rolling her eyes. She whispers to me, "C'mon, talk to him. Tell him he is wrong."

Finally Kamile says, "Abdul-Kareem, let Phyllis speak. She knows many Muslim feminists who are unhappy in their countries, who want change. Maybe America is not the paradise for women, but, really, do you think how Turkish or Egyptian brothers treat their sisters is right? They steal their inheritance money and their property and then try to marry them off for more money to horrible men. Is that right?"

I step in as her knight, prepared to do battle for my lady. But I also smile a lot and try to find points of agreement. I even propose toasts.

I raise my tea cup and say, "Here we still are, together and safe. May we all remain healthy for many more years. Here's to Kamile's health—and here's to many more meals together at your dinner table."

On this day Abdul-Kareem refuses to step around our differences. He launches attacks and refuses to concede a single point. The ceremonially courteous Afghan digs in his heels and dares me to protest. He says, "The so-called Westernization of Muslim women has not really led to their liberation. They dress and drink like whores and call that freedom. They are fools."

"Abdul-Kareem," I say, "are you really back to this again? Will Muslim women be free only when they wear face masks or full body coverings? Is it freedom from the West that has you mesmerized? Afghanistan was never conquered by the West, and Afghan Muslim women were never free."

Abdul-Kareem is shrewd, worldly, and jovial, but, like many Afghan men, thin-skinned when it comes to criticism. He loves to criticize others, beginning with other Afghans. He easily sees through people and enjoys criticizing them.

Abdul-Kareem praises unreservedly all the important people who have treated *him* as an important person. He praises his private high school and college in America and all his American surgeons and physicians. Other than that, he enjoys delivering scathing criticisms of America, Americans, Afghan leaders, women, and especially feminists. He is sometimes right.

I once took him along with me when a Muslim feminist was delivering a lecture. I had hoped that he would hear her on the issues that I often raised. Afterward his only comment was this: "She is an opportunist who is more interested in money for herself than in helping Muslim women. She will take no risks."

To my chagrin he turned out to be right.

As assimilated as Abdul-Kareem may be, he is incapable of praising any woman—unless she is an actress, the wife of an important man—or his daughter. Abdul-Kareem is not pro-Taliban. He is in favor of female education and careers. His daughter lives as a free woman and has a career. Yet his blind spots and prejudices about gender apartheid are typical; many other educated Afghan men share his views and his tactics.

In 2007 an Afghan American anthropologist wrote to me. He praised an article I had written about my time in Kabul as the "only objective glimpse we have of upper class urban households in Kabul during the 1960s," and urged me to "expand your account." He thanked me for my "keen observations and insights about gender relations"—and then, unasked, began to lecture me about women. He told me that women are most exploited, abused, and demeaned in America and Europe. As proof, he referred to a "growing industry" of shelters for abused women in the West, not in Afghanistan. I saved his emails, but I did not tell him what I thought. I will do so here and now.

I am one of those second-wave feminists who, for the last forty-six years, is on record opposing pornography, trafficking, and prostitution;

bemoaning the vulgar eroticization of women, including female children both in the West and worldwide.

Does this anthropologist really believe that women are not abused and demeaned in Afghanistan and in other Muslim countries? We have at least criminalized domestic violence in the West and have tried to prosecute the perpetrators; we have given some minimal shelter to victims of sexual assault, forced prostitution, and domestic violence.

In Afghanistan, with a few exceptions, girls and women are sent to *jail* when they run away from the most gruesome torture at the hands of their in-laws, husbands, and parents. Their spirits are broken, and many are victims of honor murder long before they can find shelter anywhere in the land.

I might agree with the anthropologist on one issue. The religious commitment to preserve the multigenerational family, which is true of all religions—not only Islam—is a positive and prowoman ideal for traditional women. But this is only an ideal, not a reality, and the price, female-only chastity, obedience, and a lifetime of domestic servitude and multiple pregnancies, is extremely high.

I do not believe that the antidote to Western seminudity is to force women into ambulatory body bags.

I favor modesty for both men and women, and I am aware that the Qur'an does, too. However, the burqa is not merely modest. As I've written, it is a sensory deprivation chamber, a moving prison-shroud that renders women socially invisible. Are Muslim men immodest because they do not wear burqas?

When they were young, Abdul-Kareem's children looked up to me and asked me many charming questions; they hung on my every answer. Now they are in their forties, and both they and the times have changed. I think they are disappointed by my refusal to sufficiently criticize the West and angry that I support Israel's right to exist. Jameela is suspicious of my research into honor killings and has argued with me about this once or twice.

I love them both. Once, in my home and at dinners in Manhattan, they kept insisting that I visit Istanbul. They told me that it is the best party town in the universe.

At another kind of party I meet three Turks. One is a wealthy Turkish intellectual who was "born a Muslim but is not a believer." She says, "I am afraid for my husband. We are known as proud Turkish secularists. My husband is a journalist. He is the type the 'beards and the scarves' will come for first. He refuses to consider leaving."

The other two, Turkish Jews, are grandparents who have already left Turkey. They tell me, "Our children have so many beautiful homes, such an enchanted life, that they do not see the danger coming. It is up to us to establish a beachfront in America. Perhaps one day they will have to run to us."

All three Turks are worried by the rapid Islamist gains in their country. They wonder whether they, their children, or their grandchildren will be impoverished, imprisoned, or even murdered for their intellectual or religious beliefs.

I cannot think of Istanbul as a party town—at least not at this time and not for me. I could be wrong. I have a colleague who lives there who confirms that the city is still vibrant and wonderful.

Now Kamile whispers to me, "Please find out whether what Abdul-Kareem is saying about Kemal Atatürk and Recep Erdoğan is true."

I assume she is talking about Erdoğan's increasing acceptance of Islamist fundamentalist values.

And so I ask, "Abdul-Kareem, don't you think that Atatürk [who modernized Turkey] is turning over in his grave?"

Abdul-Kareem responds rather savagely: "Let Atatürk spin. He was a fool. He wanted the West to like him so he became superficially like the West. He forced women to smoke, drink alcohol, and wear Western clothing. What is good about any of that? Granted, women deserve to go to school, but what Erdoğan is doing is much better. He is letting women go to school and allowing them to wear hijab. And he has freed Turkey from the military."

Perhaps Abdul-Kareem has a point, yet what is his real point? Kamile smokes, drinks, and wears Western clothing. Her long-ago demonstration of her ability to earn a living, drive a car, and live independent of her family is an accomplishment that signifies her hard-won dignity.

Abdul-Kareem sees these personal freedoms as forms of Western imperialism. He is saying that Kamile has been duped by Atatürk, who only wanted to please the West. What Abdul-Kareem says may be specifically calculated to challenge my feminist views or to shame Kamile, who vocally idolizes Atatürk.

But Abdul-Kareem has stood by her loyally. In his way he is quite devoted to her. They are each other's constant companions.

Abdul-Kareem usually spends hours conjuring up an Afghan feast. Today, on 9/11/11, he orders a meal from the local Turkish restaurant. As we pass around the rice dishes, Kamile is quiet and Abdul-Kareem continues to criticize American foreign policy—even as he expresses his admiration, even love, for President Obama.

As we begin to eat, I look directly at Kamile and begin to talk about my research into honor killing.

Abdul-Kareem interrupts me, stating that such research is racist in that it singles out one ethnicity when all ethnicities are equally to blame.

"If you want to tackle something important, research racism, look at America itself. That's something that the Phyllis I once knew would be doing."

As usual I say, "Abdul-Kareem, I am not talking about racism in America or about the history of African slavery in America. I am talking about honor killings."

The elegant Mr. Abdul-Kareem turns nasty. In a harsh and scornful tone he says, "Did you personally interview the allegedly murdered girls? No. Did you perform the autopsies yourself? No. Did you talk to their families, understand their point of view? No. Did you work with the police? No. So you are just guessing."

"I am not on trial," I respond, "and I do not have to answer hostile questions at a family dinner."

Whenever the subject of honor killings comes up, Abdul-Kareem always says that he has never known any to have taken place in Afghanistan.

When I name names, dates, cite a particular newspaper story (his favorite medium) on this topic, Abdul-Kareem ultimately says, "I will not talk about that."

Or he says, "Well, there are so many crimes of this nature happening around the world, this is only a very small part of that."

Abdul-Kareem pretends that he has not read my work, including whatever I have written about Afghanistan in the past. But I know that he has read every word because every so often, right out of the blue, Abdul-Kareem will either concede that I finally got something right or he'll criticize me on some small detail that I presumably got wrong.

Once, when I was studying custody battles worldwide, I asked him about custody in Afghanistan. Our conversation was hilarious but instructive.

Phyllis: Has any Afghan mother ever lost custody of her children?

Abdul-Kareem: Never. Not once. Not that I know of.

Phyllis: According to the Sharia, a father is entitled to his children when the boy is seven and the girl is twelve.

Abdul-Kareem: No, no. It is only "at puberty." But what father would remove children from a good wife? What would he do with them?

Phyllis: What if the mother did something unheard of—like commit adultery?

Abdul-Kareem: Under Sharia women can also sue for divorce if their husbands commit adultery or are impotent or refuse to support them or are cruel.

Phyllis: I don't think this is true, but you have not answered my question. Alright, when the rare divorce does occur, who keeps the children?

Abdul-Kareem: Divorce never occurs. It doesn't have to. Even when the men of my father's generation took a second wife, they didn't divorce or abandon their first wives and children. That would be too Western.

Phyllis: What if a woman really disobeys her husband? Can that lead to divorce or to her loss of custody?

Abdul-Kareem: Wives don't disobey their husbands. Why would they? Now, if a mother is genuinely incompetent, if she completely neglects her children—

Phyllis: Neglects her children?

Abdul-Kareem: Perhaps a mother is overly devoted to her own family. Perhaps she insists on visiting her mother every single day. Perhaps she leaves her children in the hands of servants too much. Perhaps she is not making sure that the children are being kept from evil influences. Even such a terrible mother will be given time to change her behavior. The Kauzi [the mullah] might counsel her husband to give her six months to change her ways. Our mullahs are against divorce. Everyone is.

Phyllis: There must be one Afghan woman who once lost custody of her children because she was married to a cruel man or because she disobeyed him in some way.

Abdul-Kareem: Give me some time to research this minor question for you.

He was not always like this. Once, he laughed at hypocrisy among Afghans and condemned Afghans for stupid and incompetent behavior.

Sometimes he still does. A few years ago, when I invited him to join me at Asia House to hear President Hamid Karzai speak, I was afraid that Abdul-Kareem's nonstop loudly whispered comments about the Afghan president would get us thrown out.

"What kind of costume is he wearing? He's a Pushtun, not an Uzbeck. Why is he wearing an Uzbeck coat? Is he a clown of some kind? What has America bought and paid for?"

"Shh-hh," I said, "they will ask us to leave or start taking photos of you."

But he kept grumbling all the time Karzai was speaking.

When I first saw homosexual men holding hands on the streets of Kabul, my Afghan family, including Abdul-Kareem, told me that I was exaggerating or misunderstanding what I had seen with my own eyes.

When I, and a handful of others, including Amnesty International and the author Khaled Hosseini, initially broke the stories of the gay male "dancing boys" of Afghanistan, the existence of Afghan warrior-pedophiles, orphaned Afghan boy sex slaves, and the inevitable epidemic of prison-like homosexuality in a woman-hating culture—Abdul-Kareem refused to discuss these matters with me.

But once he saw the 2010 PBS and BBC documentaries on dancing boys in Afghanistan, listened to NPR's program, and read all about it in the *New York Times,* he simply acted as if he had known about this all along. Thus, without referring to any of our previous conversations (really nonconversations) on this very subject, *he* now told *me* all about the dancing boys.

"But," he insisted, "you must realize that this is true only of Kandahar. It is true nowhere else."

I understand why he needs to disagree with me. I'm the wife who got away, the wife who delivers public lectures all over the world and who writes books. He cannot take me on in public. The only place he can argue with me and attempt to assert dominance, superiority, is privately, when I am at my most vulnerable, because I am trying to be nice, trying to honor our family-like connection.

From his point of view it is bad enough that he has lost everything. He is also saddled with a feminist first wife who insists on exposing things that are meant to be hidden, certainly from infidel and non-Afghan eyes. Internal divisions, terrorists, and the world's superpowers have laid waste to his country. Now the infidel destroyers are enjoying themselves, criticizing and feeling superior to the country they failed to help.

*W*e finish our dinner and are drinking our tea. But the atmosphere has gotten tense. It is not pleasant. I try to bring us together. Looking at Kamile, I say, "I want to toast again to your health and to our continued relationship."

Kamile beams. "You are like family, like a sister to me," she says.

In 2007, when Abdul-Kareem went back to Afghanistan to sell the best and the last of his family's land "to rich and unbelievably vulgar drug lords," he had Kamile call me right after he had called her, to assure me that he was alright. They both thanked me for my genuine concern.

In a strange way I am still a member of this family—a distant member to be sure, but my status as Abdul-Kareem's first wife is an identity that will never change and one that is never challenged. Our relationship and my relationship to his family, including his second wife, did not conclude with an annulment. We have remained in contact.

In fact my biological son has grown up knowing Abdul-Kareem's family. I attended the various graduations of Abdul-Kareem's children. They attended my son's wedding, I hosted some lovely dinners for us all.

Over the years Abdul-Kareem would always come to pick up me up to drive me back to his suburban home. If he could not do so, one of his grown children filled in for him. And then someone would insist on driving me back. Whether this was overly protective or not, it was an Afghan custom that I came to appreciate.

I was always proud that an American Jew could have a long-term tie to an Afghan Muslim.

*I*t is still 9/11/11 and Kamile is still eager to talk about Turkey. The matter has been in the news quite a bit recently, and I am interested in her views on the subject. I ask, "When will Turkey admit to the Armenian genocide?"

Both Abdul-Kareem and Kamile speak at the same time and say exactly the same thing.

"Turkey will never do it. The Turkish Republic did not commit those crimes, the Ottoman Empire did. Why would they admit to a crime they didn't commit?"

At this point Abdul-Kareem lowers his voice and says, almost in a whisper, "If Turkey does this it would be exposing itself to the kind of thing the Jews do."

He rubs his thumb and index finger together, indicating moneygrubbing and greediness.

"The Armenians would demand reparations. It would be endless."

I can barely breathe.

It gets worse—far worse—as Abdul-Kareem suddenly launches into a first-time tirade against Israel in a particularly ugly way. What he says is inaccurate, unoriginal, irrational, and practically anti-Semitic. Is this something he really believes? Or does he feel hurt by what I have said about honor killings? Is this his payback?

This is crazy. Abdul-Kareem married a Jewish woman. Many of his friends in Kabul were Jews, and most of the people who helped him escape the Soviet occupation and become established in America were Jews. What has poisoned his bloodstream against the Jewish state?

He is not a mosque goer. He gets his information only from the secular media. He reads the British newspapers, English editions of German and Arab newspapers, perhaps the Turkish press, the Afghan media, and of course the mainstream American media. He has not gotten his information from an Islamist mosque.

In many ways Abdul-Kareem is now another kind of stranger. When I first met him, he passed as Western, indeed as a version of a cultured and wealthy Brit or as an affable colonial-era chap. I had no idea he would be force marching me back into the tenth century. I am so sad we no longer talk about films and books; our most neutral discussions are about our various age-related medical problems. On politics . . . we now disagree.

It is getting dark now. It is still 9/11/11—and Abdul-Kareem has still not acknowledged the plain fact that one of Afghanistan's ruling warlords was the man who provided Osama bin Laden with shelter, a hiding place, and the time to choreograph the 9/11 attacks.

But that is not the worst of it. Once again he has managed to silence both his first wife and his second wife.

*I*n 2002 Asne Seierstad, the Norwegian journalist, published *The Bookseller of Kabul*. It is a best-selling expose of a commendably bookish and hospitable Afghan man, Shah Mohammed Rais, who liked to present himself as a Western-style liberal but who was quite the misogynist tyrant at home.

Seierstad lived with him and his two wives for four months.

At the age of fifty Rais took a second wife; she was sixteen at the time of her marriage. His first wife was inconsolable. Although he constantly preached the importance of education, Rais refused to send any of his children to school; instead he forced them to work twelve-hour days in his various stores. Seierstad notes, "The family is the single most important institution in Afghan culture. . . . Family law—decided by the men in the household—is more important than government legis-lation. . . . If we can't understand the Afghan family, we can't understand Afghanistan."

Like the bookseller of Kabul, Abdul-Kareem is a misogynist, a charming misogynist, an educated and seemingly assimilated misogynist, but awful where wives and feminism are concerned.

Abdul-Kareem is ruining the book I want to be able to write. What a triumph of the human spirit it would be if I could show that a relation-ship could flourish between an American and an Afghan, between a Jew and a Muslim, and especially between a feminist and a misogynist.

I have made it a point of honor to step gingerly around all these dif-ferences, pretending that they are not as important as my commitment to this connection. Abdul-Kareem has done so, too.

Since Abdul-Kareem came back to America, he has always called to see how I am, how my son is, how my family is, and to wish me happy holidays on both Jewish and national occasions. I rarely call him on Muslim holidays.

He remembers me as a young woman; I barely remember myself at that age. He knew my parents, now long dead. He and his wife and children came to my fiftieth birthday party. I have photos of us standing together, smiling; even my mother seems glad to see him.

Abdul-Kareem acted honorably toward me *as an Afghan husband.* I was a virgin, and he married me, and he intended to stay married to me for a lifetime. From his point of view he remained true to our young love; I betrayed it as only a Western woman can.

Why would I cut him out of my life completely?

And yet: What happened in Kabul, coupled with Abdul-Kareem's growing conservatism about women, is now getting in the way of our having an enjoyable time together.

Perhaps Abdul-Kareem sees me as also having become more conser-vative, more of a patriotic American, less a citizen of the world. Maybe he views my feminism as a betrayal of the kind of young woman I once was and whom he once loved.

It is a miracle we can talk to each other at all.

I fought against my captivity in Afghanistan—yet here I am, still talking to my jailer.

The Kabul I once knew and the Kabul that existed from the mid-1960s to the late 1970s, a Westernizing Kabul, is no more and is not likely to return anytime soon. All those who worked toward and instituted a modern constitution were either murdered or driven into exile.

This country, which once held me captive, remains a country and a region in which—incredibly—America is now trapped, just as I once was.

THIRTEEN

America in Afghanistan

My visit with Abdul-Kareem on 9/11/11 saddened me. He was not his usual hospitable self.

We were first torn apart by how Abdul-Kareem mishandled what happened in Kabul. Now feminism seems to be dividing us.

Many people, including Abdul-Kareem, believe that Americans profile Afghans and Muslims for racial reasons. In my view Islam is a religion whose adherents represent all the colors of the human race.

Are Americans prejudiced against Afghans, whether because of 9/11 or because they are Muslims?

Not at all, according to Suraya Sadeed, an Afghan American businesswoman, author (with Damien Lewis) of *Forbidden Lessons in a Kabul Guesthouse,* and the founder of Help the Afghan Children (HTAC). Sadeed was born in 1952 in Kabul, where her father was the governor. They fled the country in 1982, four years after Abdul-Kareem did.

Sadeed began her humanitarian missions to Afghanistan in 1993. She brought blankets, medicine, cash, pencils, food—and walked right into Taliban Hell, where anything and everything was for sale: "Anti-tank missiles, a kilo of heroin, a thirteen-year-old virgin, a contract to assassinate someone."

With daring compassion a naked-faced Sadeed challenged the Taliban fiends who used bayonets to rip up blankets meant for widows and orphans. In the Afghan refugee camps in Pakistan, Sadeed discovered that the camp directors were pimping out widows and their children. Those involved in this heartless operation also sold the food and supplies intended as payment to these women and their families.

By 9/11 Sadeed's organization was out of funds. Afterward she feared that Americans would never send money again. But she sent an e-mail begging for help to the thousands of Americans already in her database. She writes, "Barely a week [after 9/11] we had nearly $500,000 in the HTAC account. All I could think was: *God, America—what a country.*"

I think that Abdul-Kareem (and others who share his point of view) are wrong about Americans' disliking or "racially profiling" Afghans.

After 9/11 other North American and European activists began traveling to Afghanistan. They exposed the plight of Afghan women; worked in prisons, hospitals, and underground schools; trained Afghans as artisans and gemologists; and raised money for supplies. Some went to criticize American military policy, but others went to witness and to serve. Physicians, nurses, educators, beauticians, social workers, filmmakers, feminists, and sympathetic journalists arrived in droves.

Nasrine Gross has been living in America with her American husband for more than forty years; her mother once was a member of the Afghan Parliament. Gross founded a survival gardening project for Afghan women and a literacy project for married Afghan couples. (This was the only way that wives were allowed to attend classes.) I heard Gross speak in New York City a few years after 9/11. She showed a film about her work in Kabul—and she was surrounded by the Americans who support her financially.

The Afghan American doctors Nafisa and Qudrat Mojadidi and their filmmaker daughter, Sediqua Mojadidi, traveled back to Afghanistan in dangerous times to train physicians. Sediqua's important 2007 film about their work is titled *Motherland Afghanistan.*

The Doctors Mojadidi specialize in family planning and obstetrical and gynecological issues, including post-childbirth fistulas. According to the film, 100,000 women in Afghanistan have unhealed fistulas. This means that feces passes through the vagina and that urinary and bowel incontinence or constant soiling occurs. Fistulas may also lead to serious and painful infections. Those afflicted are ashamed and often shunned by their families. Afghanistan also has the highest maternal death rate in the world and the world's second-highest infant mortality rate.

(As I write this I pause. I might have given birth to a stillborn, and I might also have died in childbirth, had I not managed to get out of Kabul.)

According to the Mojadidis, the substandard hospitals in Kabul had literally no medical supplies. The promised American aid had not materialized. But eight hours from Kabul, in a Hazara tribal region, the Mojadidis, who are Hazara in origin themselves, found a clean well-stocked hospital: Dr. Simar Samar's Shuhada (The Female Martyr) Hospital.

Perhaps the most heroic woman is Afghanistan's own Dr. Simar Samar. In her book, *Veiled Threat: The Hidden Power of the Women of Afghanistan,* and in her film, *Daughters of Afghanistan,* Sally Armstrong, a Canadian author and humanitarian, honors Samar. I met Armstrong at her book launch party in New York City. Once again the rooms were filled with pro-Afghan Americans.

Armstrong traveled to Afghanistan in the late 1990s and bore witness to incredible atrocities. She describes a protest organized by women in Herat against Taliban rule. "According to eyewitnesses, the Taliban surrounded the women, seized the leader, doused her in kerosene and burned her alive."

The Taliban guarded the single hospital in Kabul. Female physicians were not allowed to remove a woman's burqa to perform surgery. According to Armstrong, "when one woman arrived with burns to three-quarters of her body, the Taliban allowed no burqa removal. 'If I don't remove the burqa, she will die,' the doctor told the guard. He refused permission. The woman died shortly afterwards."

Against all this stood Samar, who said, "I have three strikes against me. I'm a woman, I speak for women, and I'm Hazara—one of the most persecuted tribes in Afghanistan."

Hazaras are Shi'a, not Sunni, Muslims. The religious war between these two branches of Islam has been—and remains—hot and heartless. Also the Hazaras are considered to be the descendants of the Mongol destroyer Genghis Khan.

Samar is a formidable woman. She rebelled against her family's traditions and attended medical school. Under Soviet rule she opened a medical clinic in Ghazni. Under Taliban rule Samar refused to veil her face. When they told her to close her schools for girls or face death, she replied, "Go ahead and hang me in a public place. Then tell the people my crime: I was giving papers and pencils to girls."

Samar ran a medical clinic in the refugee camps in Quetta, Pakistan, and in Kabul. The Taliban kept threatening her. She said, "You know where I am. I won't stop doing what I am doing." Instead of killing Samar, Taliban members secretly began to bring their mothers and wives to her for care.

Other than through sheer will and character, how did she keep going? Samar *had international support*. She contacted "international women's networks who rallied round," Armstrong reports. "They pressured their governments to channel funds to the Afghan Woman's Ministry," a ministry that Samar headed from 2001 to 2003.

Unfortunately, under President Karzai, the fundamentalists managed to have Samar ousted from her elected position as vice chair of the Loya Jirga (a high-level council of the tribes) and dismissed from the cabinet. They also "called for her execution." Since 2005 Samar has remained chair of the independent Afghanistan Human Rights Commission and a UN Special Rapporteur on Sudan.

Consider the Afghan activist and politician Fawzia Koofi, who has been deputy speaker of the Afghan Parliament since 2005. Koofi has continued to fight on behalf of Afghan women and plans to run for the presidency in 2014. (I'd vote for her if I could.) In her book, *Letters to My Daughters,* she makes it clear that she will not relinquish her political ambitions despite tremendous intimidation and hatred. She writes, "During the latest elections, there were even more threats on my life: gunmen trailing my car, roadside bombs laid along my route, warnings that I would be kidnapped. On the day of voting, two people were arrested who admitted they had planned to kidnap me, take me to a different district and then kill me. They had links to another local politician."

In the summer of 2012 Hanifa Safi, the acting head of women's affairs in eastern Afghanistan, was killed by a bomb that exploded under her car; undaunted, Najla Sediqi took her place. In December of 2012 she was shot to death on her way to work. The bravery of these women is stunning and their executions tragic and infuriating.

Even before 9/11, Americans provided hospitality and informational networks for Afghans who had fled the Soviets. The American author Rosanne Klass, who is the former director of the Afghanistan Information Center at Freedom House, seems to have kept in touch with almost every Afghan she ever met—especially her male students who went on to study abroad and then returned to head academic departments and government bureaus at home. They are now either dead—murdered by the Soviets—or in exile in the West or elsewhere in the world. Klass has remained a motherly friend and networking resource for them all.

The best Western male journalists and Afghan experts (and there are many) have had little to say about Afghan women. As men, and through no fault of their own, they have had no access to them; their otherwise excellent reportage and analyses have failed to understand half the Afghan population—as well as something essential about Afghan men and Afghan society—because these reporters have had no entrée to family life.

Post 9/11, some Western women, including journalists, have had access to Afghan girls and women. Many of these Western women have taught in the underground schools, worked in the hospitals, and visited women in prison. They have done compassionate social work but have not often analyzed Islamist jihad. Thus women's reportage about the tragic plight and extraordinary heroism of Afghan women has also missed an essential part of the story. Ann Marlowe, in countless articles, and Saira Shah, in her book and film, *Beneath the Veil,* are exceptions. They cover gender apartheid but in the context of the larger political, religious, and military issues involved.

In permanent exile my bon vivant former husband has become somewhat bitter—perhaps for good reason. The world—the "international community," as represented by the United Nations—did not and does not really care about Afghanistan.

The Soviets murdered approximately 1.5 to 3 million Afghan civilians and created 5 million refugees who were trapped in refugee camps in Pakistan; millions of Afghan refugees might still be there.

According to an Afghan acquaintance of mine, as of 2013 "at least one and a half million Afghan refugees [were] still festering in these camps." He lived in Kabul during the Soviet invasion and was tortured first by the Soviets, then by the Taliban, and for the same reasons: he spoke English, knew Americans, and his wife worked for an international organization. He beseeched me to understand that the "Taliban is not really an Afghan phenomenon."

"You were there, you lived with us, and you know that Afghans are not like that. This is orchestrated by Saudi Arabia and Pakistan. My son works for the United Nations. Unfortunately he cannot help Afghans."

Ah—the United Nations, that particularly naked emperor.

I have come by my disgust honestly. In 1979–80 I worked for the United Nations. It was an eye-opener. Some male diplomats sexually harassed or assaulted their female employees; some treated their home-country domestics as if they were slaves; many treated their wives in a similar fashion. They partied hard and were glad to be in Manhattan rather than in their impoverished, war-torn, and repressive countries. They were not here to represent the poor of their country but rather to represent its ruling elite.

In 1980 the UN itself claimed there were 1.6 million Palestinian refugees. This included actual refugees as well as their children, grandchildren, and great-grandchildren, most of whom were born and grew up in other Arab countries—countries that systematically denied Palestinians citizenship. But by 1980 *five million* Afghan refugees had been forced out of their country. The UN showed little interest in supporting them. Although Afghans were also Muslims and in grave crisis, there was no anti-America or anti-Israel political mileage to be gained by creating a United Nations Relief and Works Agency (UNRWA) for Afghans, as the UN had done for the Palestinians.

Afghanistan—presently the focus of so much world attention—was essentially deserted by the world in its moment of agony.

During the Taliban years, before 9/11, the plight of Afghan women symbolized our greatest feminist nightmare. The tragedy of Afghan women demanded that we at least draw a verbal line in the sand against such brutal and unapologetic misogyny.

Some American feminists took to the airwaves expressing outrage. They opposed male domination (purdah, polygamy, stoning, forced child marriage, and the like) as symbolized by the dreadful burqa. The burqa became *the* symbol of sexism for American feminists. But the issue of the burqa was hardly paramount to most Afghan women, who were without food, water, electricity, medicine, shelter, personal safety, and all peace of mind. The burqa even gave them some protection from male street harassment.

At the urging of my Afghan family, I published a letter in the *New York Times* to this effect. And anyone who knows my work knows that I oppose the burqa. I even published an academic article that calls for a ban on the burqa in the West.

As I noted previously, the burqa is not religiously mandated. In the past many Muslim countries either banned the burqa or allowed women and their families to choose how women would dress. From a human rights point of view the burqa demoralizes both the wearer and all women who see her: hobbled, hidden, invisible, unable or forbidden to join the social conversation.

Thus I agreed with the early American feminist views about the burqa. However, I feared that Western concepts of women's liberation would gain little traction in what was essentially a medieval, illiterate, impoverished, agricultural, tribal, and highly religious country, one that had now been bombed back many centuries by the Soviets and further colonized, bribed, and terrorized by the most fanatic Islamists.

In the past I had criticized some Western feminist groups for their simplistic feminism, self-aggrandizement, anti-Americanism, and wrong-headed optimism. I also shared Abdul-Kareem's feelings that Afghanistan had become a symbolic pawn in people's dramas and that the do-gooders' own operating expenses were bound to eat up most of the monies they raised—even before corrupt Afghan middlemen demanded their share of the take.

Allow me to apologize to these feminists here and now. At least they tried to do something.

For a time the Revolutionary Association of Women of Afghanistan (RAWA) was the favored group among certain feminists. Association members once had a speaking engagement in New York City. A long line snaked around the Judson Memorial Church in Greenwich Village to hear them. People were being turned away. As I turned to leave, my companion, Kate Millett, stood her ground and forcefully thundered, "Do you know who she is? This is Phyllis Chesler, and I am Kate Millett, and we have to get in." I was mortified, but Millett's audacity worked. The crowd parted for us—just like the Red Sea.

But the RAWA representatives were so young and so shy. They did their best; under the circumstances they could do no wrong. And yet—the Soviets had already tried a Marxist approach to women's liberation in Afghanistan. Resistance to that canny imperial attempt has so far led to more than thirty years of fighting with no end in sight. RAWA's message was far more popular on the American feminist left than in Kabul or Kandahar.

Some organizations have been effective in their efforts on behalf of individual Afghan women. Sunita Viswanath, a cofounder and board member of Women for Afghan Women (WAW), has rescued women in Afghanistan who have been brutally attacked. Viswanath mentioned one case, that of a girl named Mumtaz, who has recently received press attention. She was "sprayed with acid and had burns over 42 percent of her body because she refused a marriage proposal. Thanks to the graciousness of the Indian government and to generous funding from individuals, WAW was able to send her to India for treatment." According to

Viswanath, "We are committed to a grassroots approach to addressing Afghan women's human rights. We work closely with mosques, schools and other trusted community institutions, and we have developed excellent working relationships with government ministries, police and courts. As we have expanded to eight [now nine] provinces in Afghanistan, there has never been a province or community that hasn't welcomed us."

Similarly the Afghan Women's Fund, which is headed by Fahima Vorgetts, has established microfinancing projects and provided Afghan village girls with an education.

The plight of Afghan women and children troubles me deeply. I do not believe that Western feminists or activists will be able to bring about a gender-egalitarian state in Afghanistan—but I praise them for exposing the realities of gender apartheid and for trying to save individual Afghans. They are doing God's work.

I only wish that such well-intentioned feminists also understood that certain tragedies cannot be reversed through social work and education; that traditional Afghan mullahs and their followers will resist, unto death, women's freedom; and that the Afghans themselves have to choose modernization. It cannot be imposed by imperial or infidel powers.

Ironically, like the American feminists, whom he loves to criticize, Abdul-Kareem once tried to make a difference. He too was part of a group of high-minded dreamers and progressives whose accomplishments were swept away.

Can Westerners or infidels abolish misogynistic barbarism in Afghanistan, Pakistan, or Iran—and in an Islamist era? Sometimes I fear that raising women's expectations only leads vulnerable women to have unrealistic hopes that doom them to early and violent deaths or to very unhappy lives. But I strongly believe in universal human rights and reject all cultural relativism as racist and sexist. I cannot hold one standard for Western women and another, lower standard for Afghan or Muslim women and men.

But if I cannot reach Abdul-Kareem on the issue of women—and he is an educated, secular, assimilated, Afghan *American*—how can anyone hope to reach men who are uneducated and fanatically religious—and who live in Afghanistan?

As I've said, Abdul-Kareem reads the news for hours every day. Yet he claims to know nothing about any Afghan's committing an honor killing in the West. I mention a high-profile case that has dominated the world press for many months. He says he knows nothing about it.

"Abdul-Kareem, the killers are Afghans, the victims are Afghans, too. The victims are all Muslims. Are you sure you've read nothing about them?"

"Not a word. Not that interested."

I am referring to a Canadian honor-killing case. Mohammed Shafia, a wealthy and polygamous fifty-nine-year-old Afghan father, murdered his three biological daughters and his infertile first wife. His second wife, who was the biological mother of the three daughters, and their biological son, helped him do it. The murders took place at the Rideau Canal, near Montreal.

According to Canadian reporter Christie Blatchford's account of eyewitness testimony, Mohammed Shafia ran his family like a "totalitarian regime." The children were taught to spy on each other and parental or paternal permission was needed "for anything beyond breathing, and the girls were virtually under guard." An uncle said that the women lived "like political prisoners."

What crime did they commit? They wanted to wear Western clothing and have Canadian (infidel) friends. One daughter wanted to marry a Pakistani man who was deemed inappropriate. Shafia's first wife supported the daughters.

On the stand Shafia sobbed when he spoke of his daughters. Shafia "attempted to paint a picture of himself as a loving, liberal-minded, generous patriarch—a bit of a free spirit even, prone to handing out money and kisses—whose only wish for his children was happiness."

But the police caught Shafia on tape cursing his dead daughters and describing them as whores, adding, "May the devil shit on their graves!" When challenged about this, he claimed that the expression is merely an old, harmless, and meaningless Kabul refrain.

Shafia was also recorded saying that "they betrayed and violated us immensely. There can be no betrayal, no treachery, no violation more than this—by God!" When asked in court if he had killed his daughters and his first wife, Shafia answered, "We never give ourselves permission to do that. Our Koran would not allow ourselves to do that." He also said, "How could someone do that?"

In 2012 all three Shafias were found guilty on four counts of first-degree murder each, and each was sentenced to life without possibility of parole for twenty-five years—Canada's maximum sentence. In other words they were sentenced to about six years for each murder. In 2012 Mohammed and Hamed Shafia, his son, filed notices of appeal based on alleged judicial errors. Tooba Yaya, his second wife, is also expected to appeal her verdict.

Mohammed Shafia lived in the West, but he still followed Afghan tribal law, not Canadian law. In Afghanistan there would have been no arrest, trial, or discussion. Even in the postfeminist twenty-first century, in the West, for certain kinds of Afghan men, their women remain their property, to dispose of as they wish.

Abdul-Kareem has consistently denied that such killings ever took place in Afghanistan. Not when he was there, not that he knows about.

But even while I was in captivity, I was told that men had the right to kill their wives, daughters, and sisters. A female relative and a foreign wife both whispered this to me. You can imagine my disbelief and my terror. Another female relative praised a man because, although his wife had behaved badly, he had not exercised this right. I also heard stories about women who killed themselves for no apparent reason and in ways that seemed suspicious.

These are stories one does not forget.

Imagine what it might be like to grow up knowing that, if you disobey or accidentally fail even slightly to do exactly what is expected of you, your own family members might suddenly kill you. Imagine the psychological makeup of Muslim, Hindu, and Sikh girls who come from families that believe honor killing is a necessary and acceptable practice. The consequent psychological insecurity, anxiety, paranoia, self-monitoring, vigilance, and aggression toward other women are unimaginable.

An honor killings differs from Western domestic violence. It is a carefully planned conspiracy on the part of one's own family of origin to murder a daughter. Hindus perpetrate such heinous murders but only in India and mainly for caste-related violations; Muslims do so both in Muslim-majority countries and in the West—and for the slightest female disobedience, either real or imagined. Although older, married mothers are also honor murdered, the victims of a classic honor killing are teenagers or young women. Their murderers are valorized and glorified, not arrested, tried, and sentenced.

In 2009, 2010, and 2012, I published studies of honor killings. From that moment on, women who had escaped being honor killed and their immigration lawyers began turning to me for help as an expert witness in their asylum cases. Muslim feminists reached out to thank me.

But talking to many of my non-Muslim Western feminist friends was as frustrating as talking to Abdul-Kareem. They feared that my research would be used by racists to target Muslims. Even those feminists who despised the burqa initially failed to oppose honor killings because for them too racism continued to trump sexism—even femicide, even human sacrifice.

I have nevertheless continued to reach out to all feminists *because they run the shelters for battered women* in America and Canada. For example, when Seyran Ates, a Muslim Turkish lawyer from Berlin, came to stay with me, I suggested that we meet the director of a shelter for battered women. Seyran (whom I have mentioned before) was eager to do so. Seyran is a lawyer who was nearly murdered for her work with battered Muslim immigrant women: A fifteen-year-old client of hers *was* murdered in Seyran's office. Seyran was also shot and nearly died.

Everyone in the shelter office is welcoming, excited to meet with both of us. But when *Seyran* tries to explain how an honor killing is different from Westernized domestic violence, the director (who is a smart, warm, and fiercely passionate feminist) does not agree.

"There are honor killings in Brazil due to machismo, and they get off with light sentences. I don't see why Islam should be targeted or why our concerns should be with Muslim honor killings. Look around. There are so many women here who have been savagely battered to within an inch of their lives. They come from all backgrounds. Recently I was able to rescue a Muslim woman because her mullah and her brother stepped in and helped me."

Both Seyran and I tried again to explain why battered women's shelters in the West had to understand the difference between an honor killing and Western domestic violence. I said, "In Toronto a shelter worker sent a seventeen-year-old girl, Aqsa Parvez, home when her mother called, crying, to say she missed her. Within hours the girl was dead; her father and her brother killed her. What was her crime? She did not want to wear hijab. Certain kinds of Muslim families in the West are not the same as Christian, Hindu, Sikh, or Jewish families in the West. This must be understood if we want to help the girls save their own lives. An American-born non-Muslim battered woman may have her husband after her. Her Muslim counterpart may have her mother, father, sister, brother, uncles, grandfather, cousins, and husband all after her. She may require the equivalent of a federal witness protection program and a Muslim adoptive family."

Seyran quickly backed me up.

"German fathers don't routinely batter their teenage daughters or kill them, either. German brothers do not monitor and micromanage their sisters' behavior the way Turkish or North African brothers do in Europe. Even a violent German family is not as violent as a violent Muslim family. I am a religious Muslim. I am not proud of these terrible behaviors. My family is not like this. I believe that the good Muslims must speak out."

Everyone smiles a lot, but we get nowhere at this time. I would have to be obsessed with this subject in order to make even the slightest bit of difference.

Abdul-Kareem may hold views with which I disagree, but he is now a white-haired man in his late seventies who walks slowly and carefully. Like me, he has fallen, broken bones, endured surgeries. He is his invalid wife's caretaker.

Their grown children also take care of their parents. Their daughter, Jameela, lives at home; their son, Mansour, is there every weekend. They are *Afghan* adult children and are used to spending time with their parents, whom they will never desert. They bring their friends home with them. This is truly a civilized and enviable custom.

Abdul-Kareem and Kamile have, commendably, raised completely assimilated children. Both are secular, chic, and successful. Abdul-Kareem is safe in America, and I am glad of it—but his dreams have all turned to dust. This is the one subject we never discuss. The destruction of his country destroyed his career and ended his life as an honored and progressive Afghan.

I am glad that he got out before the full Soviet military invasion and long before the Taliban started their savage reign against women, before the Taliban began their cross-amputations with the grisly public displays of severed limbs, and before they began publicly stoning women to death. In short, Abdul-Kareem got out before the Taliban implemented Sharia law.

Abdul-Kareem has only one brief and grainy video of a garden party that his family gave on a sunny afternoon in Kabul many years ago. I have watched it with him a number of times. His children wave as they splash in the swimming pool; guests hold drinks and cigarettes. He has no photo albums. He does not even own a copy of the film that he wrote and directed.

I have known him for fifty-four years. Can this single relationship shed a useful light on the relationship between Americans and Afghans or between the West and the increasingly Islamist East?

Is my unexpected captivity in Kabul something of a cautionary tale about what can happen to any Westerner who believes she can enjoy a Western or modern life in a Muslim country?

In terms of Afghanistan here's the question: Can a tribal, religious, impoverished, corrupt people, beaten down by war and without an industrial infrastructure; a country with a strong warrior and anti-infidel tradition; a country theologically and geographically vulnerable to al-Qaeda and other Islamist groups become modern and Western? Can infidel Westerners help them to do so? Especially when the West is in the grip of an economic crisis and when we are despised and murdered for trying to help?

What are some of the hard lessons that I've been privileged to learn?

FOURTEEN

Hard Lessons

s soon as we arrived in Kabul, my Westernized husband became another person—one whom I had never before met. Thus I learned that even a well-read scholarship student can be easily fooled by the man she loves and that a man who can easily pass as a Westerner in the West can just as easily revert to Eastern ways when he returns home.

At a young age I understood how little in life is personal. We may experience everything as if it is, but this is not necessarily true. My husband's betrayal was not *personal*. It was cultural. He merely treated me as an Afghan wife, not as an American college student with serious intellectual and artistic aspirations.

Abdul-Kareem had no personal animosity toward me—he loved me—but because I was a woman, he could not show me any affection in Afghanistan. He had to behave the way his father and brothers and countrymen behaved toward women.

I was young and arrogant—that is the Jewish American author and descendent of Egyptian Jews, Lucette Lagnado's, apt phrase for her younger self. I had expected to be treated like a queen. Imagine the shock to my pride and innocence. I would soon have to wage a struggle for my very existence in a psychologically wounded state.

I learned that my immune system was not invincible. I never fully recovered from hepatitis. Secretly it weakened me, rendered me vulnerable to a lifetime of subsequent illnesses. Afghanistan had humbled my mortal frame forever.

Perhaps this was a small price to pay. After all I had briefly slept in the arms of ancient history in a city that is more than 3,500 years old. People had been farming and raising animals there since the dawn of recorded history; by the sixth century BCE the region already boasted thousands of cities, royal courts, famed artists, poets, and religious mystics.

At the time I knew nothing about this history, nor did most Afghans. Thus I learned that most Eastern peoples do not necessarily treasure or resurrect their past. People constantly revise history. They build their houses of worship right over their predecessor's, or enemy's, houses of worship and then wipe out all traces of what came before. I learned to value the search for origins: one's own and those of the entire world.

I learned the importance of research. When I blindly, stubbornly followed Abdul-Kareem back to Afghanistan, I had not carefully researched the country. I did not seek out other American wives of Afghan men. I was not suspicious. I was ambitious; I wanted to have an adventure. I did not take marriage seriously. I took books seriously. I thought I would triumph, no matter what adversity I might face.

I learned that being a woman placed me at a great disadvantage. I had never thought of it this way. After Kabul this way of thinking continued to make sense to me.

I learned that, like women everywhere, Afghan women have also internalized the sexism that legitimizes their own mistreatment. Oppressed daughters and oppressed wives in turn oppress their daughters and daughters-in-law and their female servants. This helped me to see variations on this theme in the West and globally. In 2002, after twenty years of research, I published a book about this long-denied, and at the time still-controversial, subject. The title? *Woman's Inhumanity to Woman.*

I learned that people take what they want without understanding the consequences of their actions, without caring whom they hurt along the way. Both Abdul-Kareem and I did this. I broke my family's heart. Abdul-Kareem offended and perhaps endangered his family and himself by a love marriage to a Jewish American. We hurt each other deeply.

As a Jew and a woman, I was drawn to Abdul-Kareem's marginality *in the West.* I identified with it and thought it made us kindred spirits. I was wrong.

After Kabul—long after Kabul—I read Betty Mahmoody's riveting book, *Not Without My Daughter,* in which she describes how her Westernized Iranian physician-husband unexpectedly trapped her in Iran under hostile conditions and held her there against her will. Betty finally escaped with her daughter, Mahtob—and a wild and dramatic tale it is. But the story did not end there.

In 1991 Betty's husband, Sayyed Bozorg Mahmoody ("Moody"), released his own film, *Without My Daughter*, in which he rebutted each of Betty's points. On camera he says, "My only sin is [in] loving my daughter, my only child. Betty knows she has done me wrong. She has wronged all Iranians." He then goes on to blame his loss on the CIA, Zionism, and Betty's desire to get rich by telling sensational lies.

I suppose Abdul-Kareem can now write his own book about his difficult and faithless American wife who caused him great suffering. Perhaps I did, perhaps that is true.

I thought Abdul-Kareem was worldly and understood everything. I was wrong. He minimized the dangerous reality of Afghan history and customs, especially gender apartheid and Sharia law. He failed to understand that a hard and radical Islamism might rise again.

In 2008, I interviewed a prominent Egyptian businessman who was the first Arab chair of a global oil company and the founder and chair of a Middle Eastern oil company. He is also a prolific writer and human rights activist. The following year this man called me, weeping. His childhood city of Port Said was no more.

"The women are wearing black sheets down to the ground, and loudspeakers are blaring hate from every mosque. Believe me, this was such a cosmopolitan city, there were people of all religions and from so many countries here. I am afraid of what is coming."

Indeed by 2012 the Muslim Brotherhood had come to power legally. Even as I write, the Brotherhood has taken over the military, the media, and the judiciary; an Islamist constitution has been passed. For some time now women have been wearing black hijab and, increasingly, face masks (niqab) in most Egyptian cities, including Cairo.

And now, Egyptian military nationalists have taken over and imprisoned many Muslim Brotherhood leaders. Protests continue.

I wonder how my business friend is now. I wonder how all Egypt is as the Muslim Brotherhood and the Salafists battle to retake the country and to abolish women's rights, human rights, and freedom of expression.

In 2005, I delivered a keynote speech at a feminist conference. The moment I stopped speaking, the first woman on her feet was someone with whom I once worked; she was a friendly colleague. She insisted that both Iraq and Afghanistan would have been better off as communist and secular countries, that women's lives would have been better.

"Oh," I say, "Women seemed to have more freedom. But what about the Iraqi women who were raped to death by Saddam Hussein's goons or the Afghan men and women who were jailed and tortured by the Soviets? What about the Kurds Saddam Hussein killed with poison gas?"

"Look," she argued. "Whatever is wrong with those countries was caused by us. First the West went and colonized the world, and then it made crooked deals with tyrants or just invaded it again for oil. Admit it. The West has ruined the developing world."

I will not admit this because it is not exactly true. The gender and religious apartheid I encountered in Kabul is indigenous to the region; it was not caused by Western imperialism, colonialism, capitalism, racism, or military occupation. And Islamist dictators may be far more dangerous than nonideological dictators.

But she may also have a point.

In 2012, I am talking to a man from Libya. Like so many exiles from the Islamic world—and like the Russian aristocrats in Paris before them—he is driving me in his limousine. He is a trim, relatively young, and good-looking man. I open the conversation.

"What a disaster in the Middle East! The world stands by, the tyrants attack their own people, the Islamists pile on, and the people die."

He takes off his sunglasses, turns around, and looks at me.

"Madam," he says, "I blame the media and the Internet. They are driving the tragedy. Let me ask you something. Do you believe that the Tunisian man who set himself on fire is the real cause of the Arab Spring? No, he was not normal, maybe he was on drugs. Everywhere people suffer but they do not set themselves on fire. The media coverage: Al Jazeera, CNN, have encouraged radicals, al-Qaeda. Now they are everywhere."

He pronounces al-Qaeda in Arabic. I say, "I thought the Tunisian man's ultimate humiliation—being insulted and slapped by a woman police officer—was the final straw."

"He is not important. Qaddafi was a hard man, maybe a crazy man, but he kept al-Qaeda out of Libya. Now Libyan women are not safe. They cannot go out. No one is safe. They are kidnapped and their families are forced to pay money for their lives. After Mubarak, Egypt went radical too, just like Syria will once Assad is gone. Al-Qaeda and other groups like them are all over the place."

"Are you saying that Arabs need a ruthless dictator in order to stop more extreme criminal forces—Muslim radicals—from taking over? You mentioned women. What if you were one of the women or men whom Qaddafi's men plucked off the streets to rape and murder?"

"You are right," he says. "But that does not compare to the much greater suffering the people are undergoing now without their strong leaders."

His English is good, his nails are carefully manicured, it is clear that he has traveled throughout the Arab world. Perhaps he once held an important position under Qaddafi.

I fear he may have a point. If so, America's past support for such dictators was not absolutely wrong. And America's current hands-off policy as radical extremists take down or profit from a people's genuine desire for freedom may not be absolutely right. Refusing to recognize the Green democrats in Iran was wrong, as is America's current policy of recognizing Islamist coalitions. I add, "The UN is useless, and America does not have the financial means or the political will to take on the policeman's role in the entire Arab and Muslim world. Either the people themselves will have to do it—and they have really tried and failed to do this in Iran—or they will suffer a terrible fate under the Islamists. Unless there is a miracle, I fear this tragedy will last for a long while. I am so sorry."

I say this expressly to offer my condolences to him on the loss of his country and the suffering of both his family and his religious compatriots.

In turn in classic Arab fashion he must also comfort me. He says, "Madam, there is always hope. One must always have hope."

But the information is in. Islamists want to turn the global clock back to the seventh century. The Afghan Taliban would rather their children die of polio than be inoculated against it. The Pakistani Taliban are shooting young girls in the head for attending school. As I have written many times, and as Leon Wieseltier has recently said, "The struggle for gender equality is the campaign against totalitarianism." One cannot reason with evil; one must defeat it.

Between 2009 and 2010 eighty-five humanitarian workers were murdered in Afghanistan. In July 2004 Doctors Without Borders recalled all their physicians after the Taliban killed five of the organization's doctors. As I write this, Afghan soldiers being trained by American soldiers to replace them are murdering their American teachers and then either blowing themselves up or hiding among the Taliban and al-Qaeda.

The American army has proposed giving soldiers a handbook that includes a list of taboo conversation topics. Americans in combat must avoid "making derogatory comments about the Taliban," "advocating women's rights," "any criticism of paedophilia," "mentioning homo-sexuality and homosexual conduct," or saying "anything related to Islam."

How can Afghan men who never fail to impress foreign visitors as sweet and funny and humble—men who giggle so girlishly—nevertheless treat women and young children so cruelly? So many Afghan men I have met were modest people, not monsters; they were simple, kindhearted, and eager to please. They loved a good joke. They accepted their fate as part of God's plan for them.

These men believe in God—yet they think that women, who are also created by God, are subhuman, nonhuman: property that must be jealously guarded, fields that must be continuously plowed. Can they be educated to think otherwise? In 2007, after Abdul-Kareem visited Kabul for the last time, he said this:

> It was a terrible, terrible experience. The country has fallen apart, it was worse than I expected. There is no electricity, no roads, and no water. One can't breathe the air or eat the food. It took me a quarter of a million dollars in bribes to get my deal finalized. It is corrupt, from the very top to the bottom. There are lots of massage parlors and prostitutes. I saw only turmoil, with no future. Everyone is paying lip service in terms of women's rights, but no one is helping. By the way— why has no one ever seen Karzai's wife? Why does he hide her? Even on International Women's Day she was nowhere to be found.

I am cheered by Abdul-Kareem's sudden concern for the ladies.

But he is right about the country's corruption. According to the *New York Times,* in 2013, the Kabul bank turned out to be a nine hundred billion dollar Ponzi scheme. Revenge drove Sherkhan Farnood, one of the bank's founders, to turn on his co-conspirators before they could turn on him. Those who had purchased villas in Dubai received minimal sentences; those who did not know what was going on received long prison terms.

Ah, and what about the women in Afghanistan? As a feminist can I just abandon them to their fate without a backward glance?

The British Afghan author Saira Shah belongs to a distinguished family of writers; her father is Idries Shah, her brother is Tahir Shah. They are all the descendants of Afghan warriors and diplomats and the Scottish writer Elizabeth Luiza MacKenzie, aka Morag Murray

Abdullah. Saira Shah traveled to Afghanistan in the 1980s and 1990s. In *The Storyteller's Daughter* she recounts what she saw in the 1990s: "People were starving. One woman crept out in a lull in the fighting. She was caught by a gang of former mujahidin and raped by twenty-two men for three days. Finally, she staggered home to discover that her children had died of hypothermia. . . . Bodies and body parts turned up everywhere in Kabul—stuffed down wells, in brick kilns, in abandoned buildings. At the Institute for Social Sciences, a group of armed men raped and killed sixty women."

Western feminists and journalists, both men and women, continue to cry out against the savage mistreatment of Afghan women—outraged by the chopped-off noses and ears, the acid-disfigured faces, the torture and murders in the name of honor. Paradoxically this signals that, despite years of being taught that everything is culturally relative, Westerners still understand that women's rights should be universal. People everywhere are offended, perhaps even threatened, by how women are being treated in Afghanistan.

Afghan (like Pakistani) girls are given in marriage to violent older men who already have a wife or two. In protest and in despair young girls are setting themselves on fire. Unlike the self-immolation of the Tunisian vendor, which presumably set off the wintry Arab Spring, the drastic and terrible actions of these young girls have had no ripple effect.

In Afghanistan in-laws confined a daughter-in-law to the basement, where they tortured her for months in order to force her into prostitution. Recently an Afghan mother-in-law beheaded her daughter-in-law for refusing to become a prostitute.

In 2010 *Time* magazine put beautiful but noseless eighteen-year-old Bibi Aisha on its cover—a poster girl for atrocities against Afghan women. With the help of the Taliban her husband, father-in-law, and other family members had chopped off her nose and ears. Women for Afghan Women sprang into action. They offered this young woman asylum, surgical repairs, and psychiatric treatment. The do-gooders soon ran into posttraumatic stress symptoms that are somewhat off our Western charts.

But she is only one of millions of Afghan, and other central and east Asian, Indian, and Arab women in similar distress. Can we relocate them all? Or fund a Marshall Plan to educate Islamists about human rights—really?

While I praise the courage that has led so many Westerners to try to help Afghans survive day by day, I am also frustrated beyond measure that so many of these humanitarians continue to blame America and the West, and refuse to understand the realities of indigenous gender and religious apartheid and the totalitarian evil we are facing.

In my opinion America should not have stayed on in Afghanistan. I also thought that America should have cut into the enormous Saudi funding of worldwide propaganda and terrorism by either refusing to buy Saudi oil, taking over their oilfields, or investing in other sources of energy. I have been saying this for nearly a decade. The West has funded the war against itself by buying Arab oil. It is as simple and as tragic as that.

Still, I am also shaken by the inability of many people to understand that evil and injustice truly exist and that one cannot win every single battle against them. I am even more shaken by the refusal of educated and progressive Americans to understand that the concept of a global caliphate is fueling thousands of Islamist terrorists, all of whom have explosives and some of whom have nuclear weapons.

We are infidels, and as such our help is feared and despised. The author Rajiv Chandrasekaran tells the story of a farmer who observed American do-gooders at work back in the 1950s, when Afghans and Americans were optimistically engaged in the Helmand River Project. The farmer had a "strange expression on his face." When Dr. Abdul Kayeum, the head of the project, questioned him, here is what he said: "'As I looked at the Americans the thought came to [me] that the land upon which they were standing was cursed because the infidel had touched the land' . . . the farmer predicted that within twenty years, the entire Helmand Valley would be a wasteland because of the tinkering of the infidels."

*I*n the context of this anti-infidel history, can Americans save the women and girls of Afghanistan?

No, I fear we cannot. This pains me but passion must yield to reason. Yes, we can and should rescue girls and women one by one and relocate them either within Afghanistan or externally; some groups are doing this. But we cannot rescue every woman in Afghanistan—or stem the tide of Islamist violence against civilians everywhere, not only in Afghanistan, without first defeating the Islamists ideologically, politically, economically, and militarily.

Are we our sisters' keepers? Yes, we are—theoretically, morally. But we cannot keep trying to do something that cannot be done. As outsiders we cannot save anyone so far away; indeed we cannot seem to save girls from honor-related violence right here in the West.

There are many things we must and are beginning to do—in the *West*. Honor killings are being prosecuted here and long or life sentences are being handed down. However, America lags behind Canada and Europe in terms of arresting collaborators or accomplices, who are often women as well as men. We have not yet committed the resources necessary to rescue women who are at risk of being slain in an honor killing in America or who seek asylum here for this reason.

Honor-related violence and gender apartheid are human rights violations and cannot be justified in the name of cultural relativism, tolerance, antiracism, diversity, religious custom, or political correctness.

The battle for women's rights is central to the battle for a Judeo-Christian, post-Enlightenment civilization. It is a necessary part of Western democracy, along with gay and lesbian rights, and freedom of speech, religion, and dissent. Here, then, is exactly where the greatest battle of the twenty-first century is joined.

In 2002 Rory Stewart, an author and member of the British Parliament, walked on foot from Herat to Kabul; he wrote a wonderful book about his travels, *The Places in Between*. Stewart has said, many times, "Instead of pursuing an Afghan policy for existential reasons—doing 'whatever it takes' and 'whatever it costs'—we should accept that there is a limit on what we can do. And we don't have a moral obligation to do what we cannot do." In 2012 Stewart wrote, "Foreigners have not forged a political solution, and now can't."

Formerly progressive cities like Teheran, Beirut, Istanbul, Damascus, and Cairo (Kabul too, from 1964 to 1980) have fallen into Islamist hands. Everywhere women are veiled, men are wearing beards, the press is censored, propaganda rules the airwaves, torture is rampant, Islamist Muslims are killing both infidels and, mainly, other Muslims; the body count remains fearfully high.

What, if anything, do I owe Afghanistan, a country where I once lived and where I nearly died? I was there. It remains a part of me. I am now a tiny part of the country's history. I remember Kabul, Istalif, Paghman, and the Pamir mountains with love. I remember my Afghan family. I will never forget my time there, the people I met, the natural splendor that I at least glimpsed.

This is an accounting of sorts. A young Jewish American woman once came to this wondrous Asiatic country and fled harem life. She finally uncovered the history of what happened to the Jews of Afghanistan, and she has told their story in order to redeem her soul. A young Jewish American woman once loved a Muslim Afghan man, and although it could never work out, they continued talking to each other down through the decades of their lives.

Each time I see him I vow to never do so again. Then, whenever he calls, we make a plan to meet.

It is more than fifty years since we first met, and Abdul-Kareem and I are sitting in a Jewish delicatessen on the Upper West Side, near one of the many summer or winter break sublets we once lived in so long ago. We are there because Abdul-Kareem said he was "just dying for a good Jewish pastrami on rye" and suggested we go to Fine and Schapiro's.

Like his father before him, he cuts a rather dapper figure. His hair is still thick, but it is now entirely white, he sports a fashionable moustache, wears an expensive watch, and carries a polished wood-topped cane. He still wears dark glasses that match his black turtleneck sweater, black suit, black cashmere coat.

I ask, "So how are you today?"

He answers, "I'm glad you asked me that question. Do you remember Minister A? You know, the one who flew me to Cumballa Hill in Bombay—the view was fantastic, divine—to consult on that cultural project? Anyway I recently got a call from one of his nephews."

Abdul-Kareem takes the long road toward every subject because along the way he must tell me about the ambassadors, presidents, film stars, prime ministers, royalty, and film directors he has met in his world travels, all of whom have shown him the greatest courtesy, sent embassy cars, arranged sumptuous dinners, seated him next to the most important people at every banquet.

Oh, the villas, palaces, hotels, fountains, gardens, feasts, and parties he has known! He never speaks without making sure his listener knows that he has moved in circles of power, among celebrities, heads of states, great artists, and beautiful women. He is a man of many peak moments.

What he says may be true. He says he knows all the major filmmakers. Perhaps he does. Perhaps this is how he manages to endure being in exile: by hugging all his former glories close. He has no country, no summer and winter villas, no working farms, no chauffeur, no gardener, no houseboys—no Ministry post left.

To hear Abdul-Kareem tell it, only he has the solution for Afghanistan. If America-which-funded-the-Taliban gets out, stops supporting Karzai-the-damn-drug-lord; if America forces Pakistan-which-also-funded-and-trained-the-Taliban to also get out and forces Pakistan to close the permeable border across which fresh Arab- and Pakistani-trained terrorists enter; if the Chinese are allowed to invest in Afghan gas and minerals (Afghanistan may have as much or even more oil than Saudi Arabia, if it can be mined and transported), then Afghanistan can climb up out of the Middle Ages and take its rightful place among the nations of wealth and so on.

Abdul-Kareem loves America, but he has high standards for us. I think he expected his adopted country to rescue, not abandon, his country of origin and then not just pile on for its own purposes.

I listen. I keep listening. I finally say, as I always do, "If you have a solution, why not write an op-ed piece, write a long article? I will help you in any way I can."

He resists. He says he is not a writer. He says that he has too much to say. He says that were his views known, he might get in trouble. We have had this same conversation for more than thirty years now. Perhaps he is right. I suggest he publish anonymously. I tell him that Muslim and ex-Muslim friends of mine do just that. He asks me whether we can share a byline. As usual I agree. But nothing ever comes of it.

"Why not at least write up your family and personal memories for your grown children so that they will know their ancestry, their heritage?" I suggest.

"Well," he softens. "Maybe for them, I might do it for them."

Abdul-Kareem does not need me to speak. He needs me only to listen, and he allows his much-relished sandwich to just sit there, uneaten, for nearly an hour. I finally break into the monologue.

For the first time I ask him why he thought that someone like me could ever have adjusted to life in Afghanistan. He responds by telling me what a great life Kamile, his second wife had, the ambassadors, prime ministers, royalty, and film stars that she too met—"and she also worked." He then says something new and astounding.

"I had hoped that you would be as ambitious as I was, that you would see the promise, the hope, the challenge involved in helping this small country progress, become modern, independent."

"Are you saying that I am not ambitious?"

"Yes. I am. You were young, you did not yet know what you wanted to do, and you turned tail and ran home. So you did end up writing a few books for a small circle of people. But that does not compare to what I had envisioned for us."

He still views his dream of modernizing one small country as more noble than my dream of freedom for women. I am stunned that he still views me as the wife who failed him—not as the feminist who got away. I was meant to help him realize his dreams. Poor man: He cannot acknowledge that I would have sacrificed myself in vain for a dream not my own—one that even he was unable to accomplish.

Perhaps another kind of woman might have flourished as the wife of an Afghan deputy minister and theater director. I am not that kind of woman. He is blind to—perhaps he despises—who I am and what I have accomplished.

I have not been able to achieve my dream of freedom for all women; but that vision is fully underway in the world. It is a work in process. Also, it was not my destiny to remain in Kabul, to set down roots only to see them destroyed by the Soviets and by the Taliban.

Yes, he is both larger and smaller than I imagined him to be. He is stubborn, selfish, and given to monologues, but he is also courtly, gracious, and strong. Through him I gained an unsentimental education, the kind that cannot be acquired through books.

As I've said, my fiery American feminism was really forged in Afghanistan.

Abdul-Kareem turned out to be one of my muses, as did Afghanistan itself. I have turned my brief sojourn—and my subsequent lifelong interest in the Islamic world—into a writer's treasure.

I experienced what it was like to live with people who were permanently afraid of what other people might think—even more so than in Small Mind Town, USA. I knew there were political prisoners and torture chambers in Afghanistan. I knew that Afghans who wanted any progress were arrested and punished in medieval ways.

Therefore I became an intellectual who views conformity and censorship as dangerous; one who deeply appreciates the importance of dissent, a free press, the First Amendment, and the separation of religion and state as crucial to any democracy and to woman's freedom.

Did I ever love him? How would I know? I was a virgin in this matter as well. But writing this book has put me in touch with the long-buried tenderness that I still feel for him—especially now that he has become a character in these pages.

I could not live with him. But what's that got to do with love?

It is a privilege to know someone this long, a man who comes from a far-distant country and culture, someone who still regularly calls me to see how I am and to tell me his family news.

I am still the first wife. As he said, he does not believe in divorce. We remain connected in our own unspoken ways.

Acknowledgments

and Dedication

I thank Karen Wolny, my editor at Palgrave, who has been impressively enthusiastic, editorially deft, and tremendously responsive. I am privileged to have found such an editor. The entire Palgrave team has been an incredible asset to this book: Christine Catarino, Donna Cherry, Lauren Dwyer, Polly Kummel, Lauren LoPinto, and David Rotstein. I also wish to acknowledge Mark Lerner and his wise counsel.

I believe I was guided to my literary agent "from above"—Jane Dystel, of Dystel and Goderich, has been fiercely devoted to bringing this, and many of my other books, to life. I am grateful for her invaluable support and guidance. I thank Miriam Goderich, who believed in this book immediately and passionately. I have likewise benefited enormously from the encouragement and expertise of my publicity team at Goldberg-McDuffie: Lynn Goldberg, Angela Baggetta, Jeff Umbro, and Kathleen C. Zrelack.

My research assistant, Adriann Agle, first came to me as an intern from Barnard. Her work was spectacular, I inevitably hired her; without her intellectual skills, "can-do" disposition, discipline, devotion, and maturity, this book could not have been written. I owe her a great debt of gratitude.

I am deeply indebted to those who funded my work both for this book and my work on honor-related violence, including honor killings: Susan L. Bender, Esq., Abigail L. Rosenthal, Bruce Stevens, Cornelia Foster

Wood, the Middle East Forum Education Fund, and those funders who prefer to remain anonymous. I thank "JB" for her political friendship.

Many travelers and authors, some long dead, others very much alive, have helped me gain precious knowledge about Central Asia, Afghanistan, and the Islamic world. They are credited in the bibliography. Those who have become friends, whose words, views, and life stories have become intertwined with mine, are especially dear to me. They know who they are.

I also thank the Columbia Universities Libraries for their excellent collections; Rosanne Klass for her generosity and her knowledge of and love for Afghanistan; and Roy Abraham and Sara Y. Aharon for introducing me to the history of the Jews and Hindus of Afghanistan.

I must acknowledge my internist, Dr. Tina Dobsevage, for her tender, professional care; when necessary, she even makes house calls. On that same note, I would like to thank all my physicians, surgeons, dentists, and alternative health care practitioners, especially Cherlyn Smith, who have taken me out of agony and kept my mortal frame in good-enough working order.

I am grateful to those friends and colleagues who were "there for me" in good times and when the going got rough, especially Joan Casamo, Linda Clarke, Rivka Haut, Merle Hoffman, Barbara Joans, Meryle Kates, William Myers, Daniel Pipes, Jennifer Roskies, Na'ama Sandrow, Fern Sidman, and Ibn Warraq.

I am moored to earth by my immediate, extended, and intergenerational family: Susan, my son Ariel, my daughter-in-law Shannon, my son's in-laws, Pearl and Harvey, and our two precious, darling granddaughters, Lily Diana and Kate Leah. And that's Diana for Diana Prince aka Wonder Woman and Leah for Princess Leia of *Star Wars*. I wish to thank my parents of blessed memory, Lillian and Leon, for having given me life and for having stood by me. I thank my long-time housekeeper and friend, Joanna Wilczynska, who surrounds me with beauty and coffee and keeps me going.

I humbly acknowledge both the suffering and the strength of the people of Afghanistan and my extended Afghan-Turkish family, especially my Afghan husband, whose friendship I value deeply. I hope my attempt to recreate a place and a time long gone will meet with their love and approval.

This book is dedicated to K., my sister, my friend. She was a very good person. May God bless her and have mercy upon her soul.

Bibliography

Abdullah, Morag Murray. *My Khyber Marriage: The Best-Selling 1920 Account of Life among the Pathan Tribesmen.* London: Longriders Guild Press, 1920.

———. *Valley of the Giant Buddhas: Memoirs and Travels.* London: Octagon Press, 1988. (This volume has been updated to the Soviet era and as such, cannot have been entirely written by Abdullah [Saira Elizabeth Luiza Shah] who died in 1960).

Aciman, Andre. *Out of Egypt: A Memoir.* New York: Picador, Farrar Straus and Giroux, 1994.

Afkhami, Mahnaz, ed. *Faith & Freedom: Women's Human Rights in the Muslim World.* Syracuse, NY: Syracuse University Press, 1994.

Aharon, Sara Y. *From Kabul to Queens: The Jews of Afghanistan and Their Move to the United States.* New York: American Sephardi Federation, Decalogue Books, 2011.

Ahmed, Qanta A. *The Land of Invisible Women: A Female Doctor's Journey in the Saudi Kingdom.* Naperville, IL: Sourcebooks, 2008.

Ali, Ayaan Hirsi. *Infidel.* New York: Free Press, 2007.

———. *Nomad.* New York: Free Press, 2010.

Ali, Latifa, with Richard Shears. *Betrayed: Escape from Iraq.* Sydney: New Holland, 2009.

Alireza, Marianne. *At the Drop of a Veil: The True Story of an American Woman's Years in a Saudi Arabian Harem.* 1971. Reprint, Boston: Houghton Mifflin, 1991.

Alrabaa, Sami. *Veiled Atrocities: True Stories of Oppression in Saudi Arabia.* Amherst, NY: Prometheus, 2010.

Alvi, Hayat. "Women in Afghanistan: A Human Rights Tragedy a Decade after September 11." *RAWA News,* November 12, 2012. http://features.rr.com/article/03rC0ilfv3buK?q=Afghanistan.

Amin, Qasim. *The Liberation of Women: A Document in the History of Egyptian Feminism.* Cairo: The American University of Cairo Press, 1993.

Angel, Marc D. *Foundations of Sephardic Spirituality: The Inner Life of Jews of the Ottoman Empire.* Woodstock, VT: Jewish Lights, 2006.

Ansary, Tamim. *West of Kabul, East of New York.* New York: Picador, 2002.

———. *Games without Rules: The Often Interrupted History of Afghanistan.* New York: Public Affairs, Perseus Book Group, 2012.

Anwar, M.H, ed., with an afterword by Keith Anwar. *Memories of Afghanistan.* Bloomington, IN: Author House, 2004.

Armstrong, Sally. *Veiled Threat: The Hidden Power of the Women of Afghanistan.* New York: Four Walls Eight Windows, 2002.

Ates, Seyran. *Der Islam braucht eine sexuelle Revolution.* Berlin: Ullstein, 2009.

Badran, Margot, and Miriam Cooke, eds. *Opening the Gates: A Century of Arab Feminist Writing.* Bloomington: Indiana University Press, 1990.

Baker, Deborah. *The Convert: A Tale of Exile and Extremism.* Minneapolis: Graywolf Press, 2011.

Baran, Zeyno, ed. *The Other Muslims: Moderate and Secular.* New York: Palgrave Macmillan, 2010.

Barfield, Thomas. *Afghanistan: A Cultural and Political History.* Princeton, NJ: Princeton University Press, 2010.

Bergreen, Laurence. *Marco Polo: From Venice to Xanadu.* New York: Vintage, 2008.

Bin Ladin, Carmen. *Inside the Kingdom.* New York: Warner, 2004.

Bin Laden, Najwa, Omar bin Laden, and Jean Sasson. *Growing Up Bin Laden: Osama's Wife and Son Take Us Inside Their Secret World.* New York: St. Martin's Griffin, 2009.

Bin Laden, Osama. "Bin Laden's Fatwa." *PBS News Hour,* August 26, 1996. www.pbs.org.

Blanch, Lesley. *The Wilder Shores of Love.* New York: Simon and Schuster, 1954.

Blatchford, Christie. "Father in Honour Killing Trial Makes his Case for World's Greatest Dad." *National Post,* November 12, 2009. http://fullcomment .nationalpost.com/2011/12/08/christie-blatchford-father-in-honour-killing -trial-makes-his-pitch-for-worlds-greatest-dad/

———. "Shafia Trial Testimony Ends with an Abrupt Whimper." *National Post,* January 18, 2012. http://fullcomment.nationalpost.com/2012/01/18 /christie-blatchford-shafia-trial-testimony-ends-with-an-abrupt-whimper/

———. "No Honour in 'Cold-Blooded, Shameless' Murder of Shafia Girls." *National Post,* January 29, 2012. http://fullcomment.nationalpost.com /2012/01/29/jury-reaches-verdict-in-shafia-trial/

———. "Shafia Defence So Quick to Strike Righteous Pose." *National Post,* February 4, 2012. http://fullcomment.nationalpost.com/2012/02/04/shafia -trial/

Bostom, Andrew G., ed. *The Legacy of Islamic Antisemitism: From Sacred Texts to Solemn History.* Amherst, NY: Prometheus, 2008.

Bowen, John. *Plain Tales of the Afghan Border.* London: Springwood, 1982.

Brauer, Erich. "The Jews of Afghanistan: An Anthropological Report." *Jewish Social Studies* 4, no. 2. Indiana University Press (1942): 121–38.

Brooks, Geraldine. *Nine Parts of Desire: The Hidden World of Islamic Women.* New York: Anchor Books, 1995.

Burton, Sir Richard. *Personal Narrative of a Pilgrimage to Al-Madinah and Meccah (3 Volumes).* London: Longman, Brown, Green, Longmans, and Roberts, 1857.

———. *The Jew, the Gypsy and el-Islam.* London: Hutchinson and Co., 1898.

Byron, Robert. *The Road to Oxiana.* New Preface by Rory Stewart. Oxford, NY: Oxford University Press, 2007.

Cassandra. *Escape! From an Arab Marriage.* Philadelphia, Xlibris, 2006.

Chandrasekaran, Rajiv. *Little America: The War within the War for Afghanistan.* New York: Alfred A. Knopf, 2012.

Chayes, Sarah. *The Punishment of Virtue: Inside Afghanistan after the Taliban.* New York: Penguin Books, 2006.

Chesler, Phyllis, *Woman's Inhumanity to Woman*. Original Publication. New York, Thunder's Mouth Press, Nation Books, 2001. Re-published. Chicago, IL: Lawrence Hill Books, 2009.

———. *The New Anti-Semitism: The Current Crisis and What We Must Do About It*. San Francisco: Jossey Bass, a Wiley imprint, 2003.

———. "Are Honor Killings Simply Domestic Violence?" *Middle East Quarterly*, spring 2009.

———. "Worldwide Trends in Honor Killings." *Middle East Quarterly*, spring 2010.

———. "Ban the Burqa? The Argument in Favor." *Middle East Quarterly*, fall 2010.

———. "Hindu vs. Muslim Honor Killings." *Middle East Quarterly*, summer 2012.

Churchill, Winston. *The Story of the Malakand Field Force*. Originally published: London and New York: Thomas Nelson & Sons, Ltd., 1916. Mineola, NY: Dover Publications, Inc., 2010.

Dannin, Robert. *Arms against Fury: Magnum Photographers in Afghanistan*. New York, NY: Magnum Photos, Powerhouse Books, 2002.

Darwish, Nonie. *Now They Call Me Infidel: Why I Renounced Jihad for America, Israel, and the War on Terror*. New York: Penguin, 2006.

———. *Cruel and Usual Punishment: The Terrifying Global Implications of Islamic Law*. Nashville: Thomas Nelson, 2008.

De Baer, Oliver Rudston. *Afghan Interlude*. London: Chatto & Windus, 1957.

Dunsheath, Joyce, and Eleanor Baillie. *Afghan Quest*. Toronto: George G. Harrap, 1960.

Eberhardt, Isabelle. *The Oblivion Seekers*. San Francisco: City Lights, 1972.

Eichstaedt, Peter H. *Above the Din of War. Afghans Speak about Their Lives, Their Country, and Their Future—and Why America Should Listen*. Chicago: Chicago Review Press/Lawrence Hill Books, 2013.

Elliot, Jason. *An Unexpected Light*. New York: Picador, 2001.

El Saadawi, Nawal. *Woman at Point Zero*. London: Zed, 1975.

Esman, Abigail. *Radical State: How Jihad Is Winning over Democracy in the West*. Denver: Praeger, 2010.

Fallaci, Oriana. *The Rage and the Pride*. New York: Rizzoli, 2001.

Federal Bureau of Investigation. *Robert F. Kennedy Assassination: Report of Independent Special Counsel Thomas F. Kranz*. Washington: Federal Bureau of Investigation, 1977.

Fernea, Elizabeth Warnock. *In Search of Islamic Feminism: One Woman's Global Journey*. New York: Doubleday, 1998.

Fernea, Elizabeth Warnock, and Basima Wattan Bezirgan. *Middle Eastern Muslim Women Speak*. Austin: University of Texas Press, 1977.

Follett, Ken. *Lie Down with Lions*. New York: William Morrow, 1986.

Forbes, Rosita. *Women Called Wild*. New York: E. P. Dutton, 1937.

———. *From the Sahara to Samarkand: 1919–1937: Selected Travel Writings of Rosita Forbes*. Edited with an introduction by Margaret Bald. Mt. Jackson, VA: Axios Press, 2010.

Fradkin, Hillel, and Lewis Libby. "Egypt's Islamists: A Cautionary Tale." *Commentary*, April 2011.

Girardet, Edward. *Killing the Cranes: A Reporter's Journey through Three Decades of War in Afghanistan*. White River Junction, VT: Chelsea Green, 2011.

Goldberg, Jeffrey. "In the Party of God." *New Yorker,* October 14 and 21, 2002.

Goodwin, Jan. *Caught in the Crossfire.* New York: E. P. Dutton, 1987.

———. *Price of Honor.* New York: Plume, 1995.

Gordon, Lucie Duff. *Letters from Egypt: 1863–65.* London: Virago, 1983.

Goulianos, Joan. *By A Woman Writ: Literature from Six Centuries by and about Women.* New York: The Bobbs Merrill Company, 1973.

Gregorian, Vartan. *The Emergence of Modern Afghanistan.* Stanford, CA: Stanford University Press, 1969.

Hakakian, Roya. *Journey from the Land of No.* New York: Crown, 2004.

Harris, Ellen. *Guarding the Secrets.* New York: Scribner's, 1995.

Hodgson, Barbara. *Dreaming of East: Western Women and the Exotic Allure of the Orient.* Berkeley, CA: Greystone Books, 2005.

Hosseini, Khaled. *The Kite Runner.* New York: Riverhead Books, 2003.

———. *A Thousand Splendid Suns.* New York: Riverhead Books, 2007.

Hunter, Edward. *The Past Present: A Year in Afghanistan.* London: Hodder and Stoughton, 1959.

Jasser, Zuhdi M. *A Battle for the Soul of Islam: An American Muslim Patriot's Fight to Save His Faith.* New York: Simon and Schuster, 2012.

Jenkins, Robin. *Dust on the Paw.* New York: G. P. Putnam's Sons, 1961.

Jones, Ann. *Kabul in Winter.* New York: Picador, 2006.

Karsh, Efraim. *Islamic Imperialism: A History.* Updated ed. New Haven, CT: Yale University Press, 2007.

Karsh, Efraim, and Inari Karsh. *The Empires of the Sand: The Struggle for Mastery in the Middle East, 1789–1923.* Cambridge, MA: Harvard University Press, 1999.

Kashani, Reuben. *The Jews of Afghanistan.* Jerusalem: Institute for Research on the Jews of Afghanistan, 2002.

Khouri, Norma. *Honor Lost: Love and Death in Modern-day Jordan.* New York: Atria Books, 2003.

Kipling, Rudyard. *The Man Who Would Be King.* 1888. Reprint, Middlesex, UK: Echo Library, 2007.

Kirkpatrick, David D. "Morsi Says He Will Work for Release of Sheik Jailed in U.S." *New York Times,* June 29, 2012.

Klass, Rosanne. *Land of the High Flags: Afghanistan When the Going Was Good.* 1964. Reprint, Hong Kong: Odyssey Books and Guides, 2007.

———, ed. *Afghanistan: The Great Game Revisited.* New York: Freedom House, 1987.

Konishi, Masatoshi. *Afghanistan: Crossroads of the Ages.* Vol. 7, *This Beautiful World.* San Francisco: Kodansha, 1969.

Koofi, Fawzia. *Letters to My Daughters.* Quebec City, Canada: Douglas & McIntyre, 2011.

Korbin, Nancy Hartevelt. *The Banality of Suicide Terrorism: The Naked Truth about the Psychology of Islamic Suicide Bombing.* Foreword by Phyllis Chesler. Washington, DC: Potomac Books, 2010.

Krastev, Nikola. "U.S.: Afghan Jews Keep Traditions Alive Far from Home." *Radio Free Europe,* June 19, 2007. http://www.rferl.org/content/article/1077209.html

Kressel, Neil J. *The Sons of Pigs and Apes: Muslim Antisemitism and the Conspiracy of Silence.* Washington, DC: Potomac Books, 2012.

Kuntzel, Matthias. *Jihad and Jew-Hatred: Islamism, Nazism, and the Roots of 9/11.* New York: Telos Press, 2007.

Lagnado, Lucette. *The Man in the White Sharkskin Suit.* New York: HarperCollins, 2007.

———. *The Arrogant Years: One Girl's Search for Her Lost Youth, from Cairo to Brooklyn.* New York: Ecco/HarperCollins, 2011.

Lamb, Christina. *The Sewing Circles of Herat.* Originally published: Great Britain: HarperCollins, 2002. New York: Perennial HarperCollins, 2004.

Lawrence, T. E. *Seven Pillars of Wisdom.* New York: Penguin, 1926.

Lazreg, Marnia. *Questioning the Veil: Open Letters to Muslim Women.* Princeton, NJ: Princeton University Press, 2009.

Lee, Felicia R. "Coping; Afghan Jews Look Back in Sorrow." *The New York Times,* December, 30, 2001. http://www.nytimes.com/2001/12/30/nyregion /coping-afghan-jews-look-back-in-sorrow.html

Legh-Jones, Alison. *English Woman, Arab Man.* London: Paul Elek, 1975.

Leonowens, Mrs. Anna H. *Siamese Harem Life.* 1873. Reprint, New York: E. P. Dutton, 1953.

Lewis, Bernard. *The Jews of Islam.* Princeton, NJ: Princeton University Press, 1984.

———. *Notes on a Century: Reflections of a Middle East Historian.* London: Viking, 2012.

Lewis, Reina, and Nancy Mickleford. *Gender, Modernity, and Liberty: Middle Eastern and Western Women's Writings: A Critical Sourcebook.* New York: I. B. Tauris, 2006.

Lichter, Ida. *Muslim Women Reformers.* Amherst, NY: Prometheus, 2009.

Littman, David. *Mission to Morocco (1963–1964).* Offprint from *The Century of Moses Montefiore.* Edited by Sonia Lipman and Vivian David Lipman. Oxford: Oxford University Press, 1985.

Loti, Pierre. *Jerusalem.* Translated by W. P. Baines. Philadelphia: David McKay, 1878.

Lott, Emmeline. "The 'English Governess' in Egypt: Harem Life in Egypt and Constantinople, 1865." In *Gender, Modernity, and Liberty: Middle Eastern and Western Women's Writings: A Critical Sourcebook.* Eds. Reina Lewis and Nancy Mickleford. New York: I. B. Tauris, 2006.

Macintyre, Ben. *The Man Who Would Be King: The First American in Afghanistan.* New York: Farrar, Straus and Giroux, 2004.

Mackworth, Cecily. *The Destiny of Isabelle Eberhardt.* Avon, 1977.

Mahmoody, Betty, with William Hoffer. *Not without My Daughter.* New York: St. Martin's, 1987.

Mahmoody, Betty, with Arnold D. Dunchock. *For the Love of a Child.* New York: St. Martin's, 1992.

Manji, Irshad. *The Trouble with Islam: A Muslim's Call for Reform in Her Faith.* New York: St. Martin's Press, 2003.

Mansur, Salim. *Delectable Lie: A Liberal Repudiation of Multiculturalism.* Brantford, Canada: Mantua Books, 2011.

Marlowe, Ann. *The Book of Troubles: A Romance.* New York: Harcourt, 2006.

———. "A Heritage in Ruin." *New York Times,* June 6, 2011.

———. "End the Costly War in Afghanistan." *Daily Beast,* June 11, 2011.

———. "Much Ado about Afghan War Photos." *Wall Street Journal,* April 23, 2012.

Martineau, Harriet. *Eastern Life, Present and Past.* London: E. Moxon, 1842.

McDermott, Kerry. "Girl, 15, 'Beheaded' in Afghanistan after Her Family Turned Down Marriage Proposal." *Daily Mail,* November 29, 2012. http://

www.dailymail.co.uk/news/article-2240220/Girl-15-beheaded-Afghanistan
-family-turned-marriage-proposal.html

McKinley, James. "Islamic Leader on U.S. Terrorist List Is in Brooklyn." *New York Times,* December 19, 1990. http://www.nytimes.com/1990/12/16 /nyregion/islamic-leader-on-us-terrorist-list-is-in-brooklyn.html

Mernissi, Fatima. *Dreams of Trespass: Tales of a Harem Girlhood.* Reading, PA: Addison-Wesley, 1994.

Michaud, Roland, and Sabrina Michaud. *Afghanistan.* 1980. New York: Thames and Hudson, 1990.

Michener, James A. *Caravans: A Novel of Afghanistan.* New York: Random House, 1963.

Millet, Kate. *Going to Iran.* New York: Coward, McCann & Geoghegan, 1981.

Mire, Soraya. *The Girl with Three Legs: A Memoir.* Chicago: Lawrence Hill Books, 2011.

Nafisi, Azar. *Reading Lolita in Tehran.* New York: Random House, 2003.

———. *Things I've Been Silent About.* New York: Random House, 2008.

Naggar, Jean. *Sipping from the Nile: My Exodus from Egypt.* New York: Stony Creek Press, 2008.

Nawa, Fariba. *Opium Nation: Child Brides, Drug Lords, and One Woman's Journey through Afghanistan.* New York: HarperCollins, 2011.

Nemat, Marina. *Prisoner of Teheran: One Woman's Story of Survival Inside an Iranian Prison.* New York: Free Press/Simon and Schuster, 2007.

Newby, Eric. *A Short Walk in the Hindu Kush.* New York: Penguin, 1958.

Nissenbaum, Dion. "Draft Army Handbook Wades into Divisive Afghan Issue." *Wall Street Journal,* December 11, 2012.

Nomani, Asra Q. *Standing Alone at Mecca: An American Woman's Struggle for the Soul of Islam.* New York: HarperCollins, 2005.

Pardoe, Julia. "The City of the Sultan 1837; and the Domestic Manners of the Turks in 1836." In *Gender, Modernity, and Liberty: Middle Eastern and Western Women's Writings: A Critical Sourcebook.* Eds. Reina Lewis and Nancy Mickleford. New York: I. B. Tauris, 2006.

Pazira, Nelofar. *A Bed of Red Flowers: In Search of My Afghanistan.* New York: Free Press/Simon and Schuster, 2005.

Polo, Marco. *The Travels of Marco Polo.* Introduction by Colin Thubron. New York: Alfred A. Knopf, 2008.

Poullada, Leon B. *Reform and Rebellion in Afghanistan: 1919–1929, King Amanullah's Failure to Modernize a Tribal Society.* Ithaca, NY: Cornell University Press, 1973.

Rachlin, Nahid. *Married to a Stranger.* New York: E. P. Dutton, 1983.

Rashid, Ahmed. *Taliban: Militant Islam, Oil, and Fundamentalism in Central Asia.* New Haven, CT: Yale University Press, 2001.

———. *Descent into Chaos: The U.S. and the Disaster in Pakistan, Afghanistan, and Central Asia.* New York: Penguin, 2008.

Reiss, Tom. *The Orientalist.* New York: Random House, 2006.

Rejwan, Nissim. *The Last Jews in Baghdad: Remembering a Lost Homeland.* Foreword by Joel Beinin. Austin: University of Texas Press, 2004.

Rifaat, Alifa. *Distant View of a Minaret: And Other Stories,* London: Quartet Books, 1983.

Rodriguez, Deborah. *Kabul Beauty School.* New York: Random House, 2007.

———. *A Cup of Friendship.* New York: Ballantine, 2011.

Rosenberg, Matthew. "Trail of Fraud and Vengeance Leads to Kabul Bank Convictions." New York Times, March 6, 2013.

Ross, Mary Laurel. *Veiled Honor.* Lee's Summit, MO: Fathers Press, 2009.

Rubin, Barnett R. *The Fragmentation of Afghanistan: State Formation and Collapse in the International System.* New Haven, CT: Yale University Press, 1995, 2002.

Ruete, Emily (born Salme, princess of Omar and Zanzibar). *Memoirs of an Arabian Princess from Zanzibar.* New York: Markus Weiner, 1996.

Sadeed, Suraya, and Damien Lewis. *Forbidden Lessons in a Kabul Guesthouse: The True Story of a Woman Who Risked Everything to Bring Hope to Afghanistan.* New York: Hyperion/HarperCollins, 2011.

Sahebjam, Freidoune. *The Stoning of Soraya M.* New York: Arcade, 1994.

Said, Kurban (Lev Nussembaum). *Ali and Nino.* 1937. Reprint, New York: Anchor Books, 2000.

Salbi, Zainab, and Rennio Maifredi. *If You Knew Me, You Would Care.* Forewords by Meryl Streep, Annie Lennox, Ashley Judd, and Geena Davis. New York: Powerhouse Books, 2012.

Sasson, Jean. *Princess: A True Story of Life behind the Veil in Saudi Arabia.* New York: William Morrow, 1992.

Schmitt, Arno, and Jehoeda Sofer, eds. *Sexuality and Erotocism among Males in Moslem Societies.* New York: Harrington Park/Haworth Press, 1992.

Scroggins, Deborah. *Wanted Women: Faith, Lies, and the War on Terror: The Lives of Ayaan Hirsi Ali and Aafia Siddiqui.* New York: HarperCollins, 2012.

Seierstad, Asne. *The Bookseller of Kabul.* Boston: Little, Brown, 2002.

Shah, Saira. *Beneath the Veil (Film).* Channel 4 UK, 2001.

———. *The Storyteller's Daughter.* New York: Alfred A. Knopf, 2003.

Shah, Tahir. *The Caliph's House: A Year in Casablanca.* New York: Bantam, 2006.

———. *In Arabian Nights: A Caravan of Moroccan Dreams.* New York: Bantam, 2008.

Simpson, St. John. *Afghanistan: A Cultural History.* Northampton, MA: Interlink Books, 2012.

Skaine, Rosemarie. *The Women of Afghanistan under the Taliban.* Jefferson, NC: McFarland, 2002.

Souad, with Marie-Therese Cuny. *Burned Alive.* New York: Warner, 2004.

Stark, Freya. *East Is West.* London: John Murray, 1945.

———. *The Minaret of Djam: An Excursion in Afghanistan.* London: John Murray, 1970.

Steegmuller, Francis. *Flaubert in Egypt: A Sensibility on Tour (A Narrative Drawn from Gustave Flaubert's Travel Notes and Letters).* Boston: Atlantic Monthly Press/Little Brown, 1972.

Stewart, Rhea Talley. *Fire in Afghanistan, 1914–1929: Faith, Hope and the British Empire.* New York: Doubleday, 1973.

Stewart, Rory. *The Places in Between.* Orlando, FL: Harcourt, 2004.

———. "Afghanistan: What Could Work." *New York Review of Books,* January 14, 2010.

———. "Time to Be Honest About Afghanistan." *Financial Times,* September 21, 2012.

Sultan, Wafa. *A God Who Hates: The Courageous Woman Who Inflamed the Muslim World Speaks Out Against the Evils of Islam.* New York: St. Martin's, 2009.

Tanner, Stephen. *Afghanistan: A Military History from Alexander the Great to the War against the Taliban.* Philadelphia: Da Capo, 2002.

Tomsen, Peter. *The Wars of Afghanistan: Messianic Terrorism, Tribal Conflicts, and the Failures of Great Powers.* New York: Public Affairs, 2011.

Tortajada, Anna. *The Silenced Cry: One Woman's Diary of a Journey to Afghanistan.* New York: Thomas Dunne Books/St. Martin's Press, 2004.

Tuson, Penelope. *Playing the Game: Western Women in Arabia.* New York: I. B. Tauris, 2003.

Twain, Mark. *The Innocents Abroad.* 1869. Originally published as letters in *Daily Alta California* (San Francisco), *New York Tribune,* and *New York Herald.* New York: New American Library Signet Classic, 1966.

United Nations. "Global Issues: Refugees." n.d. http://www.un.org/en/global issues/refugees/

Van Dyk, Jere. *In Afghanistan: An American Odyssey.* New York: Coward-McCann, 1983.

Wallach, Janet. *Desert Queen.* New York: Anchor, 1996.

Waller, John H. *Beyond the Khyber Pass: The Road to British Disaster in the First Afghan War.* New York: Random House, 1990.

Warraq, Ibn. *Leaving Islam: Apostates Speak Out.* Amherst, NY: Prometheus, 2003.

———. *Why the West Is Best: A Muslim Apostate's Defense of Liberal Democracy.* New York: Encounter Books, 2011.

Wharton, Edith. *In Morocco.* 1920. Reprint, Los Angeles: Aegypan Press, 2011.

Wieseltier, Leon. "The Schoolgirl's Lessons." *New Republic,* November 8, 2012.

Wilson, G. Willow. *The Butterfly Mosque: A Young American Woman's Journey to Love and Islam.* New York: Atlantic Monthly Press, 2010.

Ye'or, Bat. *The Dhimmi: Jews and Christians under Islam.* Preface by Jacques Ellul. Rev. English ed. Madison, NJ: Fairleigh Dickinson University, 1985.

———. *Europe, Globalization, and the Coming Universal Caliphate.* Madison, NJ: Fairleigh Dickinson University, 2011.

Zafrani, Haim. *Two Thousand Years of Jewish Life in Morocco.* Jersey City, NJ: KTAV, 2005.

Index